The Guilded Pen

The Power
of
Ten

Tenth Edition – 2021

The Guilded Pen, Tenth Edition is a publication of the
San Diego Writers and Editors Guild
2307 Fenton Parkway, Ste. 107-266
San Diego, CA 92108
www.sdweg.org

The Guilded Pen, Tenth Edition was published by Grey Castle Publishing. Copies are available on www.Amazon.com, www.sdweg.org, and www.greycastlepublishing.com.

Rivkah Sleeth, Managing Editor, Compilation
Marcia Buompensiero, Managing Editor, Design/Publishing
Sandra Yeaman, Asst. Editor/Copyeditor
Irene Flynn, Asst. Editor (Poetry)

Cover design by Leon Lazarus
Ebook creation by Sarah Faxon

Paperback price $21.95

Print Book ISBN: 9780578987149
Ebook ISBN: 9780578993263

The Guilded Pen

The Power

of

Ten

Tenth Edition — 2021

Contents

Authors   Works

(continued)

Authors Works

For all the members of the

San Diego Writers and Editors Guild

who braved COVID-19 restrictions to keep the meetings,

workshops, and all other online Zoom events relevant, fun,

and excitingly alive in 2021, this anthology is dedicated to

you.

Introduction

What is the "Power of Ten"?

The San Diego Writers and Editors Guild published its first collection of short stories, essays, and poetry offered by its members in 2012. We called it *The Guilded Pen*—an apt title we thought—a cute play on words—and the title stuck. And so did the idea of publishing an annual anthology to encourage and promote the writing arts in San Diego. We could not have foreseen the impact that such an anthology would have on the San Diego writing scene.

As Guild membership has grown, so has the anthology. It has become a powerful platform to display the talent and skill of our diverse membership who represent a variety of cultures and life experiences, races, ages, and genders. They are high school and college students braving public scrutiny for the first time, as well as experienced writers exercising their craft and leaving a legacy of wisdom for those who follow. All stories, whether real or imagined, have something to offer the reader.

It has been said that writing is a lonely struggle. Telling the story, whether it be fiction, a life memory, or a poetic path of travel, is an art. Like all art, masterpieces come easily for the few and, for others, masterpieces are worked over tirelessly until perfect.

Although the act of writing is a singular effort, a team is needed to share impressions and evaluations of the work. Getting that story ready to print is a learned skill and one to which our team of reviewers, editors, and coaches is dedicated. Each writer receives impartial review, guidance and coaching, and unwavering encouragement to persevere in honing their craft. Acceptance is granted only after rigorous standards have been met. Good grammar, a plot that hooks the reader, and a cast of interesting characters moving the story forward to its conclusion is essential.

For over a decade, the annual publication of *The Guilded Pen* has brought recognition to the Guild and its members and has been a successful promotional tool for recruitment. In those ten years, more than 565 entries written by our members have been published. Copies of these anthologies repose on the shelves of public and private libraries and welcome newcomers to *The Guilded Pen* to peruse their pages.

The SDWEG has been providing its members with this wonderful opportunity for ten strong years. We look forward to future decades of printing great writing in *The Guilded Pen,* an opportunity offered as one of the many benefits of Guild membership.

—Rivkah Sleeth
Managing Editor, Compilation

—Marcia Buompensiero
Managing Editor, Design/Publishing

Acknowledgments

The Guilded Pen — Power of Ten, 2021 is the tenth edition and owes its existence to the SDWEG Board of Directors. Their dedication and foresight fostered the creation of a venue to showcase members' works and continue to carry on the mission to support the local writing arts.

Board of Directors 2021

Sarah Faxon, President
Bob Doublebower, Vice President
Laurie Asher, Secretary
Kelly Bargabos, Financial Officer
Marcia Buompensiero, Treasurer
Melody Kramer, Membership Chair
Patricia Bossano, Newsletter Editor
Directors-at-Large:
Janet Hafner
Rick Lakin
Leon Lazarus
Rivkah Sleeth
Penn Wallace
Sandra Yeaman

We are grateful to our editorial review panel who read, critiqued, and edited the submissions. Special thanks and appreciation goes to Laurie Asher, Gered Beeby, Bob Doublebower, Corinna Goold, Janet Hafner, Mardie Schroeder, Jack Sleeth, Ruth Wallace, Nico Waters, and Ken Yaros.

Rivkah Sleeth, Managing Editor, Compilation
Marcia Buompensiero, Managing Editor, Design/Publishing
Irene Flynn, Asst. Editor (Poetry)
Sandra Yeaman, Asst. Editor/Copyeditor

San Diego Writers and Editors Guild

~ Mission Statement ~
To Promote, Support, and Encourage the Writing Arts for Adults and Youth

We are a nonprofit local group of writers and editors dedicated to improving our skills and helping others to do the same. Since 1979, the Guild has played an important role in furthering the goals of both novice and accomplished authors. No matter what your writing skill, we can help you get to the next level. Our members come from all over the region in search of support and to share their talents.

Benefits of membership include:
- Monthly meetings with informative speakers
- Marketing Support Group
- Monthly Newsletter (*The Writer's Life*)
- Workshops focusing on specific aspects of writing/publishing/marketing
- Membership Directory
- Manuscript Review Program
- Opportunity to publish your work in *The Guilded Pen*
- Opportunity to list yourself and your work in the SDWEG Members' Works pages on our website
- Active Website and Social Media Presence
- Access to Online Resources for Writers
- Access to discounted space at the Annual Festival of Books
- Periodic presentation of awards: "The Rhoda Riddell Builders Award" — recognizing efforts to build/expand the Guild; "Special Achievements Awards" — for extraordinary service; and "The Odin Award" — to those who have been major stimulators of the writing arts in San Diego as evidenced by their body of published work.

Guild membership is open to all, and guests are welcome to the meetings for a small donation. Visit: www.sdweg.org.

An Unwelcome Review

John Yamada

10/10, a masterpiece in a class of its own.
Best new writer of this generation.

I read the words from the review again and again as I glance over to my other monitor featuring a blank Word document, still unceremoniously titled *Document1*. I look at the date in the lower right corner and despite all the Power of Positive Thinking I could muster, it's still only two months before my deadline.

"What an *asshole*," I say, unable to hold in the anger any longer.

"What did you say, baby?" Alexandra says from the bed in her thick Italian accent that I thought was so inspiring and transcendent just a few weeks ago.

"Nothing, babe, go back to bed. This is just part of my process—I say stuff out loud, it's how the magic happens," I say, cringing. This is my new persona now. I've written a bestseller. I've moved from Queens to a fancy apartment in Manhattan. I've spent weeks wooing a beautiful Italian woman with fancy dinners and lavish gifts because I thought she could be my muse. I'm such a fraud.

She squints at me, trying to gauge my reaction and then shrugs her shoulders and lays back down, pulling the covers over her head until all I can see is the top of her unruly dark hair.

I click through the reviewer's text again. *Brilliant characterization.* I feel my skin crawl. *Tight pacing.* I want to vomit. *With this masterpiece, Brian Boston stands among the giants of the fantasy genre.* I grab my hair with both hands and

1

pull until my fingers go numb.

I exhale deeply, sighing for what feels like the hundredth time. I glance over at Alexandra who makes a muffled noise of complaint and pulls the covers over her head until I can't see her at all anymore.

How am I supposed to ever write again after a review like this? None of the other reviewers were so glowing with their praise. *Great work* I can handle. *Pretentious drivel* I can handle too after punching a few walls. But *this*.

I minimize the Blank Document of Glaring Inadequacy and pull up a web page I've refreshed over a hundred times. I found out about Fr33knetz from a dozen conversations with nerds, geeks, good-for-nothings, and other friends of mine. One eventually connected me to this site on the dark web where all kinds of illegal things can be procured. There is only one thing that I'm looking for though.

As the web page loads, I read over my inquiry to make sure the requirements are clear and that I don't sound like I might be some narc looking to upend this illicit Internet society.

Need identity, location, and all available information from Amazon username.

The page flickers to indicate it has completed its refresh. A response appears below mine.

Stand by.

My heart jumps. Finally! Now I'll find out who this dirtbag George Davis is who robbed me of my ability to write the award-winning sequel that I would've been able to write were it not for his terribly inconsiderate review.

I hear my phone ring and I nearly fall out of my chair. I look at the screen and the number comes up as *unavailable*. The time on the phone says it's 3:37 a.m. — definitely not a telemarketer. My mind starts to race. I didn't provide my cell phone number. Was this the FBI? Would a stint in jail add to or detract from my number of Twitter followers? I scramble out of the room and answer the phone as soon as I close the room door.

I lower my voice a few octaves and try not to stammer.

"Go ahead," I say.

"Hi!" says a cheerful female voice with a light southern accent.

"Uh, what?" I say, unable to hold back the stutter or the girlish tone of my voice this time.

"You requested information about someone? My name is Kathleen and I'd be so happy to help you with that," she says with an A-plus customer service smile that I can hear through the phone. "I've run some analytics on your browsing history, and based on where you most frequently pause your screen, I'm thinking the Amazon username you are looking for is George Davis, is that correct?"

"Uh … yes," I say, unable to produce any other words, further disgracing the world of writers. I can barely hear my voice over the pounding of my heart. How was any of this possible? I feel as exposed as when I ask someone to read over an unfinished work, although this somehow feels worse since it feels so … uninvited.

"Okay, well, George Davis isn't this user's real name. This user actually has a number of different aliases," she says. I can hear rapid clicking and typing in the background. "Hmm, she's good this one."

"She?" I ask, my surprise overcoming my fear of interrupting the scary/friendly hacker. For the past few months I've always imagined knocking on George Davis's red door in the suburbs. The guy who answers is a tall middle-aged guy with thin wisps of brown hair combed over to try to hide the fact that he's balding. He looks like a nice guy, he has a real saccharine smile, he wears a blue V-neck sweater and some tan slacks, but I can see the stupid jerk that he is behind all of that. He has a bit of a beer belly — that no-good alcoholic — and he has a ketchup stain on the side of his mouth — the disgusting slob — and his gray eyes sparkle like cubic zirconium instead of diamonds because he sells used cars for a living, and he really knows how to turn on the schmaltz when it matters, but it's all fake. He says, "How can I help you, pal?" and then I punch him right in his stupid nose. I've never thrown a punch in my life, but this one fires

3

like a SCUD missile and sends him right down on his pompous derriere. Then I stand over him, point a finger, and say, "It's people like you that make it impossible for writers to make a living in this world."

"Mr. Boston?" says Kathleen, breaking me out of my reverie.

"Oh, um, yes. She?" I ask again.

"Yes, sir," she says without a hint of judgment in her voice. At least she can't read my thoughts. "This user actually has about 12 different Amazon accounts and her online profile is all over the place. She uses a VPN — that's a virtual private network — multiple in fact, so I'm having a hard time locking down her true IP address and location. I might need to try and spoof her account or embed a trojan horse …"

My mind starts to glaze over at the computer lingo.

"So how do you know she's a … she?" I interrupt again hoping against all odds that it's not a *she* but still just my despised sweater-wearing George Davis.

"Oh!" Kathleen says as an acknowledgment of the interruption. "These aliases don't have much in the way of browsing history that give away anything about the person's identity, but there is one purchase that one of the usernames made. Maybe she messed up and forgot she was trying to hide her identity."

"What purchase?" I ask.

"That wasn't part of the original request Mr. Boston. May I have your authorization to withdraw an extra $100 from your checking account in order to provide you with this information?"

I stop breathing for a moment. I didn't provide any payment information. "Um, I didn't know that we worked out any payment details. How much is this going to cost me?"

"Well, this phone call is $100 per minute and we've been talking for about 7 and a half minutes, so $750 plus the $100 for the purchase history — it was women's underwear by the way, bra and panty set, tan, lace, kind of fancy, really cute actually — and we're looking at $850 already deducted from your preferred checking account ending in 0895."

4

I don't know for how long I've stopped breathing, and I make a sudden gasp for air. "What?" I think about hanging up the phone and calling the FBI. This was way over my head.

"This is your first time, Mr. Boston, I understand," Kathleen says. "Some people get really frightened during their first time requesting illegal services that carry serious legal consequences. And some people think about doing something silly like contacting the authorities, but you're a bestselling author, Mr. Boston, and you're too intelligent to do that, isn't that right, *sir*?"

I perceive a slightly threatening tone to the way she says *sir*, and I take my finger away from the *end call* button where it has been hovering for the past few seconds. "Um, yes, that's right, Kathleen."

"Good!" she says. "I'm glad you're no longer trying to end the call. There's a camera on your phone by the way, remember? Nice PJs by the way—Old Navy? Oh wait, looking through your purchase history that would be … Ralph Lauren. Wow, too rich for me!"

I shake my head incredulously, both impressed and terrified, and accept the death-by-quicksand fate that I seem to have entered. "Thank you … so uh, what happens now?"

"Now, you wait a few days until I can get a definite ID on our *George Davis*. When I find her, I will provide you all of the information we have on her. The standard menu for this is name, address, phone number, social, known aliases, and points of contact. The cost for this service will be $2,000. We also have specials going on right now for more … premium packages."

"Uh, no thank you—this is more than enough," I say, uncertain of what I even want to do with this information now.

"Oh …" Kathleen says, wavering for the first time. "Well, just for you, Mr. Boston, I can offer you the accidental death package for only $20,000. This is a 67 percent savings from the regular price."

I can't believe what I'm hearing. "Accidental … death? As in murder?"

"Oh no, no, no, no," she says. "Murder is a tremendous liability. We want our clients to experience the comfort of our premium accidental death policy where the intended target will simply have an accident, like a fall or a hospital complication, and it can be as quick and painless as you like. Or … it can be less painless if you prefer of course."

I want to throw my phone in the toilet and hide in a bunker for the rest of my life. "Uh, no thank you," I say.

"Oh," she says, disappointed. "We also have a Fall in Love package if that's more what you're looking for. We arrange for a series of circumstances and encounters that highlight your best features to your intended target. If all else fails, we can use more forceful tactics like extortion, hypnotherapy, pharmacological affectation treatments …"

"No. Thank. You." I say, trying to sound firm but also appropriately respectful of Kathleen's terrifying power.

"Oh," she says again. "Well, I see that you aren't interested in these premium packages at this time. We value your patronage and respect your desire to decline at this time … but actually …" she says conspiratorially. I can hear the sound of clicking in the background. "Did you know that this *George Davis* has an Amazon alias where she gives a glowing review for another author other than yourself? She wrote, 'Best new writer in this galaxy or any other.'"

I see George Davis's stupid smile again as he poisons yet another author with his despicable praise and before I can even stop myself … "Death package please," I say. "Definitely the death package."

I can practically hear Kathleen beaming through the telephone. "You won't regret this, Mr. Boston!"

I smile, thinking I just made this nice young lady's day until I realize that I just signed over someone's death.

"Wait, can you at least make it painless?" I say, but the phone has already disconnected.

I stand there frozen, numb from the experience. Was any of that real? Could hackers even do any of this stuff? Why did I even agree to a death package? That definitely wouldn't happen, right? My mind won't stop racing, and my heartbeat won't slow down, so I do what all the great writers who came before me did. I walk over to my alcohol cabinet, do a silent toast to Hemingway, Faulkner, and so many others, and drink to try to forget what a useless piece of human excrement I am.

I wake up the next morning to pounding at the front door to my apartment. Alexandra must have left at some point because this level of noise would have made her hide herself so far under the covers she'd find herself in Narnia. I stumble groggily toward the door until the memory of last night hits me like a cement truck. It's the FBI. Wait, does the FBI knock on the door or do they just battering ram it down while agents rappel in through the windows? I stop abruptly and look for a place to hide until I realize how stupid it would be if the SWAT team found me under the covers with my feet dangling out the side.

"Uh ... who is it?" I call out.

"Honey, it's me," says a familiar female voice. My mother.

"What the hell, Mom," I say, opening the door.

She pushes past me and closes the door, locking the deadbolt and peering through the peephole like a deranged woman.

Her brown eyes are bloodshot and wild, her dark hair is patchy and matted and her clothes look like she spent the afternoon crawling through air ducts.

I give her a hug. "Mom, what happened? Are you okay?"

She pulls away. "Yes, sweetie, are *you* okay? Are you in some kind of trouble?"

I freeze and I pretend I have a sudden fleck in my eye that I need to attend to so I can avoid looking at her directly. My mother is tiny but has a commanding presence about her.

"You *are*, aren't you?" she says. She puts a hand on my shoulder and sits me down on my sofa. "What's going on? I've been trying to reach you all morning. I think someone's after you."

"What?" I stand up and I look at the door and the windows again wondering where and when the battering ram would be coming through. I reach into my pocket for my cellphone, and I see 10 missed calls and a new voicemail alert.

7

She pulls me back down and directs me to look at her. "So look, honey, all morning things have been ... *weird*," she says. "First, I step out the door and I'm on my way to work and everyone I see says *hello* to me, smiling like we're in some kind of '50s sitcom."

I nod knowingly. Definitely weird behavior in Queens.

"OK, but how does that explain ... well, all of *this*?" I ask, gesturing toward her overall appearance.

"Shush, I'm talking," she says, smoothing her hair with her hand a few times. "So then I get on the train and people keep looking at me. A lot of these people pretend like they're reading, but they're not, I can tell. Their eyes are too shifty. And the crazy thing is, they're all reading *your* book."

"Well, maybe there are just a lot of people reading my book in Queens — you know, support the hometown kid," I say, realizing how dumb it sounds as I say it.

"Oh, Brian honey," she says, putting her hand over mine. "Anyway, I get off the train and some kid, maybe 18 or 19 years old, he grabs my briefcase, you know, the heavy brown leather one with my laptop and all my legal papers? So I swing my arm back," she stands and draws her arm up mimicking the action, "and I'm ready to put this poor kid out of his misery ... and then he says 'No, no, no, ma'am, I'm just trying to help you. Your bag looks really heavy.'"

"Wow," I say. "Were you being filmed or something?"

She claps her hands. "That's exactly what I was thinking! So I put my arm down, because there might be cameras, and I let the kid grab my bag because he doesn't look like he's going to make a run for it. And just like he said, he carries the bag off the train, waits for me to get out, then helps me sling the strap over my shoulder."

"And that's it?" I say, growing impatient.

"No — get this. Then he says, 'Have a great day, ma'am. By the way, I'm a huge fan of your son. He's a great writer.'"

That part sends a few chills down my spine, but it feels like, exaggerating anything and everything.

"Okay, slightly ominous, but that's it? That's what you came rushing over here for?"

8

She nods, her face full of concern. "Yes, this is exactly how the feds get you. Haven't you seen any movies where the feds are getting ready to bust someone? Are you in trouble with the feds?"

"Wait, what—the feds?" I ask, laughing uncomfortably. Her repeated use of the word feds was too silly to take seriously.

She eyes me carefully. "So you're not in trouble with the feds?" She stands up and clasps her hands together in prayer while looking up at the ceiling. "Thank you, God."

I start to smile until I remember her disheveled appearance. "Wait—that can't be the end of the story. Why do you look like you picked up some extra shifts as a chimney sweep?"

She scowls. "That's not very nice," she says, looking down at herself. "But this? After the train left, I got to talking with some guy about how weird that kid was who helped me with my bag and then ... I somehow tripped and fell down on to the train tracks," she says the last part quickly.

I bolt up off the sofa. "What!" I shout more as a statement than a question. "Are you okay?"

She waves a hand, dismissing me. "I'm fine, I'm fine. I tried to pull myself up, but I'm so short, and I fell down a few times. That's all, no big deal," she says, looking down. She notices the top two buttons to her blouse have fallen off. As she adjusts, I instinctively look away—no son wants to be looking at his mom's undergarments—growing up I couldn't even look at the neatly folded ones in the laundry. Unfortunately I catch a glimpse before I can turn away, and just as I'm about to curse myself for my bad luck, a horrible thought occurs to me.

"Mom ... that bra," I say, pointing at her.

"Brian!" she says, quickly covering herself.

"Tan and lace, kind of fancy, really cute actually," I recite robotically, feeling the reality set in.

My mom looks down and smiles, impressed with her own bra, then eyes me suspiciously. "I'm glad you think so. Are you researching lingerie for a new book or something?"

9

I groan loudly. "Mom! You're ... George Davis?"

I can't remember the last time I've ever seen my mom this caught off guard.

"What? Wh-what are you talking about? You know that my name is Barbara Delilah Bo—"

"Cut the crap, Mom. I know it's you. *You* wrote that review for my book? Best new writer of this generation?"

She puts her hands on her hips. "Well. Some sons would be grateful to have such a proud mother." She points a finger at my chest. "Do you know how hard it was to post that? I had to slip Ivan my tech wiz at work *five hundred bucks* to hide it from you because I knew — I just knew you'd never forgive me if you knew I wrote that."

"Ugh, Mom, how could you? What's wrong with you — who does something like that?" I cut myself short because I feel like if I say any more, some hand of God will come and strike me down for my hypocrisy.

"Mom, I need to check my phone," I say hurriedly. I grab my phone and pull up the voicemail messages, deleting the frantic and nonsensical messages from my mother until I get to the one from Kathleen.

"Hello, Mr. Boston!" Kathleen says over the recording. "I have wonderful news — I've found our *George Davis*! But Mr. Boston, it seems like we may have a problem. It looks like *George Davis* is also known as Barbara Delilah Boston, and although this is quite an awkward situation this being your mother and all, unfortunately you've ordered the nonrefundable death package. Please call me at 999-999-9999 as soon as you can, and I'll see what I can do to ensure you have a satisfactory resolution. Failure to respond to this message promptly will result in continuation of the plan and the tragic, purely 100 percent guaranteed accidental demise of your mother. Thank you and hope you have a fabulous day!"

I dial the number on my phone faster than I've ever dialed a number in my life. The phone rings once and Kathleen answers.

"Mr. Boston?" she asks. "What can I help you with? Has your mother fallen victim to an accidental death to your satisfaction?"

"Cancel it!" I say it so loudly my mother jumps.

"Mr. Boston, unfortunately the order has already been put in for the absolutely accidental death package. So your mother is—"

"She's alive!" I yell. I glance at my mother who is eyeing me now, burning judgment directly into my soul. "Uh, she's alive," I say more calmly.

"Oh!" Kathleen says. "Well, in that case, yes—the order can most certainly be canceled although it is unusual that your mother did not fall victim to a completely accidental and unavoidable death as guaranteed in your $20,000 accidental death package."

I walk toward the bedroom, trying to escape the listening range of my mother. "Yes, yes, please just cancel it."

"Absolutely, Mr. Boston. I will need you to state your desired intention as such—for legal purposes, surely you understand. 'I, Brian Boston, hereby agree to cancel the accidental death package for one George Davis, also known as Barbara Delilah Boston, per provision 134—failure to adequately execute death by accidental or unintentional means to the full and total satisfaction of the customer.'"

"I, I can't remember all that," I say, glancing back at my mother. I quickly open the door to my room and go inside and close the door so she can't hear.

"Alright, that's not a problem, sir," she says. "We can say it one line at a time. I, Brian Boston," she says.

"I, Brian Boston," I repeat.

"Hereby agree to cancel the accidental death package," she says.

I hear footsteps by my door—I can almost feel my mother's presence there.

I mumble the entire speech quickly, straining to hear for any signs of surprise from the other side of the door.

Kathleen seems delighted. "Wow, Mr. Boston, I don't think anyone has ever been able to recite that all at once like that! Then, per provision 134, your death package has been canceled. And just in time too. One of our dedicated quality

11

assurance representatives was downstairs in the apartment below, about to accidentally knock over a candle next to some highly flammable polyester curtains. People sure can be clumsy these days!"

"Yes, um, thank you, Kathleen. Please withdraw whatever I owe you and take some for your, uh … excellent service also. You've been, um, great."

"Why thank you, sir!" she says. "Already done!"

I hang up the phone, barely able to breathe from all of the bated breaths.

My mother knocks and enters the room before I can respond. Classic mom move.

"I know you were at the door, Mom," I say.

She puts her hands up defensively. "No, no, I didn't hear anything. Are you okay?"

I walk over and hug her.

She shrieks in pain. "Ow, not so tight, you're killing me!"

I pull back quickly. I look at her to make sure she's alright, and she smiles back at me slyly.

"Mom!" I say.

"Yeah, yeah, maybe I heard a little," she says. "I don't know what kind of dark stuff you've been getting into, but sounds like you don't want to kill me anymore, so that's good, I guess."

"Ugh, Mom. I didn't *know*," I say. "And hey, who says you get to be off the hook for the black ops stuff you pulled to write that review?"

She nods appreciatively. "Yeah, probably shouldn't have done that," she says.

I look at her thoughtfully. "Did you mean it though?" I ask.

"The review?" she says. She looks at me for an extra half second which means she's being serious now. "I'm your mom, so of course I did. You're the best, kid."

Then I remember something and I feel a flash of anger. "*Actually*," I say. "It looks like you wrote a similar review for someone else."

I can see the guilt in her eyes. "Well, you see, my friend

12

Nancy has a son, and he just wasn't getting any good reviews on his first book so I—"

"Mom!" I say.

She comes over and pinches my cheek. "Oh, so insecure! He means nothing to me, I promise," she says, holding up her left hand in what looks like some kind of Vulcan salute. "I love you, my murderous little bubby."

"I love you, Mom," I say, feeling exhausted and relieved and still terrified all at the same time.

Later on that night, alone in my room sitting in front of my computer, I smile with sudden realization. I'm not a brilliant writer after all. I sigh with relief. Now I can write that bestseller. I close my eyes and start to think of all of the directions I should go with my next book.

But one thing this all has taught me is that I'm also a pretty terrible person. I take my phone out of my pocket and dial.

"Hi, Kathleen!" I say before she has a chance to answer.

"Hi, Mr. Boston!" she responds, seemingly overjoyed by my enthusiasm.

"Do you happen to have a *premium package* that can say, make a manuscript appear on my doorstep that will be a guaranteed bestseller?"

Kathleen doesn't hesitate. "Well, Mr. Boston, I was wondering when you'd ask! You'd be surprised how many of these I've delivered. Now would you like that as an accidentally erased file from an aspiring young writer or perhaps a hallucinogen-induced work from a tortured genius? We can have it to you right in time for your deadline!"

"Option one, please!" I say and finish placing my order with Kathleen.

I lean back in my chair, unsure of what I should do now with all this time on my hands. Of course, I already know the answer. I click open the Amazon review page, sort by 1-star reviews, and start to read. I wonder how many Accidental Death Packages I can afford.

A Visit with My Dad

Janice Coy

On February 10, 2020, my dad and I hugged goodbye, neither of us knowing that it would be the last time we would see each other in person for more than a year. And that our next visit would be our last.

That February visit passed like any other year.

I arrived on a Tuesday at the Sacramento airport, took a bus downtown, and had lunch near the state capitol building with a longtime friend. When I showed up later at my dad's, we settled into the living room, as usual, with my stepmom, all with our individual, small trays of cut-up vegetables, wooden bowls of nuts, and glasses of wine to watch the sunset. The backyard trees were bare and had grown tall enough to see below the branches to the hilltops beyond. I munched on carrot sticks and peanuts as the sun sank in a final blaze of light, shading the winter clouds with golds and dark pinks. After, we watched the nightly news with Lester Holt. Delicious smells emanated from the kitchen.

"Can I help?"

"No." My stepmom shooed me away from the stove with her wooden spoon. "Sit with your dad."

Dinner was served in the more formal setting of the dining room where candles were lit, and toasts were made. Breakfast and lunch were always at the round kitchen table where we each had our unique napkin ring.

The next day, my dad drove us along winding country roads to lunch at a nursery where a greenhouse had been converted to an outdoor restaurant. His uneven driving was a contentious subject between his children and the state of California. We all thought he should no longer be driving

14

(there was debate about whether he could at least drive in their 55 + community) but the state kept giving him a license.

"As long as he passes the eye test and the written test, they won't give him a driving test and they keep renewing his license," my stepmom would say. She was in the camp that he should no longer drive. But she also was legally blind so needed him to grocery shop and take her to the hair salon.

"I'm thinking of getting an electric car like yours," my dad told me. "But I think it would make more sense at my age to lease it." He was 92 after all and unsure it was economically feasible to purchase a car. "Each morning I wake up and think *well, I'm still here* and I just see what the day will bring."

He added that he thought often about something an older gentleman at our church used to say, "This is the day the Lord has made, I will rejoice and be glad in it."

That February, my stepmom wasn't satisfied with how their front courtyard was looking with its jumble of pots and mismatched plants. So, after lunch, we spent some time wandering around the nursery, looking at all kinds of plants, plain clay and painted pots, and gurgling water fountains.

"The trees in the courtyard are leafless," my dad grumbled. "How can you imagine anything new until the leaves come out? It might already look better than you think."

My dad was never one to wander. He always had a destination, a plan, a goal in mind. He finally threw up his hands, returned to the car, and waited in the driver seat for us to return.

The next morning, I rose early, dressing warmly for the colder Northern California temperature, intending to walk on the neighborhood path referred to as the seep trail because of its distinctive geological feature. Trees and bushes thrived in the folds of the wet seep throughout the year. The scent of freshly brewed coffee drew me to the sunlit kitchen where my dad was already dressed for the day and busy preparing breakfast. Mugs were out and ready to be filled. Two individual white fluted bowls of diced fruit—melons and bananas—were on the counter. The fruit was for my stepmom and me; he had eaten.

15

"Coffee's ready," he said, pulling over a mug for me. His voice sounded gravely, and he cleared his throat.

"I'm going for a walk," I said.

"Hold on." He settled the empty mug back in its spot. "I'll join you."

He grabbed his jacket from the closet and the walking sticks he used to keep his balance. He settled his driving cap, pulling it low on his brow. He still had some hair, but not enough to keep his head warm.

The paved trail started at the end of his block and wound up a hillside with an open vista to the south of winter-brown grass and the always green seep area. Birds trilled in the thickly entwined branches providing a musical background. The air smelled clean after last night's rain. The details of our conversation escape me, but we probably talked about the topics we usually covered: his volunteer work on various community committees, my latest writing project, family, and world happenings. He had worked on engineering projects around the world, so I was always interested in his thoughts.

I offered to drive my stepmom to another nursery the following day so that my dad could rest and not be subject to our aimless poking around. Fortunately, he agreed. It was the first time he let me drive his car since my college graduation.

My husband arrived Friday and the four of us went to the community gym where we each pursued our own exercise regimens. Both my dad and stepmom had recently decided that the group exercise class was too much for them.

"Between square dancing, getting up early for swimming, and working out, we're just too tired all the time," they said. We should all be so lucky.

Saturday morning was for sourdough waffles made from scratch—a family tradition. The four-hundred-year-old sourdough starter was brought all the way from Italy on the airplane, stored in a cooler. My dad had twice gifted me with some of the precious sourdough starter but, each time, I forgot to set some aside for the next batch of waffles.

"No more starter for you," my dad said with a laugh. My dad was known for his corny jokes, but despite his chuckle, I

16

knew he was serious about this.

We talked about how we would see them in August in Los Angeles for a grandniece's wedding and, after breakfast, said our goodbyes.

Shortly after, the state was shut down due to the worldwide COVID-19 pandemic and travel was restricted. The wedding was postponed. My dad figured out how to use Zoom, and we wished each other happy birthdays over the Internet. We talked on the phone every week; we Facetimed once — my dad wasn't a fan; we zoomed at Christmas.

My husband and I planned another visit north when we were all vaccinated against COVID-19, but my dad was diagnosed March 13, 2021, with cancer that had spread to his liver. The doctors couldn't predict how much longer he would live.

We decided our visit couldn't wait, and we drove north through the spring green Central Valley where the almond trees were beginning to blossom.

My dad was just home from the hospital when we arrived. I was shocked at how thin both he and my stepmom looked. My dad considered me with curiosity.

"Where did you come from?" he said. The doctor said the cancer might affect his brain.

"We drove from San Diego, Dad," I said, trying to hide my concern at his question. Didn't he recognize me? Further conversations revealed that he was rooted in the present. Each day was new to him. Each time someone told him of his cancer diagnosis he expressed surprise.

We didn't sit in the living room to watch the sunset or gather for dinner at the dining table. Instead, we huddled around the breakfast table in the kitchen for takeout burgers and fries because it was a better fit for my dad's wheelchair. My stepmom picked at her food; she had no appetite.

My dad hadn't lost his sense of humor. When my husband presented him with an inflated plastic donut for his wheelchair, he set it on his head like a hat.

"Is this where it goes?" he said smiling his same impish grin. We all had a good laugh.

My dad slept late the next morning, and I spent some time in the redone front courtyard that was only a conversation on my last visit. The leafed-out trees formed the arch my stepmom had pictured; new pots lined the low wall fronting their street; the gravel path that wound around the side of their house to their backyard was raked and fitted with new wooden borders. A neat hedge bloomed with purple flowers that had a delicate scent and petals that were soft to the touch.

Our visit passed in a blur of setting up a hospital bed, installing a handheld shower head, signing up with hospice, and phone calls with doctors and other family members. Each night I collapsed in bed numb and too exhausted to grieve.

One afternoon, my husband and I took a break to head up the seep trail. It felt odd to walk the path without my dad, a familiar companion beside me on other visits.

The hillside was awash in green; a plethora of rabbits grazed near the edge of the wetlands; birds sang in the trees; my husband spotted a bobcat before it disappeared into the thick brush.

My dad was propped in his favorite chair in the living room, a blanket draped over his knees, when we returned.

"We saw a bobcat," I said. "It froze at the edge of the thicket and stared at us."

"A bobcat," he nodded. "I haven't seen one."

Did he mean on the seep trail or ever? I couldn't tell.

My goodbye this time was sad. My voice rough when I told him I loved him, the grief surfacing now that the rush of getting him settled was past. My lips brushed the warm skin of his forehead. This could be my last personal contact with my dad ever. I mourned the missed year of in-person visits, the way I had always assumed my dad would be around. We promised to head north again in a few weeks.

My tears flowed, stopped, then started anew as we drove home through the Central Valley speeding south to San Diego. Weathered farmhouses and scattered cows grazing on the verdant hills were mere flashes through the car window. The hours passed with memories both happy and sad, alternating between chuckles and sobs. My dad was 93, and it

18

had seemed like he would live forever or at least until 97 like his own dad.

At home, I spoke on the phone with my dad as often as possible. He spent most of his days sleeping now so our conversations lasted only a few moments. Mostly, he listened to me talk. My stepmom told me sometimes he saw fairies dancing in the garden outside their bedroom window. We didn't get to be with him again before he died April 6 while holding my stepmom's hand.

I'm going to sit in the garden on my next visit. When the sun sets over the neighbors' tile rooftops, I'll lift my wine glass in a toast to my dad. I'll walk the neighborhood trail and think of my dad ambling up the hill beside me, my memories alive as the evergreen seep despite the changing seasons.

And maybe, I'll sneak some of that sourdough waffle starter to bring home.

EMBER X

Leon Lazarus

10

The blurred lime green number was followed by garbled writing and quickly replaced by a square cursor blinking in its place. He couldn't remember. Was it words?

Ten? Ten what?

Oskar screwed his eyelids together. The room looked clearer when he opened them.

Percent? Days?

The cursor raced across the glass dome dropping letters behind it.

10 Minutes to Life Support Failure.
Cryopod O^2 Level Critical.

Then,

9 Minutes to Life Support Failure.

Somewhere, buried deep, Oskar knew what to do. He pulled the pod cover emergency release handle. The glass dome sailed up and back. He wiped at the sleep crust gumming the outside edges of his eyes. His gloved knuckle banged against the clear helmet visor and he remembered where he was, in the most general sense.

Space.

The Ember X.

The cryo bay.

There was nothing unusual about waking up disoriented. He had made the trip from Saurus to Danen and back enough times to know that the human body did not take well to stasis. Just another feature of deep space travel. The low oxygen levels in the pod seemed to have made it worse.

He reached up and snapped the latch on the restraint that

20

attached the helmet to the cryo-pod. Every suit had three magnetic restraint points. Head, hips, and knees. Protection in the event of gravity failure or sudden deceleration. He sat up, or at least attempted to. The muscles in his stomach cramped into a tight ball and twitched. He groaned and turned to the side, using his arm to leverage himself into a sitting position.

Rolling the helmet from side to side, Oskar's neck bones gave an alarming crack and his muscles ached.

"ET. Status update." His voice was dry and broke on the "a". Oskar smiled. It had been thirty-five years at least since he had sounded like that. A stream of data swept up the inside of the visor, tracking in bright trails behind the harlequin green cursor.

Route plots - locked.
Local threat level - low.
Velocity – 0.18
Reactor status –Decommissioned
Solid fuel thrusters – 4%
"ET, please expand fuel and speed."

The square pulsed twice, and a second flood of data filled the visor.

"ET, is this correct? No reactor? We're coasting?"

The visor cleared and a single word flashed in front of his eyes. *Yes.*

Oskar slapped at the remaining release points and swung his legs off the base of the gray metal pod. He leaned his helmet against the lip of the raised pod cover and closed his eyes. Even after a long food-free cryostasis, he still felt bile rising in his throat. Probably thaw-sickness.

"ET, wake the crew."

The green cursor blinked for a long time. *Does not compute. Please rephrase.*

"ET. End all cryo sessions now."

Blink.   Blink.   *Unable to initialize.*

Oskar swept an eye over the nine sealed cryopods in this bay, arranged in a semi-circle around a central workstation. Their covers remained sealed. He waited, hoping for the telltale hiss of pressure equalization as they opened.

"ET, open pods."

Blink.   Blink.   *Unable to initialize.*

He fought to focus his mind. There was an emergency release on the control station. Stretching across to the blue, powder coated steel desk, Oskar slammed his palm down on the large emergency pod depressurization button.

The loud snap of latch releases rang off the bare metal walls, leaping from one pod to the next and ending at the nearest, followed by a deafening silence. The covers rose silently on their hinge points.

"ET, where are the crew?"

Blink.   Blink.   Blink.

On board:

Arends, K – Galley

Avigdor, B – Recycling bay

Daniels, G – Stateroom 7

Denby, T – Stateroom 12

Malinowsky, D – Recycling bay

Ondongwe, C – Loading bay 3

Singh, R – Galley

Tremaine, W – Galley

Volodkin, Y – Galley

"ET, audio link to Yelena, please."

Blink. Blink. Blink. *No response.*

"ET, run a system check. Is there a problem with your code?"

The cursor flashed for a long time. Oskar nibbled at a flap of dry skin that had peeled back from his lip.

The cursor moved. *All available systems nominal.*

"Damn it. I'll check on them myself." He pushed himself up from the pod and swayed for a moment, allowing his legs to get under him. His muscles felt tired, atrophied, more than usual. Maybe he was just getting older. Probably getting too old for this shit.

Oskar gripped one thick gray glove under his armpit and pulled. The sensation of air on his skin tingled. He pulled off the second glove and used both hands to lift the helmet from his head. The air was stale, vaguely reminiscent of plastic containers that hadn't been opened in a long time.

Overcome with an urgency to shed the suit he tugged at the large fabric zipper pull, dragging it down in short bursts. "Dammit. I don't remember this being so hard." With a shrug, the heavy pressure-suit stuffed full of coolant and sensors crumpled around his ankles. Benny called it his technology turd and laughed at his own joke, every time they came out of cryo.

Oskar stepped out of the pile and stretched. His blue bodysuit had clung to his form at the start of the journey, now it was loose, hanging ever so slightly in shallow folds below his arms. The chill of metal floor plates rose through his thin gray cotton socks as he padded over to the rack on the wall behind his pod. Using two fingers, he lifted out the wrap-around data-sight glasses. As they settled on the bridge of his nose, the lenses flickered and the familiar incandescent green type rolled by in his peripheral vision.

He made for the passageway and stateroom seven. If anyone were working on the computer glitch, it would be Graham, the shipnet systems engineer.

The passage followed the curve of the gravity ring, LED clusters stretching away to the left in a graceful arc. The living quarters and cryo bays were placed in two clusters, with maximum distance between them. Space travel was dangerous. A rogue meteorite might take out a crew cluster. The intentional design ensured that at least half the crew would remain alive and capable of completing the mission. Oskar was glad B-block was close by. A trip all the way to A-block would have been painful.

A ragged buzz accompanied by a small shower of sparks snapped Oskar's head up. His eyes locked on a rip in the white cable shielding that ran the length of the juncture between wall and ceiling on his right. The edges were blackened. Burned through. A weapon discharge, perhaps. A shredded red wire swayed in the breeze from a punctured air channel and sparked intermittently.

"ET. Get me Arends."

Blink.　　Blink.　　*Unavailable.*

"ET. Open a commlink with the maintenance bay."

Blink. Blink. *Unmanned.*

Oskar stumbled into a slow jog, ignoring the pain radiating from his joints. Reaching the bulkhead door to Block-B, he leaned against the wall and fought to bring his breathing under control. He could not remember a time he had felt so exhausted and dizzy.

Pushing himself away from the red floor-to-ceiling letter "B" behind his back, he shuffled on, stopping at seven.

He knocked and waited; his hands pressed flat at either side of the door. He knocked again and listened closely. Not a whisper.

"ET. Open seven."

Blink. Blink.

The door slid away into a hidden recess. The bed was unmade. Standard issue sheets on the Ember X were white, but here, the bottom sheet was a mottled brown. Greg never mentioned bringing his own sheets from home. Anyway, Captain Singh would never have allowed it. Even a cargo vessel like the Ember X was subject to company rules.

Oskar crossed the floor, stepping over a discarded pair of data-sights. He touched the sheet. Rust flakes came away, disintegrating into a fine powder that rose on soft currents. A faintly metallic pungency infiltrated the air around him, triggering a deep, limbic response that sent him stumbling to the door, retching.

"ET, please. Get anyone on the comms."

Blink. Blink. *Unavailable.*

A truth began to scratch at the very darkest recesses of Oskar's mind.

"ET. Show me crew locations."

A floorplan scrolled out from the center of the data-sight with clusters of red pinpoints. Oskar's blood chilled in his veins. He was directly beside Gregory on the map. Not easily scared, he nevertheless spun around, expecting to see a body or a— something. He reached down and picked up the glasses from the floor. Greg's red dot radiated rings, showing movement. It was the only one. Oskar dropped it to the floor.

Oskar's face flushed and he felt a tightness in his chest. He ran from the room, his hand slapping against the passage wall as he faltered and stumbled onward. He dropped back against the wall outside stateroom twelve and barked the open command. A knot of apprehension wound tighter in his gut. The door slid away. Another vacant room. Shipshape, this one. Neat edges to the bed. Denby's kitbag was on the nightstand. His data-sight hung from a loop on the front pocket.

"Holy mother of — where is everybody?" Oskar hissed under his breath. He turned to the empty passage and screamed, "hellooooo…"

The ship's white noise deadened the yell.

Tears burned his eyes. He wasn't sure if it was frustration, or fear, or the growing sense of isolation that had begun to suffocate him. Staring at the crew tracker, he waited for any sign of movement. Just one ping. That would be good. Then the grip of a firm handshake. Perhaps a hug. How are you doing after cryo? Can I get you a bite to eat? You've got mail from home, bud. Mail. Mail from home. Heia would be waiting for word. Max would be turning ten about now. They would have sent him messages, regularly. This far out, his family's messages might be a few months out of date, but he'd have them on screen.

Running again, Oskar made for the elevator. Most of the crew were in the galley on level two. The two mail bays were there, alongside the food rehydrator. Say a quick hi, then grab a plate of something hot and eat while he caught up on news from home.

The yellow elevator doors set into the tube-shaft snapped open as Oskar approached. He stumbled in, collapsing to the floor against the far wall and sitting with his legs out in front of him, marionette style. Accelerate. Decelerate. Stop. The doors opened. He clambered up and lurched out into the atrium behind the bridge. No one in there. No one out here.

He cocked his head. Music. It was faint, but familiar. *Songs For Drella,* Yelena's favorite album. Unmistakably Lou Reed, the voice was streetwise and tired and pissed-off.

Oskar struggled to remember the words and sang *Starlight* in snippets as he walked, following the source of the song. He and Yelena had listened to the album a hundred times at least. She had a playlist to accompany her on EVAs, sort of a good luck charm. She floated more than any of the crew. As the ion drive engineer, she spent a lot of time fine tuning those reflector blades. If you went extra-vehicular, you were on her turf.

"It's the only music fit for a walk among the stars," Yelena would say.

Oskar's steps quickened as he approached the galley, and the music became louder. The sliding automatic door, jammed by an overturned chair, closed, and opened, closed, and opened, closed, and opened. The song ended, leaving the shuh-dunk, shuh-dunk of the door to expand into the quiet. Then, the song began again.

Oskar stepped over the chair and kicked it into the passage. The door slid closed with a soft, grateful hiss.

Three of the four round-top tables that once were artfully arranged in a diamond pattern, three chairs to each, now lay scattered. Only one remained standing. Yelena sat beside it on a chair, her head on her folded arms and her long auburn hair covering her face.

"Yelena?" Oskar whispered, and crept forward, keeping a wary eye on the room. "Yellie, you okay?" He reached out to place a friendly hand on her back.

His fingers brushed the arm of her overall. With a muffled click, her shoulder dislocated. The overalls sagged and, with a dry clatter, folded in on themselves and slipped from the table. Bones scattered across Oskar's feet. He screamed, but only a choked gargling sound left his throat. Yelena's head rolled to the side and flakes of ancient, desiccated skin dropped from white bone, salting the table. Her sockets stared across the room. The jaw released and clattered to rest alongside a seven-petawatt sidearm. One bony knuckle remained lodged in the trigger guard.

* * *

26

Oskar awoke to Lou Reed. *Starlight*. His head hurt. He felt around the back of his skull and came away bloodied. A swelling had formed. It throbbed. He remembered and scrambled back, sending bones skittering away in every direction. A desperate sob broke free and he doubled forward, clutching his knees. Drool dripped from his chin onto his legs, and he slapped the strands away with a feral cry.

Pitching forward onto his knees, Oskar stood and forced himself to look again. To see. Wiping away tears, he reached for a strip of white plastic that lay in the folds of Yelena's overalls. Tightly written hand script covered the surface. As an afterthought, he slid the sidearm off the table and tucked it into his waistband, leaving the knuckle bone spinning on the tabletop. An involuntary shudder wracked him.

Setting the table nearest the entrance on its base, he laid out the long strip. The permanent marker was hard to read on the textured surface and it had faded in places.

In his mind, Oskar could hear Yelena's voice, loud, above the din of the blaring music.

"Dear Ozzie,

I'm sorry I left you such a mess. We hit a patch of space dust. The plasma burst killed our fuel rods and the ion drive failed. Also, ET was fried. Two banks had holes burned through them. I failed. There's no way to get us past 0.2 light speed and not enough power for outbound quantum signaling. We'll be behind ULAS J0744+25 for about eight hundred years at this speed, so normal comms is useless. I managed to set ET to pick up stray inbound signals on the bend, so we do get some messages.

I woke Greg and he brought ET partially back online. He wrote some code and rerouted as many circuits as he could. ET can't manage cryo or reset course now, so your pod is autonomous, and we aren't turning around.

When the food ran out, Greg fought me. He hurt me bad. I was locked out behind the bulkheads, so I came in the airlock and got him in his bed. Dumb systems engineers, you know. Sorry, I remember you were friends. There was no choice,

27

though. I was hungry.

I made sure it was quick for each of them and rationed them carefully. Apart from Greg, I got them as they came out of stasis.

Anyhow, I left you to sleep until your cryopod runs dry. We had some good times.

Hopefully help is on the way and when you wake up, you'll be rescued.

Love,
Yellie
April 1, 2210

* * *

Oskar carefully rolled the plastic strip into a tight spiral and gripped it to his side. Numb, he walked over to the mail bays and crumpled into a seat. "ET, open my mail." His tongue stuck to his teeth.

A hologram of forty or fifty clusters of mail items floated in the air above the desktop. Oskar tapped one near the top left.

August 7, 2209.

A fragile holograph of his son floated up. "Daddy, mom bought me new shoes. Look. They have Captain Fi—" The image splintered.

He tapped another, closer to the middle.

January 22, 2214

His wife's face was lined and weary. "Hey darlin'. If you get this, we miss you. I'll keep sending these for as long as it takes. Come home soon, okay. Max is doing good. He asks about you."

Oskar's hand shook as he reached out to tap a message lower down.

November 19, 2231

"Hey Dad. It's Max."

Max? His son. A man with graying temples.

"I'm sure you'll never see this, but Mom asked me to send it anyway. She said she loves you. She— well, she died, you

28

know. She was sick, and old. I'm sorry. This is stupid." Max's lip quivered, and he turned away as the image blinked out.

March 1, 2250

Max's face, old and deeply worn, stared impassively. He sat, quietly, looking through Oskar at something far beyond. He said nothing, but Oskar knew. This would be Max's final communication.

Oskar reached out and touched the message at the very bottom of the last cluster.

August 10, 2691

The message flickered in and out. Mostly static and garbled shards. Then it ended.

Oskar slowly pushed back the chair and stood, hunched. Thirst and hunger were now pushing to the fore. Adrenaline had squelched it earlier. He shuffled over to the row of portholes that lined the wall between the rehydration equipment and food storage. Stripped of dreams, and hope, he stared out into the black void that lay beyond the outer halo.

His hand slipped down to his waistband and felt for the comforting bump of the sidearm as *Starlight* played one more time.

THE END

An American Gathering

Al Converse

Expecting a ten-minute wait, the old man, still spry, entered the austere waiting room. The less than comfortable chairs stood arranged in strict order. Early, in order to expedite his blood work and be out of the damn place, the old man approached the ticket number dispenser and turned toward the only other occupant of the room.

"Guess we gotta take a number, huh?" he said.

The middle-aged Latino man glanced up. "Oh, yeah."

"You wanna take one?"

The middle-aged guy moved up to the counter and pulled B-1.

The old man pulled the next, B-2. "Just like Bingo."

Another man, bedraggled, shuffled in as the VA worker turned on the light in the blood draw room.

"Take a number," she yawned and sat down.

The guy, limping and moving slow, reached the number dispenser and pulled B-3.

"Good morning," the old man said.

The gimpy black man ignored him.

At seven o'clock the VA worker slid open her little window and called the guy with number B-1. He went inside, came out a few minutes later, looked around and picked up his urine sample cup and went to the head.

After a few minutes fussing with paperwork at the front desk the VA worker, trim, black, and moving deliberately called the old man's number, her no nonsense officious tone muffled by her downcast head.

The old man entered and sat in the chair.

She began, "Name and date of birth."

30

She could have at least said please, the old man thought. Instead, he said, "It's a beautiful morning." After a pause he added his name and birth date.

"I'd rather not be here this morning," She rubbed the vein in his arm with antiseptic.

She's human the old man thought. "Yeah, they got ya covering the desk and coming back here to draw blood. They ought a give you some help."

She drew the blood, pushed a gauze pad on the spot, and said, "Pressure."

The old man, detecting some softness in her voice, pressed his fingers on the pad.

"Okay, you're finished," she said with an uptick in warmth.

"You have a good day," the old man said smiling.

"You too, sir."

The VA worker had served as a hospital corpsman with a Marine company in Afghanistan and got her VA job after mustering out. The old man had served as a watch officer on a Navy ship in Vietnam. The middle-aged man had served in the First Gulf War as a tank driver, and the gimpy black man had served as a Marine, in country, Vietnam.

Dalia's Swan Song

HR Goold

"If you only play ten notes over and over again, is it still a song?" Dalia murmurs. Leaving the corner and her blanket, she approaches the dusty grand piano sitting on a raised platform in the middle of the hall. The large skylight filters muddled moonlight over the area.

"I think even two notes could make a song, even if it is rather repetitive. After all, aren't most things repetitive?" She argues with herself, leaning over the keys.

The heavy clouds that scatter across the sky begin to let go the rain. The soft pattering noises on the old panes make her think of all the history that could have happened in this one hall. Her eyes drift back to the piano.

"I wonder ... "

Sitting on the matching, rickety stool, Dalia presses her fingers into the first chord. The piano is a little sour but still somewhat in tune.

Though she was unsure when or how she had left that dreary home for the elderly, she guessed there was always a reason one ends up where they do. She took a breath, appreciating the petrichor that drifts through the oilskin-covered windows. She begins to hum along with the chords.

"When was the last time someone played you?" Dalia asks. The piano wheezes in response. Another sour note. She laughs. It has been a while for her as well.

"My true love, the rain, brings my body pain." She sings aloud. "Sleep deserts me, attempts at sleep are in vain." She laughs at her feeble attempt at poetry.

"I haven't slept in so long," she continues, "it's always so hard. How can I sleep tonight, when my companion is like a bard?"

She pauses for a small interlude. She opens her mouth to start another joking verse when a male voice queries, "Like a bard?"

Dalia lets out a squeak and her fingers slam onto the keys.

"Oh sorry, did I startle you?" The kind tenor voice apologizes.

Dalia whispers a small apology to the piano. She grimaces as she turns slowly, surprised to see a drenched traveler. "Ah, I suppose so. Who, uh. Not to be rude, but who are you?"

Dalia evaluates what she sees. He isn't terribly tall, but a good height for a working man. His khaki pants and tan shirt covered by a worn leather jacket indicate he is not wealthy. His hair is long and whips around his face in wet, blond curls. Carrying a pack too small for workmen's tools but heavy nonetheless, he hefts it onto his sloped shoulders with practiced ease.

Below the platform, leaning against one of the linen-covered tables, he replies, "Phinn. What are you doing here?" he asks with some concern in his voice.

"I guess I don't know." She gazes around at the old hall, a shadow of its vibrant history. She begins to feel rather underdressed in her light yellow shift. "I woke up here." She shivers, her bare feet suddenly cold.

"I liked your song."

Dalia laughs. "It wasn't much of a song, was it?" The corners of her mouth tremble good-naturedly. "You don't have to lie. I'm not very good."

His grin is crooked and friendly. "Nonsense. I can't play a single note! Teach me?"

Warmed merely by the gesture, she nods with a smile. "Okay, Phinn, but only if you tell me what you were doing in that storm?"

"Deal. How about in song form?" His eyes glimmer playfully.

The two can't contain their giggles. "Okay, come up here, I'll show you some of the basics I know."

Phinn drops his pack onto the floor by the tables and

rushes up the few steps to where she sits. He settles on the old stool next to her.

"I'm Dalia," she introduces herself to her new pupil.

"I know," he answers, his eyes betraying a wisdom beyond his age.

Letting his revelation rest within, Dalia directs his fingers to play a few chords. *He was right. He isn't very good. And his memory of the keys seems a little shoddy. How much is he actually focusing on my teachings?*

After he starts to get the hang of it, she surprises herself by laying her head on his shoulder. "If you only play ten notes over and over again, is it still a song?" She hums her new tune under her breath.

Phinn halts his playing. He wraps an arm around her. "I think even one note can be a song, even though it's repetitive."

Dalia frowns and pulls her head up, just enough to look at him properly. "One note? Don't you need at least two?"

Phinn's brow furrows. "Yeah. Just one. See?" He presses down on one key. "It's beautiful all in itself."

Dalia begins to play the old piano once more. "But accompaniment, rhythm, melodies and backgrounds ... "

Phinn places his hands over hers.

"Dalia, think of one note as a person." He plays the one note again. "That one person, note, is also beautiful in their own way. One note can't be a complicated song, it needs other notes." He presses a chord. "The same is true for people. One person can be their note, but only by being with others can they create a chord." He begins to play again. "Or a song. See?"

Dalia's shoulders grow tense, her hands hover over the keys, unsure if she should stop him. Or, maybe she should encourage him?

Phinn continues. "But without that one note, that one person who is off trying to be their own song, cheats both themselves and the symphony." He hits an incomplete chord and looks at Dalia, who winces at the soured finish.

She withdraws her hands from the piano.

34

"But remember, it's one note to one person. One beat to one heart. We can't play anyone's note but our own."

Exhausted, she slumps. "Oh, I guess you're right." Dalia's vision blurs.

His hands cover hers which rest in her lap. They sit together quietly for a time.

Her voice quivers. "Phinn, where am I?"

Taking her hands, Phinn presses them to his lips.

The heavy pattering on the window panes worsens. She looks to the skylight, afraid the old hall is under too much stress.

"Dalia. Dalia." Phinn releases her hands and draws her face toward his own.

Their eyes meet and her tears overflow. Her head falls into his chest, and he holds her there.

"Do you not see, Dalia? You are exactly where you are supposed to be right now." He kisses the top of her head.

"And you … ?" She whispers.

Phinn looks away, gazing at the keys again. "May I play you a song? One that might help you sleep? You sound like you haven't slept well in a while." With no reply, he teases, "You said so in your song."

Dalia offers him a watery grin, instinctively trusting the stranger. "Sure."

Dalia rises and walks off into the darkened corner where she finds her blanket. She wraps herself inside it and lays on the carpeted floor.

Phinn begins to play again. His skills are still subpar, but to Dalia, they produce a masterpiece — more than adequate to soothe her. When she finally falls asleep, Phinn stops.

* * *

The figure contemplates the now-empty blanket. "I didn't realize how lost she would be," he whispers. "Others that find this hall as their waypoint are often more secure in themselves." He smiles softly, "I'm glad she sang one last song."

35

He walks to the table where he'd dropped his pack when he first met Dalia. "She'll be okay now. She's home." He still found it curious that Dalia's exit was so broken and abandoned.

Scooping up his pack, Phinn glides across the grand floor and out of the hall. He situates his pack properly on his sloped shoulders and begins to walk down his path. He stops and turns to watch as the hall slowly fades behind him. Resuming his trek through the woods, he approaches his next assignment, hoping the well-lit cabin appearing in front of him will be a simpler task.

I Bow to You in Honor, America

Dora Klinova

Ten years have passed.
Ten long, short as a blink, saturated and
*   meaningful years.*
America gave me the greatest pleasure: my precious
*   grandson, Dennis.*
America gave me many outstanding friends.
America gave me inspiration and made me a writer.
My stories and articles have been published in many
*   newspapers and magazines.*
America gave me a Merit Award for my poetry.
This silver cup and a few medals crown my
*   intensive ten American years.*
America gave me so much.
I bow to you in honor, America.

I came to America on July 20, 1992. Now is the year 2021. About a year later, on July 20, 2022, I hope, I will celebrate 30 years since my immigration to America. I do not feel these 30 years. It was as if it happened yesterday.

But it doesn't matter how I feel. I am an American for a long time, according to my passport. In my soul, I am still a foreigner and perhaps will feel like this for the rest of my life. The roots we are born with we carry forever. This is the price of immigration.

The first ten years became an intense search for my own place in this new country: years of learning, accepting, denying, welcoming new friends, crying, laughing at myself, and again, continuously searching and studying.

My most important goal was learning English. I didn't let

myself read any book in Russian or watch any movie in Russian, or any Russian TV program. I deleted Russian from my life!

The second important goal was searching for God. Growing up in an atheistic country, I tried to find my way to the Highest Ruler of the Universe. Being Jewish, certainly, I started in Synagogues: Orthodox, Conservative, Reform. Eventually, I became a member of the Temple Emmanuel Reform Synagogue and was for many years. I tried my best with all my willingness and desire, but I barely knew English. They prayed mostly in Hebrew, and I was blank in Hebrew. I finally left.

Somehow, I found Paramahansa Yogananda's teaching and the Self-Realization Fellowship Temple. How I found these teachings, feeling that they are my spiritual path, do not ask me. It is somehow a miracle. There are many thousands of Russian immigrants in San Diego, but as far as I know, I am the only Russian-speaking devotee in our big Temple.

New country and people and various experiences opened wide horizons. Thoughts and ideas swirled in my head. A current of electricity flowed in my body, persistently demanding a discharge. I started to write. To my surprise, essays, poetry, and stories appeared on paper in English, not in Russian! Where and how did I find the exact English words to describe what I felt? What inexplicable power pushed me from inside to write in a barely known language? It is still a big puzzle and a miracle for me. Was it God's insistent will? This wonder is beyond my understanding. Perhaps I will never know the answer.

Many of my stories I read from the stage at San Diego's famous theaters — Old Globe Theater, Old Town Theater and others. I tried many things. Believe or not, I sang with David Letterman, in his show.

Trying to improve my English, I became a member of Toastmaster International Club Saturday Savants, and I was with this club for about 10 years. They asked to prepare speeches, and I did. They were different: serious, funny, sad, or entertaining. Perhaps, they were good; many of my speeches earned awards. One of them I would love to present to your attention.

This speech was presented at the San Diego Toastmasters meeting on October 28, 2006:

"In the beginning of August, I spent 6 days in Los Angeles. I stepped into the Hotel Westin Bonaventure in downtown LA on August 6. On August 12, I stepped out from this gorgeous 35-story building. During 6 days I didn't put my nose out of the hotel, not for a second. I didn't have a need to go beyond the hotel. I permitted myself a complete detachment from the entire world. What magnet kept me in this hotel during this week? It was the worldwide Convocation of Self-Realization Fellowship (SRF). What is SRF? It is a huge organization, a fellowship of followers of Paramahansa Yogananda's teachings.

"In my opinion, these teachings accumulate all the wisdom in the world and really give the followers a clear sense of self-realization. Religious and scientific knowledge, Albert Einstein and Bible, Kabala and Torah, Christianity and Bhagavad Gita, — all are included in these teachings. The more I try to understand, the more I am amazed how deep is this knowledge and how simply it is written. The more I try to follow it, the more I understand how this is not easy. It is awfully hard, because we need to change ourselves. And who are the most stubborn in our entire world? There is no doubt, it is our own selves.

"Each year about five thousand people come to this event from all over the world seeking reinforcement in the SRF teachings. France and Switzerland, Germany and England, Australia and India, Brazil and Canada, Moscow and Argentina — I cannot enumerate all the countries I saw on attendees' name tags. This year for the first time I even saw a group from Japan.

"If people travel from so far to participate in this Convocation, it must be valuable for them. Every year since 1998, I have rushed to the Convocation for wisdom. It is my best vacation that gives me tremendous spiritual uplift and renewal. I am immersed in this energy, I drink these vibrations, they fulfill me so much that I don't want to mix it with anything else. I want to keep it pure. I adore the logic and wisdom of Yogananda's teachings. It teaches me what I should do right now. Here are some principles:

"*SRF teachings believe in reincarnation and in karma*. We are not the bodies, we are souls. This body is our temporary vehicle. This Universe is a perfect balanced system. No debts in the Universe remain unpaid. We come here to work out our karma and to learn.

"*Don't blame your life. You are its creator*. Thought is material energy. It produces everything in the Universe. Each moment we create our own karma. We must be careful how we think and how we act right now.

"*We are not sinners*. Each of us has his own unique talent and came to this Earth for a purpose.

"*Love yourself and love God*. Trust him. God loves each of us, his children, as much as He loved Jesus.

"*Don't be a beggar*. Talk to God persistently, because He is your Father.

"*Do not be afraid of suffering*. Even Jesus suffered. An easy life is not a victorious life.

"*Don't fear death*. When you are alive, you are alive. When you are dead, it is all over. So, what is to fear?

"*Asking for forgiveness is not a disgrace*. Only a strong person can ask for forgiveness.

"*Everything that exists is God*. As you look into the face of each person you meet, think: 'It is God, who has become this form.' So, you are all God in your own form.

"*Power of positive affirmations*. Avoid negative thoughts about yourself forever. As I give this speech, here is what I am thinking: *I am the most beautiful, wonderful me right now. This is my best speech; you are my most charming listeners, and you, all of you, adore me.*"

Yes, there was laughter! Then, I continued.

"The centerpiece of these teachings is Kriya Yoga. Officially, to practice Kriya you need special permission and must go through an initiation. Kriya Yoga initiation is a beautiful ceremony in the Indian tradition, with an ocean of flowers and beautiful peaceful music.

"I-have participated in the flower committee for many years. We prepare three thousand roses and two thousand carnations for this ceremony. The ceremony is just outstandingly touching and beautiful. At the end of the ceremony all two thousand participants were showered with rose petals. The petals are blessed with a special prayer. And people chant: *Roses to the left, roses to the right, roses in front and behind.* Two thousand people softly sing this chant. And you literally feel that you are your own wonderful, sweet, outstandingly incredible, dear self, the most fragrant, gorgeous rose among others. At the end of my Convocation speech, I showered my audience with the rose petals. What a marvelous experience."

That was my speech. You should have seen my toastmaster fellows' shining eyes!

The Maya

Cary Lowe

Under a summer sky streaked with clouds left over from a morning shower, I stood at the edge of a clearing in the Yucatan jungle, ten miles up a rough dirt road leading in from the coast. Where I saw nothing a moment earlier, a figure appeared to my right, just an arm's length away.

Five feet tall, with a bronze complexion and a high forehead sloping back from a prominent nose and deep-set eyes, he looked like he had stepped out of one of the stone friezes I viewed on the side of a temple at Tulum the previous day. Other than his clothes — white cotton shirt, dark slacks, and black leather sandals — he could have been a Maya who confronted Spanish *conquistadores* 400 years ago.

My wife, son, and mother-in-law, meanwhile, had walked over from our rental car. We drove to this remote spot in 1982 to see the partly excavated ruins of Cobá, once a thriving city of 50,000 that dominated the region and built a pyramid a hundred forty feet high, taller than the more famous one at Chichen Itza to the north. On that warm, breezy day, we were the only visitors.

We came on a tip from a friend in Los Angeles, after I related to him a visit the previous year to the thoroughly excavated and well-curated cities at Chichen Itza, Uxmal, and Tulum, also once deep in the jungle and forgotten by all but local villagers. My friend had been a Catholic missionary in Yucatan thirty years earlier, riding burros on dirt trails along the coast and into the jungle to visit villages where locals with ancient-looking rifles stood guard over sacred sites off-limits to outsiders. He urged me not to miss out on visiting this place at the next opportunity.

42

The Maya (as I will call him, since I never learned his name) pointed his left index finger at his chest, spread his arms in our direction, and finally extended his right hand toward the start of a leaf-strewn path leading into the jungle. He spoke a few words in a language I didn't understand, very different from Spanish, and which I assumed to be one of the many native dialects still spoken in the region. I surmised he was offering to guide us.

Apprehensive, I turned to my wife, Joan, and asked in a whisper, "What do you think? Are you okay with following him?"

No taller than the Maya, she looked him in the eye, shrugged, then waved toward the path, which disappeared after just fifty feet or so into the dense, shaded forest. Brett smiled and nodded, showing the excitement of a twelve-year-old on his first adventure trip. Bonnie grimaced but didn't object. With their acquiescence, I turned back to the Maya and gestured for him to proceed.

In moments, the forest enveloped us. Thin trumpet and dogwood trees mingled with sturdy ceiba and mahogany trunks. Plumeria vines burst with ivory blossoms. The path occasionally narrowed to a thread where the wet jungle encroached amid the smoky aroma of rotting vegetation.

While we walked, our guide pointed out stone ruins scattered about in the undergrowth. On our own, we would have missed most of them. Tree roots had broken them up and vines obscured them. Occasionally, he pointed to small hills, no more than ten feet in height, where centuries of jungle growth covered the remains of toppled structures. And, at every turn, he showed us the barely visible remnants of stone paths that once connected Cobá to outlying communities throughout the region.

The Maya spoke neither Spanish nor English, and we didn't know a word of his language, yet I felt like I understood everything he explained using hand gestures, facial expressions, and occasional sounds. Those forms of communication apparently are universal, I thought. A pocket guidebook we purchased at Tulum helped too, allowing us to attach names and detailed identities to the more prominent ruins.

A steady breeze off the ocean kept the humidity down. It also kept the mosquitos away. Instead, the jungle teemed with butterflies—many sizes and colors, but mostly a striking variety with a four-inch wingspan, black with iridescent blue markings.

A half hour into our walk, we came upon Ixmoja, the central pyramid. Unlike the fine stonework and intricate decoration of its counterpart at Chichen Itza, this one looked as if constructed in a hurry. Its hundred twenty stairs, running the entire width of the structure on all four sides, were uneven and narrow, with varying heights and rough surfaces. Roots snaked out from between the stones and randomly draped the steps.

Climbing El Castillo at Chichen Itza, allowed in those days, felt safe. This pyramid looked much less stable and a lot riskier. Still, when the Maya gestured for me to follow him, I couldn't resist the challenge. The others waved to me to go, though Joan's smile looked pained.

I understand today a heavy rope provides some security for climbers. Not then. I watched where the Maya planted his feet and tried to follow closely. I assumed he had made this climb many times. Despite a few slips, we ascended without serious incident. From the flat top, where a ceremonial structure probably once stood, we looked out over a jungle that reached to the horizon in all directions—except the east, where we could see the turquoise blue of the Cozumel Channel in the distance. The shallow limestone shelf of the Yucatan Peninsula kept trees from sinking deep roots, limiting their height to about half that of the pyramid. From the edge of the platform, I waved at my family, who looked as small as jungle bugs.

Then, the Maya motioned to me to follow him back down. The stairs seemed scarily steep, much steeper than they looked or felt on the way up. A misstep could be disastrous. Seeing me hesitate, the Maya pointed at his eyes, then at his feet. The trick, I understood, was to focus precisely on where one stepped and avoid looking farther down the stairs.

With that, the Maya began one rapid step after another. Most stairs were uneven and just a few inches deep, too narrow to plant our feet firmly. Trying hard to focus on each next step, I followed close behind him. But, as we picked up speed, my caution evaporated, and I felt like we flew down the face of the pyramid, our feet barely touching the stones. By the time we reached the bottom, sweat soaked my shirt and my heart pounded like that of a sprinter at the finish line. My rubber-soled athletic shoes had performed admirably. I marveled that he could make that descent in loose-fitting sandals.

Joan and the others applauded our feat. The Maya, deadpan serious until now, gave me a big smile.

After a brief rest, we continued on what turned out to be a roughly circular path. As we passed through an area of particularly large trees, the Maya paused, reached down, and picked up two round, brown seeds, each the diameter of a quarter coin but a half inch thick and circled by a pale white band. He held them close to his eyes, then acted out a person seeing visions or experiencing an altered state of mind. Finally, he conjured an image of a ceremony set there in the jungle. I wondered if the contemporary Maya still used these hallucinogenic seeds in religious or cultural rituals. He handed me the seeds and indicated to me to keep them. As I placed them in the pocket of my shorts, he nodded.

The path soon led us back to the road, within sight of where we had entered the jungle. I tried my best to express appreciation to the Maya for the unexpected adventure he provided us. I thanked him in English and Spanish, hoping he knew those words in one language or the other. Wanting to reward him, I looked to Joan, standing behind me, and asked for some Mexican currency.

I then turned back to the Maya, only to find him gone, disappeared, as quietly and suddenly as he had appeared two hours earlier. Confused, I asked the others, "Where is he? Did you see where he went?"

No one replied. They all looked equally puzzled.

45

"Did this really happen?" I asked. "Was he really here?" They all nodded. As we walked back to our car, I glanced back over my shoulder several times, thinking I might glimpse the Maya at the edge of the jungle, but I saw nothing.

Two days later, we flew back to Los Angeles. As we unpacked, I came across the seeds given me by the Maya. I still have them. One of these days, I'll overcome my inhibitions and try them. Then maybe the Maya will reappear and guide me on an even more mystical adventure.

Three Past Midnight

Richard Peterson

His Movado Swiss watch read 2:10 a.m. Elliston Trevor smiled and gunned the Mercedes-Benz CLS-Class. He couldn't help himself. What a sweet ride, he thought. He looked to his left and examined the small gray Toyota idling next to him at the stoplight. Drab and generic, he thought sourly. A sorry way to live.

The light changed and he pulled out. Just then the Mercedes comm setup buzzed.

"Hey, E, what's cookin'?" The soft female voice was almost a purr.

"Nothing much," he said. "Just an emerald and diamond brooch, and a sapphire ring."

"Jackpot!"

He laughed. "You love your jewelry, don't you?"

The purr again. "You know I do, E."

He leaned over, popped open the glove compartment, and fished out the bottle. "I'll be there in a few. Time to celebrate, eh?"

"You know it! Mama's waitin' for her jewels!"

Yeah, celebrate, he thought. No more nighttime trips. Mrs. B's cousin and spouse were flying in from Chicago next week; they planned to stay about a month. Too many eyes, too many people who somehow might notice him and the silver Mercedes slipping off the Del Mar estate in the early hours.

Elliston raised the small Helmut Lang cologne bottle and gave his throat two quick sprays. He loved this particular cologne. Joyce did too. It was an expensive blend of fruit and citrus, but gave off a musky masculine vibe—at least that's what she said.

47

2:10 a.m. The stoplight turned green. Roy Dobbs watched as the large silver car went forward, aggressively pulling ahead. Roy hung back. He knew the kid wouldn't speed, even though the Mercedes no doubt had impressive horsepower. The kid would obey all the speed limits and not pull some stunt that would catch the eye of any bobbies.

Sorry, old sport, Roy mused. Being cautious won't do you any good tonight. Tonight you'll bloody well lose your pretty baubles. Keeping a reasonable distance, Roy followed the Mercedes toward the freeway.

Even if the Mercedes driver had done a jack-rabbit and sped out of sight, it wouldn't matter. Roy knew exactly where the kid was going: his girlfriend's place in Ocean Beach on Narragansett. And he knew what the kid and girlfriend, Joyce, were up to. Months ago, posing as an electrician, Roy had carefully placed an electronic "bug" in her condo. The kids liked to talk. After several months and multiple nighttime visits, their overheard chit-chats had revealed their scheme. Now Roy knew it—all of it.

At the stoplight he had looked over as well, and noted the kid's scowl at the Toyota. Exactly what Roy wanted: a pedestrian vehicle that few people would give a second glance. Great cover for a professional thief, and Roy considered himself an excellent one. And he would prove himself again, tonight, when he "relieved" the kids of their stash.

Roy switched off the radio. Bloody well time to focus. He reviewed his plan. He'd follow the silver car as it traveled Route 5 south, then he'd peel away and arrive at the condo complex by an alternate route. With so little traffic he didn't want the lad to become suspicious of a tail. He would then get his Ruger P85 pistol—carefully stashed in a camouflaged bag beneath a jasmine bush near the complex's main entrance—and confront the kid just as he would be entering the place. That was the real tricky part, and required excellent timing.

48

But Roy felt confident. He carefully pulled on a pair of latex gloves, then flexed his hands. "Nosirree, pardner," he muttered, lapsing into an American accent. "This ain't my first rodeo."

* * *

Her taxi dashboard read 2:10 a.m.

"Showtime, right, Harrie?" said a deep voice from the back seat.

"Oh you know it, lieutenant," replied Harriet Palmer, a.k.a. Harrie, retired San Diego PD detective. "It's what we PIs live for, don'cha know?"

The man chuckled softly. Then, "The department's been good for you, Harrie."

She glanced at him through the rearview mirror. "Yes, indeed."

"Gotta admit," he continued, "With all the connections you made over the years, Samantha Brin is a damned good one."

The light turned green and Harriet pulled out, following the gray Toyota. Per tonight's operation she would quickly pull ahead of it, then enter the freeway and fade into the night. After all, she knew where the Toyota was going, as well as the silver Mercedes. And she knew how important tonight would be. That's why she had her passenger.

And his SWAT team.

"She's a wonderful lady," said Harriet. "Despite being a widow and all, she's carried on pretty well with the Judge's charity work. I probably never told you, but I first met her at a St. Jude's Hospital fundraiser. She and the Judge were both staunch supporters of law enforcement, we had some things in common … ." She shrugged. "We hit it off."

"So she called you first and not us."

His tone sounded wounded, but she knew better. They both laughed.

She pulled around the gray Toyota and sped toward the freeway. "Hey … girl power." Pause. "Ya know, if this were a

49

Sherlock Holmes mystery I'd call it, 'The Tale of the Sensitive Nose.'"

"So your notes show. And leaving her tennis lesson early."

"For sure."

* * *

Elliston slowed his speed to just under the limit. These nighttime runs, which he'd been doing for months, required caution. Even though he would miss them, there was a lot of money to be had with these jewels. Besides, he was ready to move on to another victim and place. Maybe Dallas?

Besides, Joyce seemed ready for a change. Their partnership was a good one, and he intended to keep it going — at least for a while. As for old lady Brin, she'd never catch on. She was even showing signs of senility, which was good news. He figured her chances of discovering their scheme were practically zero. Elliston gave verbal signals to activate his music list; he chose smooth jazz and began humming along.

* * *

Dobbs hummed one of his favorite songs, "Luck Be a Lady Tonight." He sure had been lucky that night he left Archie's place in Del Mar early in the morning. Good old Archie and his insomnia. But the bloke was a social media whiz, and had located two good leads: a couple in Eastlake who were fretting about where to house their two terriers while they explored Yellowstone; and someone up in L.A. — Pacific Palisades. Dobbs had been to that area before. Those hillside estates made for some juicy targets.

Luck, if you've ever been a lady to begin with, luck be a lady tonight.

So there he was, driving east on Del Mar Heights Road months ago when a big silver beauty of a car slid past. Dobbs checked out the driver, turned out to be some kid, maybe late 20s. But what was this kiddo doing driving a car more suited

50

to a CEO or Hollywood producer … at that time of night, no less? Being a highly curious fellow, Dobbs couldn't help himself. He had to follow. Maybe it was a lucky sign.

So they both traveled south, took a turnoff, and ended up in Ocean Beach. The kid parked and walked into a condo complex. He carried a medium-size box tucked into one arm like a football. Dobbs's curiosity flared. Who was the kid visiting? What was in the box?

That's when Dobbs got lucky again. The kid must've forgot something, because he returned to his car. Dobbs quickly left his own car double parked, slipped into character, and followed the kid into the complex. The kid stopped in front of a door, then looked back at Dobbs.

"Helluva night, eh, pal?" Dobbs slurred. He stumbled past, seemingly drunk. "Havuh gud un." He noted the condo number. After a few yards he glanced back. The kid was entering the open door. Bingo.

Dobbs hurried back to his car. Now he knew what he had to do next.

* * *

Harriet knew what she had to do.

Going the opposite direction on Narragansett, a silver Mercedes slid through the intersection on a yellow light. A small gray car scooted behind it through the red. The lighting and timing were perfect, so Harriet got a good look at the driver's face in the smaller car. It was Dobbs! Damn! *That* Roy Dobbs!

No traffic nearby so she did a tight U-turn in the intersection and began following both cars, but hanging back.

What the blazes was Dobbs doing at this time of night? After a few blocks both cars ahead of her slowed, so she followed suit. She pulled out a pad and jotted down the gray car's license number. Just as she had finished, the silver car pulled into a reserved parking spot in front of a condo complex. Harriet slowed even further and saw the smaller car squeeze itself into a spot further down. She quickly pulled

51

into a gas station almost across from the condos and parked in one corner closest to the complex. A man got out of the Mercedes, carrying something, and walked into the complex. Soon he came back. That's when Dobbs got out and followed the man back into the complex. Was Dobbs going to rob him? She didn't have to mull that over for long. Dobbs soon returned to his car and got in. Started it up and slowly drove away.

Harriet clenched her hands on the steering wheel. Should she follow? She softly ground her teeth. No go. Trying to follow in such light traffic was a fool's errand. And from reading the case file, she knew this guy was no fool. He'd immediately spot a tag. What was her next move? The time was around 2:35 a.m. and she could barely stay awake. That crazy JoAnne had roped her into another late night film fest. But JoAnne, from Narcotics, was one of her best pals from the force. And the film had gotten both of them totally engrossed.

She slowly drove out of the gas station and went past the silver Mercedes, pausing long enough to record the plate number. Tomorrow she would ring up Lieutenant Powell and convince him to run both plates. She could imagine the conversation: "Did you say Dobbs?" he would ask, disbelieving. "Oh yeah," she would say. "No doubt ... I got a good look. That was the car he was driving."

Mention the name Dobbs at the precinct, and most people would perk up their ears. "The Desert Debacle," her former partner, Frank, had dubbed it.

Quite a case, and a real embarrassment for the department. Roy Dobbs had been the prime suspect, but a lack of solid evidence as well as mishandled evidence had spoiled the case. Ruined it, actually. Expensive clothing, jewelry, watches, and the like totaling tens of thousands had been stolen from four high-end suites at the L'Horizon Resort and Spa in Palm Springs. Harriet had not been a party to the case, but she'd heard plenty of buzz and got a look at the file. The detectives in charge were convinced Dobbs was the mastermind, with several accomplices helping him in the caper.

After weeks of legal turmoil, Dobbs had walked free – a middle-aged man who didn't look at all like a stereotypical thief: handsome features, wavy chestnut hair, intelligent gray eyes, and an engaging smile you might see in a magazine ad. Quite the pretty boy, she had thought when first looking at his photo.

What was Dobbs up to? And who owned that silver Mercedes? Harriet had hopes for those license plates.

* * *

Two porcelain plates from her Williams Sonoma dinnerware collection sat on the long coffee table. One plate held a small mound of trail mix, unsalted; the other, a stack of rye crispbread and a container of red pepper hummus.

"Your green tea is almost ready, E," Joyce sang out, walking toward the kitchen.

At first she had called him Mr. E. Then, over time, the nickname switched to just "E." Elliston sat on the sofa, put the jewelry box on the table, and started in on the hummus. From the beginning it was clear she had a crush on him, but it wasn't reciprocated. As he had once told her, "I fly solo these days, and I'm enjoying the trip." Theirs was a business partnership, and he wanted to keep it that way. He glanced around the condo: decent size, two bedrooms, large living room, and so forth. But he had to keep reminding himself not to be too judgmental. When you're living large in a guesthouse on an estate, your perspective gets skewed.

"Good enough!" he called out, then settled his gaze on a large tropical fish tank across the room. Watching their languid movements was strangely relaxing.

"Here you go, E," she said. She walked around the coffee table and set down a pot of tea with a cup and saucer. She straightened and gave him a toothy smile. "So let's take a look at those goodies." She knelt in front of the table and opened the jewelry box.

As usual, her face lit up like a child's who had just opened a wonderful present.

53

Elliston poured himself some tea, glancing at her from time to time. Average looks, nice figure, whip-smart, probably a couple of years older than him. But more important, a top-notch jewelry counterfeiter. Her second bedroom had been completely converted into a workspace with the various tools and equipment necessary to her trade.

"Nice haul, E." She gently fingered the jewelry. "Not too fancy, not too complex."

He knew that was important. Some jewelry pieces even she could not duplicate. Early on she'd asked him how he had gotten access to the rich gal's jewelry boxes, but he had told her in no uncertain terms: that would remain a secret. Even though he was Mrs. B's personal assistant, he had to be careful as to where he was in the mansion and why. Of course it had taken several months of careful, brief forays through the large place for him to discover a sliding panel in one corner of her large, walk-in closet. Then how to open it. As he had told Joyce, it required the patience and perseverance of a goddamn snail crossing a road to reach grass on the other side.

They chatted while he ate his snacks, then she took the jewelry into the bedroom; she soon returned the box, which contained the counterfeit replicas of his previous "shipment." When he returned to the mansion, sometime that day he would replace the genuine jewelry pieces with the counterfeits — if possible. He had to be careful.

"We're almost done, Joyce," he reminded her. "Then it's on to the next stage."

She sat next to him and helped herself to the trail mix. "Yeah, after all this work," she said brightly, "it's gonna be harvest time."

* * *

"Really, sweet pea?" Roy Dobbs muttered. Harvest time? Right you are, he thought. Harvest time for *this* bloke, not you.

He shifted his weight in the car seat, taking some pressure

54

off his sore right hip. He was seated in his Toyota, parked across the street but near the complex entrance. At this point Roy knew quite a bit about these two. In fact, more than he wanted. But if he could get his hands on the jewelry, it was well worth the trouble. It had taken several months of data gathering, off and on, listening to their conversations — thanks to his audio surveillance "bug."

He shook his head, remembering. Two days after spotting the silver Mercedes he'd shown up dressed in what he considered an electrician's uniform, complete with phony shoulder patches and an official-looking name tag. It was 11 a.m. when he knocked on the door of Unit 109. A young woman answered. He flashed his best smile, and explained that the homeowner's association had requested an electrician begin a systematic check of all the units. Possible fire hazards, you know.

"Safety first, all the time," he said. He made sure she saw his large metal toolbox, which was full of the required side-cutting pliers, stripping tools, voltage tester and meter, insulated screwdrivers, and so forth that a legitimate electrician would carry. Fortunately, Roy didn't have to figure that out. He had kept abreast of the field, and his extensive schooling in the Royal Air Force years ago as an electronics technician had served him well. "If you have no problems," he continued, "I should be done in a jiffy."

American slang. Roy loved it.

He was surprised when he walked into one bedroom, obviously converted into a workspace, but he pretended only a casual interest. He kept up a pleasant patter of talk. Then the moment came: As he distracted her by commenting on the fish tank, he quickly stuck the "bug" underneath her coffee table.

"Mission accomplished," he said, smiling back as he walked out the door.

That, it turned out, was the easy part. The hard part would be sitting in his car listening for hours. Audio surveillance could be a bitch. But over time the details of their scheme began to emerge, as well as her daily routine. She was a creature of strict habits, always working diligently on her jewelry into the early hours. She nicknamed the guy "E," and called him every Wednesday and Saturday at 7 p.m. to give him a status report. She had no regular job, and indulged in the usual telephone calls to friends, relatives, acquaintances. Did her own cooking, went to a local fitness center four times a week. On and on.

But Roy couldn't do this full-time; he had other "irons in the fire," as the Americans would say. But within three weeks he became privy to many of her quirks, mannerisms, bad and good habits. A lot of garbage, but he still had to listen for any nuggets of information. Such as, Where was the jewelry kept? Answer: In a safe, under the kitchen sink. It was too risky to transport them outside the complex.

Finally! This phase of their little criminal enterprise was almost over. E's nighttime trips to the condo, almost done. Dobbs hunched down in his seat as the headlights of the silver Mercedes swept past. Then he sat up and used his rearview mirror to watch the car's taillights disappearing down Narragansett.

"Next time, boy-o, it'll be harvest time, all right. *My* harvest time."

* * *

"Boy, I'll bet my peanut butter smoothie tastes better than yours," said Samantha Brin.

"There's no doubt," replied Harriet, looking glumly at her large paper cup of Apples and Greens. "Peanut butter is addictive, for sure."

Lieutenant Powell forked the last of his scrambled eggs into his mouth. Amused, he looked at both women and shook his head.

"And she would know," said Harriet, nodding toward Brin. "I don't think she mentioned it, but this lady was a sous chef for many years before she met the Judge. She worked at some very posh restaurants in San Francisco, uh, Phoenix … where else?"

Samantha pursed her lips. "Hmm, Las Vegas for a while."

Powell laid down his fork and leaned back in his chair. "I am impressed. Really."

Harriet continued, "Samantha has an excellent palate, and that means a refined sense of smell. Hence our 'The Tale of the Sensitive Nose.'"

Powell raised his water glass. "That's right. A toast to the sensitive nose!"

They heard a soft buzz. Samantha pulled her phone from her chic, light brown leather jacket, looked down at the screen, then back up at her companions: "A message from Elliston. He's reminding me of my producers' meeting at the Old Globe. I'm helping with an original comedy, a bit avant-garde. So, if you'll excuse me ... ."

About five minutes later Powell and Harriet watched as Samantha's sporty yellow Alfa Romero Spyder motored past the front of the Del Mar Plaza building.

Harriet sighed, enjoying the sleek look of the vehicle. "Yellow is my favorite color."

"So you've said. On many an occasion." Powell leaned in toward her. "Our case is almost over," he said quietly. "We have enough evidence. Time to close the jaws of the trap."

Harriet took a sip of her smoothie and gazed out over the choppy, grayish blue ocean. The sky was overcast, but she still enjoyed this view from the Plaza's third level.

They both started pulling out money to pay the bill. "Yes, sir," said Harriet. "The case that almost never was."

Powell grunted. "No joke. Samantha Brin was lucky. If she hadn't left that tennis lesson early, she might never have known."

Brin had gone upstairs and into her walk-in closet to change. She must've missed Elliston by just a minute or less, because she picked up the lingering scent of his cologne. Why would he be in her closet? She checked. Everything seemed to be in place: clothes, jackets, shoes, jewelry. All of it. Both curious and suspicious, she called Harriet. The two women spoke, and one thing led to another. Harriet was given access to the mansion. At an appropriate day and time when Brin and Elliston were out, she brought along a professional jewelry appraiser. Harriet soon learned that appraising was a time-consuming, exacting business. After several hours the appraiser could only examine a portion of Samantha Brin's treasures by Bulgari, Louis Vuitton, Buccellati, De Beers, and others. But he did find five counterfeit pieces.

Also, the police had run both license plates. The plate for the Toyota was a phony; the silver Mercedes was owned by Samantha Brin.

"To cover all the bases," Harriet had told Powell, "let's ask the Wonder Wagon to check for electronic signals around the Narragansett complex. I have a hunch our friend Dobbs might have planted a bug. Cuz we know he's been staking out the place."

Powell had been reluctant. "A long shot, Harrie. I don't know if that's the best use of resources." He thought for a while, then, "But we're talking about Dobbs, aren't we."

That made the difference. The thief was an ever-present sore spot for the department.

Detectives called the mid-sized van the "Wonder Wagon" because the elite and highly effective squad of men and women—undercover officers and electronics experts—who operated the van often performed wonders of intel-gathering through surveillance. Soon the nondescript tan vehicle, which had the unique name of "A La Commode Plumbing" emblazoned on both sides, was parked in a suitable spot near the condo complex. Harriet was very pleased, because it didn't take long for the electronics wizards to pick up an audio surveillance signal; they monitored the signal and began putting the puzzle pieces together.

* * *

"I'm puzzled by something that Elliston told his gal," said Lieutenant Powell.

"Something about Samantha Brin showing signs of senility?"

Harriet pulled the taxi into almost the same spot at the gas station she did the very first time. The undercover taxi had been outfitted with all the electronics gear the police would need. Powell was now wearing a small headset so he could communicate with both the SWAT team and Wonder Wagon personnel.

"I'll take credit for that," said Harriet. "During our chitchats, Samantha told me she had minored in drama while at Berkeley, then played some low-level roles for a few Old Globe productions and even some in LA; she also did a lot of TV commercials. Keep in mind, this was before she got into cooking."

Powell held up a hand, then spoke into the headset. From the conversation Harriet could tell that SWAT was carefully moving into position around the condo complex entrance. The Wonder Wagon was closely monitoring any talk inside Unit 109, and the SWAT team leader was listening as well.

She had heard such instructions before. It's what Captain Seidman always stressed: teamwork, communication, no civilians hurt, safety.

Powell finished. "So you were saying?"

She shifted around in her seat to look at him. "I recommended she use her acting chops to make Elliston feel more secure." She shrugged. "A few little acts of forgetfulness might make him think she was going a bit ditzy."

"Clever girl," said Powell. "It worked."

Harriet rolled down her window. Moderate temperature. Quiet. Insects buzzed. A dog barked in the distance. Powell spoke into his headset, and seconds later a car slowly pulled out of its parking spot across from the complex. Harriet watched as two SWAT members, sidearms out, slipped like dark shadows through the entrance and into the central courtyard of the complex.

"Someone should be here any minute now." Powell, speaking softly now, a distinct undercurrent of tension in his voice.

Twenty seconds later the gray Toyota came into view. As planned, Roy Dobbs spied the open spot and quickly pulled into it.

"Excellent," whispered Harriet. She took a small pair of binoculars off the passenger seat and used them to watch Dobbs cross the street, then veer off toward some bushes. He crouched and picked something up. Then he walked nonchalantly through the entryway and disappeared.

Powell informed SWAT. Soft radio chatter back and forth. Harriet felt her stomach muscles starting to tense. She didn't mind. It was good thing—as long as she kept it under control. She had learned long ago, even the simplest plan could go sideways. Things could get ugly real fast.

Dobbs was barely out of sight when the silver Mercedes appeared. It slid into the usual parking space. Elliston got out. Harriet refocused her binoculars. Yep, she thought, another box of goodies tucked into his arm.

She looked back. Powell had his own binoculars now, trained on the complex entrance. Harriet could see dark figures, like ninjas, slowly creeping as they worked their way along the sides of the complex. Like pincers closing, they were converging from both sides of the complex entryway.

"He's gotta gun," whispered Powell. "Dobbs has a gun."

"Damn fool," Harriet said. "We need him alive."

Seconds ticked by. Harriet slowly unclenched her jaw. Flexed her hands. *Open, close.*

A minivan drove past on Narragansett. She firmed her lips, irritated. *Who the hell would be out now?*

"They're inside now. All three are inside," Powell reported.

Open, close. Breathe deep.

Powell kept listening, then ordered the SWAT team leader to hold off until someone exited the condo. Apparently there was a lot of talk in the condo, some arguing, but no violence…yet.

Open, close. Open, clo —

"They're executing!" exclaimed Powell.

Harriet listened intently. Suddenly, shouts came from inside the complex. She heard loud voices. Then more loud voices, both male and female. But no gunfire, no explosions.

Suddenly, "Good, good!" Powell said tersely into his

mike. "Good job! I'm coming in!"

"We got Dobbs?" said Harriet.

"We got Dobbs! We got everybody!" He threw open the taxi door and began quick-walking toward the complex entrance.

Harriet exhaled, letting out a gush of air. "We got Dobbs! Hot damn!"

She took a few moments to collect herself. Then she pulled her phone from her jacket pocket and called Samantha Brin. Cursed herself. Her hands were trembling!

Hard-boiled PI? A female Philip Marlowe she wasn't. At least not yet.

Two police cars, no sirens but with lights flashing, pulled up. As she watched the action, she spoke to Samantha. It was a short call; they would talk at length tomorrow.

At the end she asked about a gratuity she'd been thinking about. Samantha readily agreed.

Soon after the call finished, Powell came walking up. "All's well that ends well," he said, grinning. "When he saw what he was up against, Dobbs dropped that gun like a hot potato."

Harriet said, "Shakespeare and a cliché. I love it."

Powell threw both hands in the air. "Who cares? I talked to Seidman, and she's one happy camper. No gunfire, no injuries. Smooth as silk. Man, oh man … *Dobbs.*" He turned, arms akimbo, to watch as the three perps were brought out and put into squad cars.

Harriet left the taxi and stood next to him. "Lieutenant, I just finished a conversation with Samantha. She's almost as pleased as you." She couldn't help adding, "And she gave the okay for a little gratuity."

"Uh-huh."

He was only half listening. She waited.

"So, uh, what's this about a gratuity?"

"Well, since I love the color yellow … ."

Now she had more of his attention. "Harrie, don't tell me she *gave* you the Alfa Romero."

She chuckled. "No, no. Nothing like that. But, I do have an

61

invitation to *drive it* pretty much whenever I want." They both stood there, watching the scene. "By the way," she added, "You, the Wonder Wagon, and everyone else involved are invited to a luncheon at Samantha's estate in the near future. And she's cooking."

"Harrie, I'm putting you in for a letter of appreciation for this. Seriously."

She felt a warm flush of pride. "Why, well…well, thank you." Moments later she turned toward him. "You know, Lieutenant Powell … ."

"Yeah?"

"I think it was in that film 'Casablanca.' Humphrey Bogart had a great line, and I'll borrow it." She paused for dramatic effect. "Lieutenant, I think this is the beginning of a beautiful friendship."

It had been a stressful night. They both enjoyed the laugh.

Get Thee to a Punnery!

Richard Lederer

At the end of this small disquisition, I'll present what in my opinion are the top ten puns of all time. I hope your response will not be, "Lederer tried to impress us with his best puns, but not one pun in ten did!"

In America we celebrate just about everything, so it may come as no surprise to you that early each January, pun-up girls and pun gents observe National Save the Pun Week. I've been a punographer all my life and truly believe that the pun is worth celebrating all year round. After all, the pun is mightier than the sword, and these days you are much more likely to run into a pun than into a sword.

Scoffing at puns is a conditioned reflex, and through the centuries groan-ups have aimed a steady barrage of libel and slander at the practice of punning. More than three centuries ago, the playwright and critic John Dennis sneered, "A pun is the lowest form of wit," a charge that has been butted and rebutted by a mighty line of pundits and punheads.

Henry Erskine, for example, has protested that if a pun is the lowest form of wit, "it is therefore the foundation of all wit." Oscar Levant has added a tagline: "A pun is the lowest form of humor — when you don't think of it first." John Crosbie and Bob Davies have responded to Dennis with hot, cross puns: "The pun has been said to be the lowest form of humus — earthy wit that everybody digs" and "If someone complains that punning is the lowest form of humor, you can tell them that poetry is verse." To those who contend that a pun is the lowest form of wit, I counter with the truism that a bun is indeed the doughiest form of wheat.

Punning is a rewording experience. The inveterate (not invertebrate) punster believes that a good pun is like a good steak—a rare medium well done. In such a prey on words, *rare, medium,* and *well done* are double entendres, so that six meanings are crammed into the space ordinarily occupied by just three.

Punnery is largely the trick of compacting two or more ideas within a single word or expression. Punnery surprises us by flouting the law of nature that pretends that two things cannot occupy the same space at the same time. It is an exercise of the mind in being concise.

Pun for all! And all for pun! Using the criteria of verbal pyrotechnics, humor, and enduring popularity of the play on words, I present my picks for the top ten blue-ribbin' puns of all time:

Sharpen your pun cells, O pun pals. Let's get to wit:

10. What do you get when you cross a gorilla with a clay worker? A Hairy Potter!

9. What do you get when you cross an elephant with a rhinoceros? Elephino!

8. As one frog croaked to another, "Time's fun when you're having flies!"

7. Outside of a dog, a book is a man's best friend. Inside of a dog, it's too dark to read. — *Groucho Marx*

6. Satan has started a wig manufacturing business. It's called Devil Make Hair, and its most popular product is the Hell Toupee.

5. Two ropes walked into an old western saloon. The first rope went up to the bar and ordered a beer. "We don't serve ropes in this saloon," sneered the bartender, who picked up the rope, whirled him around in the air, and

tossed him out into the street.

"Oh, oh. I'd better disguise myself," thought the second rope. He ruffled up his ends to make himself look rougher and twisted himself into a circle to look bigger. Then he too sidled up to the bar.

"Hmmm. Are you one of them ropes?" snarled the bartender.

"I'm a frayed knot."

4. Twenty-five years ago, we had Steve Jobs, Johnny Cash, and Bob Hope. Now we have no jobs, no cash, and no hope. Let us pray mightily that Meat Loaf, Kevin Bacon, and Jon Hamm don't die!

3. One of the greatest men of the twentieth century was the political leader and ascetic Mahatma Gandhi. His denial of the earthly pleasures included the fact that he never wore anything on his feet. He walked barefoot everywhere. Moreover, he ate so little that he developed delicate health and very bad breath. Thus, he became known as a super-callused fragile mystic hexed by halitosis!

2. You better watch out, or my karma will run over your dogma.

And the numero-uno pun of all time, created by the incomparable Dorothy Parker: I'd rather have a bottle in front of me than a frontal lobotomy!

Wingless Flight

Ty Piz

These precious moments fly by
 as the cool breeze fills our sails
carrying us away for ten days or more
—a flash in time.

We drift silently
upon the gentle waves
of the mystical sea
—no direction in mind.

We see a lighthouse
far away on a distant shore
shining brightly to guide our ship,
safely to port.

No longer floating alone on the open sea,
we now have one another,
our solid rock to cling to
To get us through the dark of the storm.

When the sun rises in the east
with all its warmth and love to greet us,
this rock is still here to hold onto
—tightly.

Friends are the treasure we found
sharing the uncertainty of rough waves,
the calmness of tranquil waters,
and they remain steady by our side
through the lonesome times as well.

Now we celebrate
the gift of our love
its light radiates outward to the entire world
showing true harmony in this life.

What Really Happened

Mardie Schroeder

On October 10, 2010, Xavier Knox, ten years old, was found floating in the pool of his friend, Jose Rodriguez, also ten. According to the police, he drowned.

Everybody believes that because that's what it said in the newspapers. Of course, I know what really happened. I didn't hear the shots because I'm deaf. Just deaf. Not dumb. I'm really smart, and there is nothing wrong with my eyes. It was nothing like the paper said. Xavier Knox was murdered.

The woman who married my father shortly after my mother died is very strict. I have to keep my room neat and tidy at all times. Today she sent me to the attic and locked the door. Either I had done something to tick her off, or she was going shopping and didn't want to take me with her. But I really like being in the attic because I have all my stuff around and I don't have to keep it neat and tidy like my bedroom. And I don't have to be around my stepmother. She's a bit scary.

One of the windows in the attic overlooks the pool area of the Rodriguez home next door. There is always something going on in the pool area, especially in the summer, and I can watch it all. I guess you could say it's my one means of entertainment. Well, that's not exactly true. I have newspapers, my diary, my lesson book, and a mirror to practice signing.

The man who calls me *daughter* is away a lot. My name really is Mimi but I can't remember the last time he called me that or if he ever did.

I have a lot of thoughts in my head and I write everything down in my journal that I see from that attic window. It keeps me very busy.

The woman who sends me to the attic spends a lot of time at the Rodriguezes. There's a gate between our properties, and I've seen her cross the pool area and enter the house.

I don't think the Rodriguezes know I exist because my parents have never taken me to their neighborhood pool parties. Lots of drinking and other stuff goes on.

One day Jose looked up and saw me in the window. His jaw dropped open. I think that was the first time he ever saw me up there. He ran into the house and came out with his father and pointed up to where I was. Then they both went into the house. But nothing came of that, which I think is a little strange.

About a week later I was sent to a camp with other deaf children. It turned out to be one of the best experiences I ever had. Everyone had lots to talk about and we all had our own way of speaking or I should say, signing. At the end of the first week, I was recognized as the person who improved the most in signing.

All the girls were in one big cabin and the boys in another. The counselors had separate living quarters but were close enough if they were needed.

Of all the activities offered, including canoeing, volleyball, swimming, tennis, crafts, and cooking, my favorite is horseback riding. I even enjoy mucking out the stalls. My friend Lara and I decided we'd be cowboys when we grow up. So I spent most of my time with the horses in the barn.

Each night around the campfire one person would talk about their family. I was really wondering what I would say about mine. I thought maybe I would make up a fairy tale story of my life.

My turn finally came. *What to do?* I signed, "I saw a murder. Nobody knows I saw what happened, but I wrote in my journal what I saw. Two young boys were in the pool area next door to me. They started fighting and the neighbor boy, Jose, went into the house and returned with a gun. They played around with it, and then Jose shot the other boy, Xavier, who fell into the pool."

Everybody started signing me.

"Where were you?"

"Then what?"

"How long was the boy in the pool?"

"When did someone come to get the boy?" and on and on.

I signed, "I was upstairs in the attic when I saw them. I don't know anything else because I had to go downstairs for dinner. I only know the notice in the newspaper just said the boy drowned. Nothing about being shot."

I guess you could say I became a sort of celebrity after that. But my month at the ranch was coming to an end. Somebody who I didn't know came and indicated they were to pick me up. The head counselor said it was okay to go with him. But I had never seen him before.

The ride home was not the route I remembered. When we pulled up to a house I didn't know and which wasn't in my neighborhood I panicked. *This guy is kidnapping me, I thought.* When he stopped, I shot out of the car and ran as fast as I could, terrified. I zigzagged at every corner—first left, then right, then left. I don't remember how long I ran but I finally saw an open garage and ran to it and found a hiding place behind some trash bins. I had to catch my breath.

A car was in the garage so maybe someone was home. I didn't want anyone to find me so I was very quiet. I had to figure out what to do next.

I realized all my personal stuff was left in the car. *Oh no. My diary. Oh my gosh. Now what?*

The most important thing in my life was now gone. I started to cry. What a mess. I was crying so hard I didn't see the car come into the garage.

Suddenly a dog was all over me wagging his tail. Two men looked at me with startled expressions. I looked at them terrified. I started to run out of the garage but the door had already closed. I just sat down and covered my face and cried.

* * *

70

A gentle hand touched my shoulder and handed me a tissue. I was given a glass of water. I sipped slowly wondering how I was going to get through this mess.

I saw them talking to each other and to me but I just shook my head. They helped me up and brought me inside the house and sat me down at the dining room table.

I indicated I wanted to write something. They brought me a pencil and paper and I wrote that someone tried to kidnap me but I escaped. I wrote my address down and they looked it up and wrote they would take me there.

The drive took about an hour and when we arrived, they walked me to the front door and knocked. There was no answer and we looked in the windows but the house was completely empty. The door was locked and none of us knew what to do next.

One of them started to go next door but I grabbed his arm and indicated not to go. I could see he didn't understand my extreme reluctance but he decided to trust me.

The two men had a long conversation before we got back in the car. I knew it was about me and eventually some decisions were made. They wrote *hungry?* on the pad. I nodded so we went back to the car and drove off.

* * *

We put our orders in at The Hungry Hunter. Then the questions started. They took turns writing. "Any sisters or brothers?" "What does your father do?" "What is your last name?"

They had so many questions. It's hard to explain everything exactly right when someone doesn't know how to sign so I wrote very brief answers which only brought more questions.

"Why didn't you want us to go next door?"

How could I answer that I saw a murder there? More talking back and forth. It was so tiresome I just wanted to go to bed and make this go away.

When they asked me why I didn't know we had moved I

explained I was at camp for a month. The counselor had told me it was okay to go with the man who came for me. They called the camp but it had closed for the season so they left a message for someone to call them.

After we ate they wrote if I would be okay going back to their house. I nodded yes. Oh, I learned the tall blond guy was George and the slender dark haired one was Tom.

* * *

By the time we returned to the house I was really tired. They settled me in the guest room. *What a day.*

* * *

In the morning I saw they left an English muffin for me and a note that they went to work and to make myself at home. I got the lay of the house. The dog, Willy, wouldn't let me out of his sight. *That was nice.*

I'm so worried about my journal missing. It has very important stuff in it. Everything about the murder is in that journal. I still haven't told George and Tom about it, but I did tell them I missed having my journal. I'm getting better reading lips too because they talk so much. There never was much conversation at my home.

* * *

Tom came back to the house at noon to take the dog out and to bring me lunch. Apparently there had not been a missing person report on me.

That night we went out to dinner. I don't think these guys do much cooking. But it's fun because I don't get out much as you know. We are all more relaxed around each other and I think they really like me. After dinner they said they had a present for me. They wanted me to guess what it was but I couldn't. I knew the minute they handed it to me that it was a new journal. I hugged it even before I took off the wrapping.

72

It's even nicer than my old journal. I made my heart sign and they made it back at me.

The next day we went shopping for some clothes for me. That night they were having a dinner party and I was the star attraction they said. I was so excited. They bought me a ton of clothes. Even the saleslady had a good time with these guys since they didn't have any idea what would suit me. So the saleslady and I got to choose my outfits.

* * *

Don't think I wasn't nervous that night. Someone brought all the food in to cook for us. About ten people came. I didn't get everything that was said, but I did know everyone wanted to help me find my family. They all took pictures of me.

I can tell you I was really beginning to like living with George and Tom. They lead such an exciting life and are willing to include me in much of it.

But now I'm in trouble. The camp people called and there was a long conversation about me. Tom and George sat me down. Serious faces all around.

"What's this about a murder, Mimi?" Tom asked. "Why didn't you tell us about this before?"

"This is very serious." George chimed in. "This should be reported to the police."

And so on. Oh, the camp also said that my family had moved, but they didn't have an address.

I wrote, "I wrote everything I saw in my journal which now I don't have. I saw one boy shoot another boy who fell into the swimming pool. But the papers only said it was a drowning. I told my camp group about it. I don't want to go to the police because they probably won't believe me. I have to get my old journal. Please just help me find my home."

"Of course we will, Mimi," Tom said. "But at some point the police will have to know about this."

I nodded. *I knew eventually I would have to tell them.*

* * *

Two days later they found my new home. One of the guests at the party was in real estate and she found out. The only reason I want to go home is to get my journal. It didn't take long to find the house. It was the exact house that I was driven to from the camp. We rang the doorbell and my stepmother answered. She looked so surprised to see me and pulled me in the house. Tom and George stepped inside with a bag of my new clothes and introduced themselves. They explained how they found me. My stepmother didn't say much, but it was obvious she didn't want them to stay. I ran over to them and we had a group hug. They both made hearts back at me while my stepmother tried to pull me away. Then they left and she closed the door.

I don't know about you, but I have a feeling I'll be seeing Tom and George again. And maybe even the police.

What do you think?

Extra Place Setting

Shujen Walker-Askew

At the tenth avenue stoplight, Shane adjusted his tie and ran his hand through his dark curly hair. "Looking good." He grinned at himself in the rearview mirror, admiring his polished teeth.

The light turned green, and he continued down the street through an upscale San Antonio neighborhood, following the GPS.

His phone rang, and he answered it. "Yes, sir." It was his soon-to-be father-in-law, Harold.

"What's your status? Where are you?" Harold asked.

"Heading to Mr. Roger's house. I'm a few blocks away."

"No need. Mr. Roger canceled."

"What?" Shane sucked in his teeth.

"Because of the cancelation, I rearranged your schedule and added Ms. Evelyn at the top of the list. She needs to sign the contracting agreement so that we can get started on her back yard as soon as possible. I've already emailed you the updated priorities list."

"Yes, sir."

"Doing great, young man. Your first week on the job, and I'm impressed with your dedication. Keep it going. I'll be in contact." Harold hung up.

Shane sighed at the unforeseen detour. He needed every sale he could get to buy his fiancée the perfect wedding gift. Not to mention the bet he had with her brother, Timothy, as to who could make the most sales in a week.

He reviewed the client priority list then typed Ms. Evelyn's address into the GPS. It guided him to a sketchy part of the city filled with rundown homes and abandoned cars.

75

Cracks in the driveways, untrimmed hedges, and missing fence slats brightened his eyes. He made a mental note to pass out business cards to the homeowners.

Shane pulled up to a light blue house with a chain-link fence and bars on the windows.

Old school. This is going to be fun.

After checking himself out in the mirror and patting down a stray curl, Shane grabbed his briefcase and stepped out of the SUV. He entered Ms. Evelyn's property through the front gate and went up the driveway, passing by a weed-infested lawn and dead rosebushes. He climbed the steps to the front door and pressed the doorbell.

A woman strutting a flamingo red robe with flowing gray hair answered.

"May I help you?" she asked.

"Name's Shane Rowland." He held up his business card. "I'm with Harold's Landscaping Services. Looking for Ms. Evelyn."

She glanced at his card, then at him. "Where's Timothy?"

"He's on another assignment."

"Mr. Harold?" She crinkled her brows.

"He's at the office."

"I only deal with the two. I don't know you." She moved to close the door.

"Ms. Evelyn," Shane called out. "Timothy told me you'd say that. So let me introduce myself again." He stepped back. "I'm Shane Rowland, Harold's soon-to-be son-in-law. This is my first week on the job, so you'll have to bear with me as I get this right." He put his hands in the air and clapped two times, then stomped his feet three times. The wooden porch shook as he swayed his hips. "We'll mow your lawn, trim your trees, and even wash your dishes if you say please. We're Harold's Landscaping … ing … ing." His voice croaked. "Two locations near you." He stomped two more times and a broad smile plastered his face.

Ms. Evelyn stared him up and down. "So you're the fast-talking city boy who stole little Tali away from Mr. Harold?"

Shane chuckled and pointed his thumb at his chest.

"That's me."

"Word of advice, don't ever do that jingle again. My husband used to do it to piss me off." She shook her head. "Come in. I take it you're here for me to sign the paperwork so you all can get my money?"

"So we can beautify your property. Cut that grass and water those rose bushes. Give you a nice place to relax on those warm summer days." Shane entered the home, catching a whiff of Bengay and chitterlings. He coughed.

"Close the door."

"Yes, ma'am." He sucked in fresh air before shutting it.

"You're here fairly early. I wasn't expecting you until the evening. It's my lunchtime." She headed down the hallway.

He followed her, tripping over the uneven plastic runner lining the walkway.

"Watch your step. I've been meaning to tape that down. Don't want you suing me because you fell. I know how you types are. I watch Judge Judy."

They stepped into the living room, maneuvering around the antique furniture. Sofas covered in plastic, a coffee table with stacks of Ebony and Oprah magazines, and a curio cabinet filled with angel trinkets, reminded him of his grandmother's house. In the corner was a piano and above that a picture of Jesus.

"Always trying to hustle." She continued into the kitchen. "That's how Mr. Harold got me. But it's okay. I've known him for years. He and Frank worked together on a few projects."

Shane's eyes fell on the stovetop full of boiling pots and the two place settings at the kitchen table. "I'll make this quick so that you can get to your meal." He placed his briefcase on the counter and pulled out the documents.

Ms. Evelyn hovered over the stove, checking each pot. "Hungry?" She grabbed a plate from the cupboard.

"No, thank you. Don't want to intrude." Shane shifted through the paperwork.

"Nonsense. There's plenty."

He found the highlighted areas needing her signature and held them up. "Sign here and here. That way, we can start on your yard, have it looking spectacular in no time. And if you don't mind, please hand these out to your neighbors." He placed several business cards down on the counter. "Really appreciate it."

Ms. Evelyn turned away. "I haven't had company in a while. It'll be nice if you could join me. Tell me about city life. I always dreamed about venturing out."

"Would love to." Shane pulled out his phone. "But, I'm on a time crunch. Thanks for the invite, though."

"Nothing wrong with taking a little break."

"Actually, I already ate."

"Eat some more. I make the best chitterlings in town. I'll pack some for the future in-laws."

"I'm a vegetarian." He separated the paperwork into two stacks, one for her and one for the company.

"How about some greens?" She fiddled with the lid of the pot. "Never mind, that has bacon in it." She removed the foil from a loaf of cornbread on the counter. "It's hot and moist."

"No, thank you."

Ms. Evelyn scrambled through her pans as if searching for something else to offer him. "Can never be too prepared." The tops clanked. "Can never be too prepared," she mumbled to herself. "Mama always taught me it was rude to turn down food when offered as a guest at one's house, but I guess times have changed."

Shane took a deep breath, knowing this woman wouldn't let up, like his grandmother. "How about a slice of cornbread?"

Ms. Evelyn made another place setting at the table, carefully arranging the fork, spoon, and knife on the napkin. She then hovered over the stove, scooping food onto the plates.

Shane reviewed the schedule on his phone, mapping out his next three clients.

"So, how's working for Mr. Harold?"

"It's my first week. So far, so good."

"What do you want to drink?" She opened the fridge. "Let me guess, a city boy like you likes coconut water?"

Shane's eyes lit up. "Yes, you have some?"

"No," she chuckled. "That stuff's expensive. How about my famous sweet tea? It's free."

Shane swallowed hard. If it were anything like his grandmother's, it was probably loaded with sugar. "How about some water?"

She pulled out a cup from the cabinet and ran it under the faucet water. It got full, and for a moment, he thought she was going to give it to him until she emptied the cup, filled it with ice, and handed him bottled water. "Coconut water, on the rocks."

Shane smiled. "I see you're a real comedian."

"In my former life." She laughed.

"Why do you keep calling me city boy?"

"Because that's what Mr. Harold calls you. Besides, you look like you stepped out of a magazine, dressed like that." She placed the plates on the table. "You're not from around here. Why the move?"

"It's Tali's hometown. She said it's best to raise a family. Besides, something different."

"Smart man."

A heap of food rested on the plate—greens, potato salad, cornbread, and chitterlings.

I only wanted cornbread.

He swallowed hard, thinking of a way out without hurting her feelings. "Why don't we sign the paperwork first?" He figured once done, he'd take the plate to go.

Ms. Evelyn placed a slice of cornbread on the third place setting, then motioned him to sit in front of it. "That's yours."

Shane took a seat at the table.

Ms. Evelyn sat across from him, staring off into space. "Shall we pray?" She placed her hands together.

"Aren't we waiting for someone?" He motioned to the empty chair.

Ms. Evelyn closed her eyes. "Dear God, thanks for the food on the table and the love in our hearts. Thanks for bringing this city boy here with us today to enjoy this meal. Bless every hand it came across, starting with the farmers planting the seeds, watering the seeds, and helping them grow. Bless the pickers and the sorters and the trucks that carried the food to the grocery stores. Bless the cashier and little Joe-Joe for helping me to my car on my bad foot. Bless …"

Shane squirmed in his seat, the seconds ticking away, along with the next client.

"… none of this could happen without your help, God. Amen," she said.

"Amen." Shane opened his eyes, noticing for the first time the crispy browned edges and buttery smell of the cornbread, just like his grandmother's. *Corner piece.* He grabbed the fork and knife, ready to dig in.

"Go ahead and eat," Ms. Evelyn said. She placed a napkin at the front of her dress like a bib.

"That's what I'm about to do. Smells delicious." Shane cut a bite-sized piece. As he went to stab it with his fork, Ms. Evelyn threw her napkin down.

"I said eat." She pointed to the empty seat. "Come on. Don't embarrass me in front of the guest. And don't tell me I don't care about you, either. I slaved all morning making your favorites. I even had to buy the greens since you stopped gardening."

Shane missed the cornbread and stabbed the plate. The fork clattered the Chinaware.

"Too salty?" She rolled her eyes. "Always complaining. Well, try the potato salad. I put in extra pickles."

Shane's phone buzzed, and he stood. "Um … excuse me, I have to take this." He went into the hallway. "Yes, sir," he answered.

"Wanted to let you know I'm adding two more clients to your schedule," Harold said.

"Great." Shane nodded, picturing the defeated expression on Timothy's face. "Let me get Ms. Evelyn to sign the paperwork, and I'll be on my way."

"Ms. Evelyn? Are you still at her house? I thought you'd be done by now and onto the next client. What's the holdup? Is she giving you the runaround about that discount?"

"No."

"Then what's going on?"

"She's eating lunch. She made this big meal and insisted I join her. I told her I was a vegetarian like you said to say in these circumstances, but she wouldn't let up."

"I knew I should have had Timothy take this one. She knows him."

"I don't think it's that." Shane frowned. "Something else is going on. She was talking to an empty chair. Arguing with it, saying it better appreciate the food she made."

There was a long pause followed by heavy breathing. "Darn," Harold finally said. "I forgot. Today is the second anniversary of her husband Frank's death. Good man. How could I have forgotten?"

A lump formed in Shane's throat.

"I tell you what, forget about Ms. Evelyn signing those papers. She's probably not up to it. Move on to the next client. Tell her I'll stop by later on today with a box of her favorite chocolates. Keep in touch." He hung up.

Shane stared at his phone for several moments then put it away. He sauntered the hallway, catching a glimpse of a photo of a younger Ms. Evelyn and a man he assumed to be her late husband, hanging on the wall. Kids and grandkids surrounded them, their smiles beaming with life. There were more photos Shane hadn't noticed or paid attention to earlier.

He plodded to the kitchen, not sure what to say. The space closed in on him, and his eyes fell on the plate of food and the extra place setting at the table. There was no sign of Ms. Evelyn, except for the sound of her voice coming from the backyard. It carried Shane to the porch where Ms. Evelyn sat, feeding her golden retriever.

"I can't believe Mama forgot to feed you." She rubbed her hand over the dog's brown fur. "I'm a bad mama, a bad mama."

Shane stepped outside the screen door and knelt. "What's her name?" he asked.

Ms. Evelyn glanced up, tears in her eyes. "Foxi. She's my best friend, now."

"She's beautiful." Shane patted the dog's head. "I had a beagle growing up, but it ran away when I was twelve. He was my best friend, too. I still miss him."

Shane and Ms. Evelyn remained quiet for several moments until Ms. Evelyn spoke.

"I signed those papers for you. I know you have to get going, so I won't hold you up any longer and have Mr. boss-in-law on your case. I know how he gets."

Shane took a seat on the porch next to her. "My grandmother always told me to slow down, or you'll miss it."

"Miss what?" Ms. Evelyn asked.

"Great food. How about that lunch?" Shane smiled.

Ms. Evelyn grinned. "I knew you couldn't resist my cooking the way you eyed my chitterlings. You're probably not even a vegetarian."

"I am." He chuckled.

"Okay, city boy, we'll see about that. I know Mr. Harold's trick."

Sunday Afternoons in Eritrea

Sandra Yeaman

I leaned against a building along one of Asmara's busiest streets, waiting for some men to change the tire on my friend Jewel's jeep, when a group of ten boys approached me on a pleasant sunny Sunday afternoon in spring.

"Can you help us?" one of them asked. They gathered in a semicircle around me.

The men helping Jewel didn't need my help, and I wasn't going anywhere. I welcomed the distraction from wondering whether the flat tire was my fault. Jewel had loaned me her jeep the day before, and I ended up on some unfamiliar roads that contrasted sharply with the smooth boulevard where Jewel's jeep was now parked, a street wide enough for the annual parade of tanks, military equipment, and soldiers to mark the anniversary of Eritrea's independence from Ethiopia. Eritrea gained its independence from Ethiopia twelve years earlier, though I had learned quickly that independence for Eritrea did not mean freedom for its citizens. Our two governments have never been on good terms, complicating personal relationships there.

Jewel, my unofficial sponsor at the US embassy in Asmara for the months I worked there, had invited me to attend a barbecue at the Israeli ambassador's home that afternoon. After she parked the jeep, she noticed one of the tires was flat. An eternal optimist, Jewel just smiled and suggested we go ahead to the barbecue and not worry about the tire until afterwards. She was sure she could convince some men at the barbecue to come back with us afterwards to fix the tire. And she was right. Two guests of the Israeli ambassador were at that moment at work jacking up the vehicle to replace the tire.

83

I turned my attention to the boys, most of them barely up to my shoulder in height, as they gathered around me with smiles and bright eyes focused on me.

"Do you speak English?" I asked.

The shortest one replied, "I do," while the others gently pushed him forward.

The tallest one, standing at the back of the group, said, "He's Dawit."

"Well, Dawit," I said, "what help do you need?"

"Money for our football team." He screwed up his face and pointed to the T-shirt four of the boys were holding as if it were a fireman's safety net intended to catch coins tossed in their direction. I got the impression I was supposed to understand everything from that image.

"What is the money for?" I said.

"Uniforms," he said.

"How much money do you need for a uniform?"

"Thirty nakfa."

At that time, the US embassy's official exchange rate for the nakfa, the national currency of Eritrea, was just over three nakfa per US dollar. I wasn't sure if ten dollars per uniform was a high price or a low one in the Asmara economy, but it wasn't much for me. *If this was a scam to collect money from foreigners*, I thought, *it's a very elaborate one. These boys couldn't have known I would be here at this moment. What do I have to lose by helping them?*

I pulled out a 100 nakfa bill. But before I handed it over, I said, "I'd like to know more about you before I give you this. My name is Sandra. I know Dawit's name, but I'd like to know the rest of your names."

Dawit turned to the rest and said something. The tallest one spoke up first. "I am Habtom. Captain of team."

"I Henok," said another.

Silence followed, perhaps from shyness, perhaps from lack of understanding. In order to keep them telling me their names, I looked directly at the boy closest to me and said, "What's your name?"

"Filemon," he said and turned his face away.

I kept looking and nodding at each one, and the boys answered. One boy's eyes in particular caught my attention. I felt myself being drawn in. *There's something special about him,* I thought. *But how can that be? And how can I find out?*

When I nodded in his direction, he said his name was Tekelu, the most difficult one for me to understand and repeat. The other names were simpler. Daniel and Isaias, Yohanna and Medhane. I repeated Tekelu's name several times until he nodded and smiled to indicate I was close enough.

"Thanks for telling me your names," I said. "But how will I know that you will use the money to buy uniforms?"

The boys huddled together as Dawit spoke before he turned back to face me, without saying anything.

"Will I just have to trust you?" I said to break the silence.

Dawit nodded vigorously. "Yes, trust us."

"Okay," I said. "Here is 100 nakfa for you to buy three uniforms." I handed the money to Dawit, who thanked me. He spoke sharply to the rest of the boys who had already begun to move away. The boys stopped, turned to face me, and each one said something approximating *thanks* and then made their way running down the street.

I turned to see how much progress the men helping Jewel had made with the tire when I heard footsteps behind me. Dawit and Habtom had returned.

"Where do you live?" Dawit asked.

"In the United States," I said.

"No," Dawit said. "Now. Where do you live now?"

"In Asmara," I said.

"In Asmara where?" Dawit asked.

I didn't know my address because I didn't need to. As a temporary employee at the US embassy, I lived in one of its rented properties. A driver picked me up each morning and drove me home each evening. All the Americans at the embassy knew where my house was so I never had to give anyone an address. "I know this will sound funny," I said, "but I don't know my address."

Dawit relayed to Habtom what I had said, and the two

walked back to the corner where the other boys waited.

The men were beginning to put the tools back into the jeep when Dawit and Habtom returned, this time with a pen. Dawit handed me the pen and asked me to write my name and telephone number on Habtom's hand. I did, thinking the numbers would rub off before the boys reached home. Jewel and I got into her jeep, and we drove back to my house.

I didn't give any thought to the incident until the following Saturday when my phone rang late in the evening. I answered, but I didn't understand the person on the other end and was about to hang up when the voice said, "Wait, Habtom, 100 nakfa." I heard the receiver being passed to someone else.

"Hello, Miss Sandra," the voice said.

"Yes, I'm Sandra."

"There is a group of boys here who want to meet with you. They say you gave them money to buy uniforms."

"Yes, I did. I thought they would have lost my phone number."

"They want to know where you can meet them so they can show you their uniforms. Where is a place close to your house where they can meet you?"

I mentioned a corner grocery store on the largest street near my home. The man at the other end of the phone confirmed that the boys knew that store, and we agreed to meet there the following day at three p.m.

Sleep didn't come easily that night. What had I gotten myself into? I had seen children all over Asmara playing in the streets just as I had done in my childhood. Few cars interrupted their play. But did that mean they were all that innocent? What consoled me until sleep came was the image of Tekelu's eyes and smile. If Habtom had managed to keep my phone number from rubbing off to make that phone call, surely this was a sign that what my heart felt needed attention.

The next morning I went early to the small grocery store to buy whatever snacks I could find for the boys—cookies and potato chips—as well as paper towels to serve as both plates and napkins. Even these items were not easy to find.

Before I left my house a second time to meet the boys, I told the two embassy guards outside the house that I would be returning with a group of young boys I had met the previous week. I wanted to assure the guards they did not need to worry about my safety or anything in the house. I explained that by the time the boys left, I would have written down all of their names, their fathers' names, their ages, and the schools they attended so that if anything was missing after they left, I would know whom to contact. I wasn't sure I could actually accomplish that much, but my heart kept telling me that meeting up with the boys was the right thing to do.

When I reached the corner store, there were 14 boys, 4 of them wearing matching shirts and shorts — the uniforms. Dawit moved ahead of the rest of the boys and walked with me as I led the boys like the Pied Piper without a flute. In spite of his small size and young age, Dawit was clearly a leader.

The boys lined themselves up on the sofas, chairs, and carpets around the living room of my temporary home. I served them the cookies, chips, and water while I asked them to tell me their names and the other vital details I had assured the guards I would get. I took photos of the boys in the order they sat so I could match up their faces with the names I wrote down. I learned they all attended the same school and that Habtom, their coach, was the only one in his teens. The rest ranged from nine to twelve years old. They practiced every Sunday afternoon, and they invited me to meet up with them the next Sunday at the same corner store so I could accompany them to their practice field, within easy walking distance. I agreed. Just as they were about to leave, Dawit mentioned that the 100 nakfa I gave them only covered four uniforms. The question of whether I would buy the rest hung in the air, unspoken. As the boys hovered near the door, I agreed to provide funds for the other ten, and I handed over 300 nakfa to Habtom.

Those two Sunday afternoons set the routine for the remainder of my time in Asmara. Each Sunday I met the boys and walked to the Expo grounds to watch them practice and play against other teams. At first I had expected the Expo grounds to be a stadium, and I wondered how the boys had gotten permission to play there. Once we reached it, however, I saw it was simply a large dirt field, littered with broken tree branches, stones, grazing sheep and cows, and an occasional water-filled ditch. The boys moved rocks and sticks and placed them to mark the goals and side boundaries. Habtom ran them through a variety of exercise routines. Other groups of boys in other parts of the field held similar practices, though without uniforms. After a few weeks the teams began scheduling games against one another.

Jewel joined me on many Sundays and brought refreshments for after practice. I took videos of their practice and games. We watched those videos afterwards at my house. Jewel managed to get copies of *Finding Nemo* and *Bend it Like Beckham*, and we watched them with the boys even though I am sure only Dawit could understand much of the language. From their faces, I saw they didn't need language to understand the stories.

I bought them boots, balls, a second set of uniforms, and provided whatever refreshments I could find for later. I sat on the sidelines, surrounded by the boys who weren't on the field. Over time, they sat closer and closer to me, even leaning against me as they rested, and they told me about their lives. Tekelu told me his father had died in the Ethiopian-Eritrean civil war, so he and his mother lived with his uncle and his wife and their children. Before I left Asmara, I met Tekelu's uncle, Nasser. We have kept in contact since then, a possibility only because he is no longer in Eritrea.

Dawit was my translator throughout, though several of the other boys tried to speak with me, even tried to teach me some Tigrinya. The boys invited me to visit them in their homes without specifying a date, but the week after they invited me, Dawit explained that their parents were embarrassed about their circumstances and didn't want me to see their homes. Maybe that was the truth, but it is also possible they did not want to draw attention to their sons being connected with an American from the US embassy.

Early in my assignment at the embassy, I found framed Superior Honor Awards with the names of two local staff members in the safe in my office. When I asked why the awards hadn't been given to the employees I learned the Eritrean government had arrested them several years earlier and still held them without charge or a trial, without the possibility of contact with their families. No one knew whether they were still alive. I understood why the parents of these boys might fear what could happen if others saw an American in their homes.

I prayed each night that my generosity toward the boys would not result in any harm to them. I knew that within a few years their childhoods would end abruptly when they would be required to attend the Sawa Defence Training Center, the final year of an Eritrean child's schooling and the beginning of the never-ending compulsory military service all Eritrean citizens must endure.

On my last weekend in Asmara, other observers joined me at the field. Several embassy staff and a few members of the UN development team in the country attended. Afterwards, they all returned to my temporary home where the US ambassador and his wife, his deputy and his wife, and other embassy staff also met the boys. The development team members discussed how easily they could improve the playing field for the boys, but I never heard whether they were able to do so. For the first time, leaving a country at the end of my assignment felt a very unsatisfactory ending. So many people had touched me there, and it was unlikely I would know what their future would bring. What I could predict would not be happy.

Tekelu's uncle Nasser, his wife, and his children, though not Tekelu, are now living in Syracuse, NY, having been resettled there through a Catholic refugee service. I never asked him how he and his family got out of Eritrea. I didn't want to put him in a position of having to tell me about something I didn't want to know or of telling me a lie. Since Tekelu is Nasser's nephew, not an adopted child, he does not

89

fall under the definition of immediate family and could not be resettled with Nasser. Tekelu is out of Eritrea but stranded without the support of the only family he has known.

A flat tire on a Sunday afternoon and the friendship of a remarkable optimist led me to take a leap of faith and place my trust in a band of young boys in a faraway place most people have never heard of. I was blessed to spend time with them and watch them being boys, playing together on a weekend, enjoying their time as a team of friends. I hope those days remain happy memories for them too.

A First Time for Everything

Ruth L. Wallace

There are tens of firsts in everyone's life, both firsts that come to mind when sought and memories of firsts that spring up unannounced. Some are one-of-a-kind firsts, some are first-of-many firsts. They mark and shape the flow of time. Some are common to almost everyone, some belong only to you.

There always a *first* first time ... the absolutely earliest thing you remember from childhood. My *first* first is a memory of sitting on the front porch of our house waiting for the ice man, so I could see the huge block of ice that he carried into the house with gigantic tongs and slid into the bottom section of the ice box. It was 1945 and we didn't give a second thought about not having an electric refrigerator.

I don't live dangerously, but my *second* first was breaking my leg while roller skating and the trip to the hospital when I was in fifth grade. Later came two broken wrists (one while roller skating at age 55), and a broken tailbone.

My enthusiasm for roller skating was also part of my *third* first—my first date. Gary, a fellow sixth grader, called to invite me to go roller skating at the rink. It was a first for my father too: do fathers ever *not* ask "How are you going to get there? ... Who's driving? ... What time will you be home?"

My *fourth* first, was an important milestone—my first job. I landed a job as cashier selling tickets at the downtown movie theater. Besides being one of the highest paying jobs in town for a high school student ($0.75/hour) the ticket booth had the added advantage of a view of Main Street. I could see who drove what car, who sat in the front seat, who was dating whom.

Is there ever a teen who can't wait to move away from

91

home for the first time? My *fifth* first was leaving home in Colorado and going to Oklahoma to attend Oklahoma State University. I was used to sharing a room with my sister, but not going down the dormitory hall to take a shower or make a telephone call. An extra special part of that OSU first was meeting my first husband.

Then there's the first time you run out of money, get a new job, and move into your first apartment. Along with this *sixth* first was a bed that folded up into the wall, which I'd never seen before, and a stove from the 1920s, whose oven stood at eye level on long legs beside the burners.

My *seventh* first was falling in love and marrying my college sweetheart. Our first Christmas together was in Kimball, Nebraska. For our special first Christmas, in a spurt of creativity, I scoured the highway out of town and found the perfect big tumbleweed. I sprayed it with artificial snow and decorated it with dozens of small pink glass balls. It was just right for the coffee table in our tiny living area. My *eighth* and first up-close look at death was when this love of my life was killed in an accident at work at 28 years old.

In the mid-seventies the feminist movement was in full swing and brought a set of *ninth* firsts. I joined other women and got my first credit card. For the first time I was able buy a car without permission from my father or husband. I bought my first house in Topeka, Kansas, all as a divorced, single woman.

My *tenth* first became possible when I moved to California and remarried. Our new home had a room designated as our office. For a long time I had wanted to make a contribution to life. I wanted to write a book which would draw together all the files, clippings, research articles, and my professional experience for the benefit of patients needing psychiatric care. This tenth first was published in 2008 as *Linking Nutrition to Mental Health*, a joyous first, but not the last first, to be sure.

It's a Little Taily

Amy Wall

D'Andre Williams turned down his radio just as Seacrest announced the number ten song in the charts. Pharrell William's hit song, "Happy" faded into the background as he pulled up to the curbside valet in his Lamborghini Aventador. The valet welcomed him on the driver's side, pushed the button in the handle and lifted the door.

"Hi Josh." D'Andre straightened his Italian-silk suit jacket and handed him the key fob. "Looks like you got a new guy," he said as he got out of the car, lifting his chin in the direction of the valet check in.

Josh waved the new guy over.

"Danny, this is D'Andre Williams. He's been a member of the Country Club for over 15 years."

The new guy shook D'Andre's hand. "Nice to meet you, Mr. Williams."

"Nice to meet you too, Danny." He took the key fob from Josh and gave it to Danny. "You know how to drive a paddle shifter?"

Danny looked at the key fob in his hand. "Yeah, I've parked a few."

D'Andre turned to Josh. "Let him take this one." He turned back to Danny, "Take it around the block first. You gotta feel how this thing corners."

Danny blushed; his ears turned bright red. "Are you sure? What if…"

"Of course I'm sure. No point in havin' a fun car if you can't share it."

The new guy looked at Josh, "Is it okay?"

"It's against company policy, but I'll pretend I didn't see

anything."

Danny never saw a car as beautiful as this. It was pearl white with black trim and had a chocolate brown leather interior. He sunk into the seat. "This leather is so soft and smooth."

D'Andre chuckled. "My wife says it is an exact match to my skin. Comes in handy when I'm trying to go unnoticed."

They all laughed.

D'Andre showed Danny how to adjust the seat and steering wheel. "In the center console, use that button to put the car in manual, then you can use the paddle shifter. The strata mode will give you the smoothest ride."

The new guy pushed the brake and the ignition button to start the engine. He followed D'Andre's instructions.

"Seriously, Danny, take your time and enjoy the ride. I'm in no rush."

He pulled down the door and drove away slowly, more carefully than necessary. D'Andre and Josh chuckled while they watched him moving the car forward about as fast as a few men could push it.

When he turned the corner and was out of sight, the two walked toward the valet stand.

"When does Kim finish school?" D'Andre inquired.

"In two months. Thanks for asking. She was able to take extra classes this year and is graduating early."

"That's fantastic."

"As soon as she finds a full-time job, it'll be my turn to start applying. I can start sooner than we originally planned because we don't have any school loans to pay back."

Although Josh had his suspicions, he wasn't certain if D'Andre secretly paid for Kim's two-year master's program. The week she got her acceptance letter, someone called the school and took care of it. Josh asked on two occasions if it was him, but he pretended he didn't know what Josh was talking about.

They both looked up when the Lamborghini drove down the street in front of the club. The new valet raised his hand out of the window waving to them as he drove by. He was moving at a normal speed now. He moved his finger in a circle indicating he was going to go around the block one more time. D'Andre gave a thumbs up.

Just as Danny was turning the corner and was out of sight again, D'Andre and Josh heard the noise of a car heading in their direction. They turned to the left to see a flash of yellow. A roar of an engine cut through the normally quiet street. They watched as a brand new Corvette Stingray entered the circular driveway of the Country Club. In total disregard, the driver took the turn a little too fast and hit the brakes a little too hard.

The driver of the Stingray got out before Josh could take a step in his direction. A tall man jumped out of the driver seat. He combed his hands through his stiff sandy-brown hair to make sure it was still in place. Before any words were exchanged, he grabbed his keys and tossed them to D'Andre.

"Park it in front so I don't have to wait." The man kept walking before anyone could say anything.

D'Andre's hands were in his pockets. The keys hit him in the chest and fell to the ground.

Josh bent down to pick them up whispering, "I'm so sorry."

D'Andre stopped him with a hand gesture and grabbed the keys. "Don't worry about it, I've got this." He grinned, a smile stretching across his face while he put his gym bag down next to the valet stand.

The Corvette driver kept walking toward the giant glass doors of the club. Before he moved to open the doors, he stopped and turned back toward the car. He took a few steps toward Josh. D'Andre was opening the driver door and was sliding into the white leather seat.

"Make sure he doesn't park it too close to the other cars," the Corvette owner barked.

Just as he was turning back to enter the club, the spiked haired man heard the rev of his engine. Out of the corner of his eye he saw his car lurch forward. The sound of the tires on the flagstones of the parking area sounded like the shrill of an angry bird. As he turned toward the sound, he saw the tail end of the car sway a little.

Josh and the car owner both stood still, but for different reasons. Josh's eyes opened wider. The owner of the Corvette watched in horror as D'Andre tested the machine's 495 horsepower. The car manufacturers claim the Stingray can go from zero to sixty in less than three seconds. Thankfully, there wasn't a road long enough around the Country Club to try that out.

It was unknown what the speed of the car was able to reach in those few seconds, but it was fast. As the car approached the end of the street, it fishtailed. D'Andre yanked the steering wheel round, putting the car into a spin. He knew a mid-engine car will oversteer on the accelerator lift off, so he gently eased off the power to regain control. The tires etched half circles on the road. After a couple seconds of stillness, he righted the car. The engine revved and the tires squealed again as the car accelerated back down toward the Country Club.

Back at the club, Josh looked around to see if anyone else was watching. His eyebrows were extended upwards, and his mouth opened. He saw the Stingray owner's face, bright red in fury as his hands pushed down the stiff spikes on his head.

"What the fuck is he doing?" he shouted.

D'Andre sped back toward the club. He jerked the steering wheel and let the car drift sharply into the bend. The rear end broke free and spun the car again. As the car turned, Josh and the car's owner saw D'Andre look over with a smile on his face. A small amount of smoke trailed off the tires.

When the car finally came to a stop, everything went silent again just before the angry man started shouting again. D'Andre carefully turned the car, drove past the front of the club, turned into the circular driveway and stopped right in front of the valet stand.

He stepped out of the car in one quick motion, looking up to see Josh's face with a look of shock. He winked at him. Josh let out a guffaw, making sure his back was turned to the furious car owner behind him.

The owner of the Stingray shouted something about suing

someone, stomping toward D'Andre. As he approached, D'Andre tossed the keys back to him. The man went silent and caught the keys at the last moment.

"Impressive. It was a little taily, but it handles curves alright. If you ever want to try out mine, let me know."

The Corvette owner, face the color of a cherry, stood silent, not sure how to respond.

Just then, Danny pulled up in the Lamborghini and stopped behind the Corvette. He hadn't seen D'Andre driving the yellow car. As he stepped out of the raised door, he walked straight up to him and shook his hand. "That was an awesome ride, Mr. Williams. Thank you so much."

"Any time Danny. Nice to meet you."

D'Andre picked up his gym bag, gave Josh a thumbs up, and walked past the fuming Corvette owner toward the giant glass doors. The man was shouting again, demanding to see the manager. As D'Andre approached the entrance he heard Danny say to Josh, "What's up with that guy?"

D'Andre chuckled as the door man pulled the handles to let him in.

The Dream Crow

Judith Lief

The scent of yeast wafted through the air inside Nana's
kitchen at 10 South Bellevue Avenue. Loaves of bread rose in
secret, crowded together under dishtowels caressed by a
warm summer breeze that swept across the Jersey shore into
the open window. At an old wooden table covered with flour,
Nana handed four-year-old Angela a piece of dough to roll
out on the tabletop.

"Tell me a story about when Daddy was little," Angela
said.

Nana laughed. Tiny, she wore her white, waist-length hair
in two long braids that she wrapped around her head and
anchored with amber combs. "Your daddy was little a long
time ago. He was born before the Great War. When he grew
up, he became a soldier in World War II. Then he came home,
met your mommy, and got married. But I've told you lots of
stories about your daddy. Why don't you tell me a story
today?"

Angela frowned. She rubbed the back of her hand
underneath her nose and a ballet troupe of flour dancers
pirouetted through the air. A few landed *en pointe* in her dark,
curly hair. "I don't know a story."

"Yes, you do. Everyone has a story to tell," Nana said as
she handed Angela the rolling pin.

Holding onto the pin, Angela leaned into the dough with
all of her weight. She pounded it with choppy strokes. "Once
upon a time, there was a little girl. She hated when her
mommy hollered. She got scared. Her mommy was pretty like
a princess with shiny brown hair and big, brown eyes. When
Mommy laughed she sparkled brighter than a star. But

98

sometimes what made her laugh one day made her yell the next. The little girl never knew when or why it would happen. She loved the happy Mommy, but the other one … Why did her mommy hurt her? What did she do wrong?"

Angela rolled the dough pressing hard against the two red handles of the pin while Nana watched her.

"Her mommy had a strap, an ugly brown strap. Mommy hit her when Daddy wasn't home."

Nana tipped her head toward Angela, then nodded. She moved closer as she showed the child how to divide the dough and roll it into long, rounded strips. She took Angela's hands in hers and taught her how to braid the strips together. Angela dipped a pastry brush into a bowl of beaten egg and water then brushed it across the loaf just like Nana showed her.

"Today Mommy got mad. I don't know what I did. Daddy was at the store. She took the strap, but I didn't run and I didn't crawl under the bed this time. I told her. I told her don't holler, don't hit me. I'm a person. Please, Nana, don't tell Daddy. Hide me."

Nana held out her arms and folded Angela close. "Can you show me where Mommy hit you?"

Angela nodded. Nana hugged her then slowly stood back and watched as Angela revealed the red welts on her thighs and buttocks. Nana hugged her again. "I'll keep you safe," she promised.

But how? Angela wondered.

"Wait here," Nana said. She went into the laundry room and returned with a large wicker basket. "Take off your apron and hang it on the peg in the laundry room while I bring in the laundry from outside."

Nana carried the basket out the kitchen door to the clothesline in a patch of side yard by the house. She filled the empty basket with sheets, pillowcases, and small towels. Then she brought it into the kitchen and tucked it into a corner near the silver radiator. After Nana lined the sides and bottom of the basket, she helped Angela climb inside.

Angela hid. Nana covered her with a sheet fresh from the

99

clothesline and swaddled her face with sun-dried towels.

What about my loaf? Angela worried. *Will Nana remember to cover it? If she doesn't, it might not grow. Daddy will be here soon. If I ask Nana, he might hear me. If I peek out of the basket, he'll see me. Then he'll take me home.*

Angela crouched inside the wicker basket and listened for the sound of her father's footsteps on the front porch. *When I go home, no one can keep me safe. If Daddy knows, then Mommy will get madder. She doesn't hit me when Daddy's home. He wouldn't like it. She said I better not tell or Daddy might go away. Then even Nana couldn't help me.*

"Where's Angela?" Daddy's deep voice asked.

"She must be hiding," Nana said. "You'll just have to leave her here."

Angela tucked her head against her chin and curled up inside the basket. She heard Daddy laugh. He laughed like Nana, but he was tall with curly dark hair. *Mommy says I'm just like Daddy. What does she mean? Is it my hair? Sometimes when she's mad, she calls me a bad girl. Daddy's not bad. He never yells at me or Mommy. When he hugs us both after breakfast before he goes to work, his face smells like the limes that grow in the garden.*

"I bet I could find Angela," Daddy said.

She heard the smile in his voice as she pressed her ear against the side of the basket. But soon it got quieter. *They must be in the dining room or maybe the living room now,* she thought, as she strained to hear. Daddy wasn't laughing anymore, and Nana sounded angry.

"I never thought a son of mine would let this happen. I won't stand for it. Whatever it takes, you and Myrna get help. If you need money … "

The voices went on and on, but curled inside the basket, nestled against the sheets and towels, Angela couldn't hear any more. She held her breath.

"Come out from wherever you are. You can stay," Daddy yelled.

Angela peeked out of the basket. Daddy stood in the dining room next to Nana, near the dark wood buffet, his back toward the kitchen. *Was it safe? Could she leave her hiding place?* Carefully she got out of the basket and tucked the sheets back inside. *It wasn't a good idea to show her hiding place to anyone. Only Nana knew.*

As Angela trudged toward the dining room, she stopped for an instant in the doorway. Nana walked toward her, smiled, then briefly dropped a gnarled hand gently on the child's shoulder before walking back into the kitchen.

Angela stood still. *What if Daddy's mad that I told? What if he doesn't love me anymore?* She walked toward her father dragging her feet on the faded floral carpet.

He turned around and knelt down on one knee, towering over her. "Nana said Mommy hits you, and you don't want to go home. Is that true?"

Angela didn't answer. *Maybe he won't believe me,* she thought. *What if he thinks I'm trying to get Mommy in trouble? Maybe I'm bad and Mommy should hit me. What if Daddy leaves?* Tears rolled down her cheeks, and she didn't speak.

But Nana could, and Nana did with a hoarse, raspy voice like a crow, as she rushed into the dining room. "Of course it's true. Just look at her. You're scaring her to death. Practically accused her of lying."

Her grandmother bent down. "Can I show him?" she asked softly.

At first Angela didn't understand. When she saw Nana point at her legs, Angela nodded. Carefully her grandmother lifted the hem of Angela's Sunday dress. Large red marks swelled near the elastic line of her panties.

Daddy's face turned funny. His eyes shimmered, and he rubbed them with his hand.

"I'm so sorry, Baby, I didn't know. It won't ever happen again."

He went home alone and returned after dinner holding a suitcase filled with clothes and a bag of Angela's favorite toys. "You can stay with Nana for a month. When you come back, I promise things will be different."

Every morning Nana took her on the boardwalk to watch the ocean and feed the pigeons. Angela carried a small paper

101

bag full of stale bread that she broke into little pieces and tossed onto the slanted boards. The birds gathered around her pecking at the crumbs. After a few days, they seemed to recognize her from a distance and flew right to her.

Sometimes, Nana took her on the beach. Then Angela pulled off her sandals and wriggled her toes in the sand before they gathered shells. Once, she found a perfect conch shell that Nana held to her ear. The ocean called from inside it while she watched the waves rise like a high green wall, curl around themselves, and crash onto the shore. Thick white foam bubbled up on top of the water. She tasted salt in the air.

I want to stay with Nana forever, she thought. *I miss Daddy a lot. I miss Mommy too, but Nana tells me stories, and Nana will never let anyone hurt me.*

One month flew faster than the birds Angela fed. Her mother came to pick her up on a Monday morning in August. When Angela heard the doorbell ring, she wanted to hide again. She clung to Nana's skirt as the door opened. Her tall, square-shouldered mother said hello to Nana, smiled, then bent down and kissed Angela on her forehead.

"Do you have your things together?" her mother asked.

Angela nodded.

"Good. Go check your room to make sure you didn't leave anything behind."

She started upstairs to her room, but paused in the second-floor hallway when she heard voices below.

"Don't interfere. I won't hit her again, though God knows children need discipline. Just stay out of it. It's between Michael and me."

Angela rested her head against the wall and listened to her grandmother's rusty sounding voice.

"If you ever touch her again, I'll take her away."

"You can't!"

"But I will," Nana said.

Angela imagined Nana puffing herself up like a magical crow.

"And you'll never hurt her again as long as I live."

"Angela," her mother called, "hurry up and finish

checking for your things."

* * *

The hitting stopped. By the time Angela turned eight, some Sunday mornings Daddy still took her to visit Nana like before, but not as often. Sometimes Nana wasn't feeling well. When Angela visited, she brushed Nana's hair and divided the long white strands into two braids. She wound them around Nana's head and anchored them with amber combs. Some Sundays she read to Nana, but her favorite Sundays were when Nana told her stories.

One Wednesday night the phone rang. Angela saw Daddy sitting on the black leather chair next to the telephone table. He leaned forward, his elbows resting on his knees, his head between his open fingers. Daddy was crying. She couldn't remember ever seeing him cry before. She wanted to fling her arms around his neck and tell him everything would be alright. But Mother caught her by the back of her blue jumper.

"Go upstairs."

Angela felt her heart pound. "What's wrong?"

"Your grandmother died."

She's lying, Nana isn't dead. She couldn't be. Angela raced upstairs to her room, slammed the door, and flung herself on her bed sobbing. *How could she lie? How could she say Nana was dead?*

That night she heard her parents arguing in their bedroom.

"It's a graveside service," Mother said. "She won't have to see the body."

"She's too young," Daddy said.

"No, she's not. She has to understand. No one gets out of the world alive. People die. They don't come back."

The next morning Mother called the school and told them Angela couldn't attend. Later a black limousine pulled up to the house on Delavan Avenue. It took them over the Dover Avenue bridge and across the big traffic circle to the cemetery. The limousine drove through the open gate and stopped on a stone roadway. Her mother took her hand and walked her across the grass to where a canopy on metal posts covered an area of chairs. She saw a coffin half-lowered in the ground. Mother had told her that Nana would be buried in a coffin.

Angela sat next to her parents in the front row. A few yards away from the coffin, almost hidden in the grass, a crow bobbed and wobbled as its strong black beak dug in the earth for grubs.

The congregants murmured. Clothing rustled against the chairs as the mourners rose then sat. She followed the sounds but kept her eyes away from the coffin and focused on the crow. It plumped up its body when her father stood and recited a prayer. The mourners responded amen.

The crow pumped its wings a few times as if for practice. Then suddenly it gave an awkward little hop. Angela saw that the coffin had been lowered into the open ground. She watched her father reach for something shiny, a shovel that he filled with dirt. Her eyes fixed on the crow and it stared back at her. "Caw," it warned. "Don't look."

A thud sounded as clods of earth hit the coffin. Just then the crow flung itself skyward, wingtips like fingers against endless blue.

* * *

That night Angela lay on her bed and stared at the ceiling. Outside the house, raindrops spattered on the cedar shakes of the roof. *They put Nana in a coffin and covered it with dirt. How could they?*

The wind tore the last November leaves from the maple tree outside Angela's window. She turned her face into her wet pillow then heard a raspy sound.

"Nana?"

No answer. But the sudden smell of yeast filled the room. Someone or something was with her. "Who's there?" she cried, then scrunched her eyes shut. Behind closed lids a picture slowly emerged of a crow, wingtips spread like fingers against luminous light.

Remember, the bird seemed to say. A blanket of air rippled over her, holding her gently in a current as warm as breath on a summer's day. *Nana promised to keep me safe,* she thought as she felt her grandmother's love surround her. *No matter what happens, Nana's love will keep me safe.*

Angela's body relaxed and just before she drifted off to sleep, she made a promise of her own. "I'll remember you, Nana. When I grow up and have a little girl of my own, I'll keep her safe because you showed me how."

Parnelli

Tom Leech

In the fall of 1972, several of the most active Baja roads, ten or more, were marked to transform their surfaces from the challenging dirt, sand, and rock to smoother but boring asphalt and concrete. So, with the soon-to-happen changes from the rough-road (but used by many of us) types to typical paved road drives, some of us frequent Baja off-road pleasure nuts decided to hit those roads one last time while they were still in their original conditions. I was one of those, at that time driving my 1970 VW camper, so I rounded up crony Ken, who had often hit those back roads with me. He said "sounds interesting," so we prepped for a several days rough-road journey and headed across the border. This would lead to another memorable Baja adventure, combined with exchanging dialogue with one of the most famous off-road Baja racers, namely Parnelli Jones.

We drove south on good paved roads along the Pacific Ocean Coast through Tijuana, Rosarito Beach, and Ensenada. About 20 miles further south, we pulled into the well-known Bradley's filling station and gassed up my VW. Most drivers filled up their buggies here as this is where the reasonably good paved road ended.

Now we were on the old unchanged dirt roads, and we headed southeast across Baja to Bahia de Los Angeles. That small but popular village was located right on the Gulf of Mexico shoreline, so our overnight lodging was where we camped on the beach. Next day continuing on, we drove along another dirt road so rough we rarely made it above the VW's 2nd gear (of 4), and our top speed was sometimes 15 mph.

Finally, after two more fun days of slow poking along the old-style rugged roads, we achieved our goal and arrived at one of the newly-paved Baja roads heading south. Now we drove in 4th gear maybe 30-40 mph with fewer bumps and rattles than the last couple days. We drove past a scenic small lake — not too many of those in upper Baja — then into a pretty town named San Ignacio. There we stopped at a real café to get lunch, something we'd not had for several days, if you don't count our self-prepared hot dogs.

As we were enthusiastically munching our lunch, three more gringos came in to order their own lunches. They had been checking out the roads in preparation for the upcoming Baja 1,000-mile off-road race, and one of them was the actual race driver Parnelli Jones. This was a typical activity for most of the teams as this was not a race to be taken without advance prep. We enjoyed chatting with them, and as we were intrigued by what sort of vehicle they were driving, they invited us out to look it over.

It was not the actual race vehicle but a rugged van that could easily carry three passengers and readily handle the many rough spots along the road. But what Parnelli was most proud of was a special modification he had installed with the vehicle. So to demonstrate, he reached up to the roof of the van and pulled over a gadget connected to a roof-top water tank. He then proudly pulled the water cord and showed how he and the crew could actually take a hot shower while traveling along Baja's many miles of off-road race terrains. Not a benefit Ken or I could achieve with my VW van.

Meeting them helped make ours a truly memorable journey, combining our success at driving the rough roads with meeting a Baja race crew checking out their upcoming route (and especially having the real driver show us his van's special capability). Thanks a lot, Parnelli, and good luck on the soon-to-happen 1972 Baja 1,000. (I can't recall if he won or not, but I bet he and his crew did enjoy those warm showers after each day of pre-testing the race route.)

Lady Mondegreen

Laurie Asher

I want to share ten favored songs we sang back in high school. Except we got the lyrics all wrong. Then we hear the song again, maybe a few decades later. This time we hear the lyrics differently (correctly) and think, *OMG, I can't believe I thought the lyrics were* this or that *for all those years!*

So what's going on here? Don't fret. It's not a condition you will find in some mental diagnosis manual, so you can relax. You have a lot of friendly company. This phenomenon is real and it has a name. It's a *mondegreen*! A short definition would be — misheard lyrics, phrases, slogans, etc., and the really good ones last for decades in your mind.

Where did it all start? My guess is back in the stone age when one Cro-Magnon man misinterpreted a Cro-Magnon woman grunting and rock banging. Nothing new under the sun!

In our modern world, the word *mondegreen* was conceived by Scottish author Sylvia Wright, who described an early childhood experience in an article she wrote for Harper's Magazine in 1954. As a young girl, she was listening to an old folk ballad that included these lines:

The Bonnie Earl O'Moray
Ye highlands and ye lowlands
Oh where hae you been?
Thou hae slay the Earl of Murray —
And layd him on the green. —

Ms. Wright heard the last line as this: — *And Lady Mondegreen* — So, she thought there were two murders!

108

One classic example of a *mondegreen* is a line from a Jimi Hendrix mega hit from the '70s, "Purple Haze." Now tell me truthfully, didn't you always think Jimi was singing, "'Scuse me while I *kiss this guy*?" This was so common that the lyrics eventually turned into the title of a book by Gavin Edwards, NY Times.[1] I guess not all of us realized it was "'Scuse me while I kiss the sky."[2] Then we listen to the song a few decades later, but this time we have one of those bang-your-fist-to-your-forehead, an *I could have had a V8* moment, and you say to yourself — *I can't believe I thought the lyrics were* this and that *for all those years!*

Want more? Here are some common ones:

1. "Bad Moon Rising." Creedence Clearwater Revivial[3]
   Mangled: "There's a bathroom on the right."
   Actual Lyrics: "There's a bad moon on the rise."
2. "Blowin' In the Wind." Bob Dylan[4]
   Mangled: "Dead ants are my friends; they're blowin' in the wind."
   Actual Lyrics: "The answer, my friend, is blowin' in the wind."
3. "Lucy in the Sky with Diamonds." The Beatles[5]
   Mangled: "The girl with colitis goes by."
   Actual Lyrics: "The girl with kaleidoscope eyes."
4. "Build Me Up Buttercup." The Foundations[6]
   Mangled: "I'll be your xylophone waiting for you."
   Actual Lyrics: "I'll be beside the phone waiting for you."
5. "Tiny Dancer." Elton John[7]
   Mangled: "Hold me closer, Tony Danza."
   Actual Lyrics: "Hold me closer tiny dancer."
6. "Don't It Make My Brown Eyes Blue." Crystal Gale[8]
   Mangled: "Donuts make my brown eyes blue."
   Actual Lyrics: "Don't it make my brown eyes blue."
7. "Let's Hang On." Frankie Vallee and the Four Seasons[9]
   Mangled: "Got a lot of lucky peanuts, hang on, hang on."
   Actual Lyrics: "Got a lot of love between us, hang on, hang on."

8. "We Will Rock You." Queen[10]
   Mangled: "You've got mud on your face, front disc brakes."
   Actual Lyrics: "You've got mud on your face, a big disgrace."
9. "Takin' Care of Business." Bachman-Turner Overdrive[11]
   Mangled: "Baking carrot biscuits."
   Actual Lyrics: "Taking care of business."
10. "Hotel California." The Eagles[12]
   Mangled: "What a nice surprise when you're out of ice."
   Actual Lyrics: "What a nice surprise, bring your alibis."

And, just a few more for grins and giggles ...

11. "Smoke on the Water." Deep Purple[13]
    Mangled: "Slow walking Walter, the fire engine guy."
    Actual Lyrics: "Smoke on the water, fire in the sky."
12. "Every Time You Go Away." Hall and Oates[14]
    Mangled: "Every time you go away you take a piece of meat with you.
    Actual Lyrics: "Every time you go away you take a piece of me with you."

And my favorite:

13. "The Christmas Song." [15]
    Mangled: "Jeff's nuts roasting on an open fire"
    Actual Lyrics: "Chestnuts roasting on an open fire"

Mondegreens are also frequently found in comedy, and in our everyday lives as well.

For example, *Saturday Night Live*, back in the '70s, had the queen of malaprops and mondegreens. You may recall Gilda Radner as the unquenchable, hilarious, bubbleheaded character of Miss Emily Litella. I recall a skit where she rants on and on about Soviet jewelry and how beautiful she thought it was and blah, blah, blah.

"What is all this fuss about Soviet jewelry, anyway," she asks? At that point, she was told that the topic was Soviet

Jewry. She closed with her famous, "Oh, *never* mind."

The New York author and editor, Gavin Edwards, says he got hundreds of examples of mondegreens every year after sharing his experiences in a magazine article. Here is his story.

"My first misheard lyric came at the advanced age of six, when I learned to sing 'Row, Row, Row Your Boat.' I was convinced that the line after 'merrily, merrily, merrily' was 'life's a butter dream,' rather than the more canonical 'life is but a dream.' I wasn't sure what visions of dairy products had to do with a boat trip, but I didn't have the courage to ask anybody."

Mr. Edward's favorite: "The Pledge of Allegiance" begins *I led the pigeons to the flag.*

So, see how fun and entertaining mondegreens are. If you share some of your own, you just might be the life of the party (or the death of it)! One thing we do know is that they are not going away any time soon, not so long as we humans have selective hearing and big fuzzy brains.

Listen to your children or grandchildren sing, there should be some real doozies coming out of the mouths of babes among those in the millennial generation, a.k.a., Generation *Why?*

Citations:

1. *Sylvia Wright (1954). "The Death of Lady Mondegreen." Harper's Magazine. 209 (1254): 48–51.* Reprinted in *Sylvia Wright (1957). Get Away From Me With Those Christmas Gifts. McGraw Hill.* Contains the essays "The Death of Lady Mondegreen" and "The Quest of Lady Mondegreen."
2. *'Scuse Me While I Kiss the Guy. Gavin Edwards, Simon and Schuster, Apr 13, 1995*
3 *"Bad Moon Rising" (Lyrics by John Fogarty, performed by Creedence Clearwater)*
4. *"Blowing in the Wind" (Lyrics by Bob Dylan, performed by Bob Dylan)*
5. *"Lucy in the Sky with Diamonds" (Lyrics by Paul McCarthy/John Lennon, performed by The Beatles)*

6. *"Build Me Up Buttercup" (Lyrics* Mike d'Abo and Tony Macaulay, *performed by The Foundations)*

7. *"Tiny Dancer" (lyrics by Elton John, performed by Elton John)*

8. *"Don't It Make My Brown Eyes, Blue" (Lyrics by Richard Leigh, performed by Crystal Gayle)*

9. *"Let's Hang On" (Lyrics by* Bob Crewe, Sandy Linzer, and Denny Randel, performed by the Four Seasons)

10. *"We Will Rock You" (Lyrics by Brian May, performed by Queen)*

11. *"Takin' Care of Business" (Lyrics by* Randy Bachman, *performed by Bachman, Turner Overdrive)*

12. *"Hotel California" (Lyrics by Don Felder, Don Henley, Glenn Frey, performed by The Eagles)*

13. *"Smoke on the Water" (Lyrics by Zeke Clements, performed by Deep Purple)*

14. *"Every Time You Go Away" (Lyrics by* Daryl Hall, *performed by Hall & Oates)*

15. *"The Christmas Song" (Lyrics by* Robert Wells and Mel Tormé)

Close Calls

Gered Beeby

Nine times out of ten you get lucky. By *get lucky* I mean you stay alive. I've had my share of close calls in life, but this one remains fresh in my mind.

I was finishing my final months aboard the *Sea Fox* to complete qualification in submarines before being assigned to a nuclear sub. Located in the Southern California operating areas that lay about 100 miles southwest of San Diego, our US Navy fleet exercises could be conducted without interfering with commercial shipping routes.

One day, in the early spring of 1969, we were given a somewhat unusual assignment. It pertained to sinking submarines. Now wait, some might say submarines sink all the time. After all, that is the business submarines do. Well, not quite. The correct word, of course, is *submerge*. This means that eventually the undersea vessel with all its crew will resurface, then return safely to port. But when it sinks, the vessel will not be coming back.

The year before, the submarine *Scorpion* tragedy had played out in the Atlantic Ocean, southwest of the Azores. Sunk in over 9,000 feet of water, *Scorpion* did not return to port. Speculations emerged immediately as to the cause, some of which persist to this day. Deep sea sonar data from arrays known as SOSUS led to locating the submarine's wreckage. Overall, however, the Navy realized that detailed recordings of the sound a submarine hull makes when it collapses were too few. The Navy wanted to sink an older, decommissioned submarine with a torpedo, then collect sonar data as the vessel sank past crush depth and eventually collapsed.

This is where my ship *Sea Fox* came into the picture. As a

113

late World War II vintage ship, we were old, but not that old. We were to be part of a small task group. Our mission was to be the listening vessel and capture those noises.

The plan seemed straightforward enough. The target submarine was to run surfaced, set on a small circular course. The last men aboard would leave from a small boat, clear the area, and relocate to a supporting surface vessel. The target's interior and exterior hatches were locked shut so that watertight spaces would remain intact. That is, they would stay this way until the live war-shot torpedo blasted a hole into one or more compartments and the whole ship would go down. Our ship's sonar would record the collapse noises as the remaining spaces imploded while the old submarine sank.

As my memory serves the three submarines–the *Sea Fox*, the firing submarine, and the target submarine–formed a triangle roughly four miles on each side. The war-shot torpedo was an electric driven, Mark 37 Mod 2 fish with some enhanced and newer capabilities. In submariner slang, torpedoes are called fish. These newer features included a sonar-homing ability and also a lower depth setting, or floor, so the weapon would not run deeper than about 100 feet.

This latter precaution was to prove vital.

Sea Fox moved into position and submerged at periscope depth. Our captain manned the periscope to watch events above. Both the crews of *Sea Fox* and the firing submarine maintained sonar contact. As the target submarine circled in place on the surface, the firing submarine completed its attack procedures, and the electric torpedo was fired.

The fish was launched. Our sonar team picked up the whine of its high-speed propeller and monitored the direction, or bearing, of the torpedo closely. Events unfolded as predicted for a short time.

I was off duty at the time in the officer's quarters when I felt our submarine take a large down angle. Something had gone wrong. Probably less than 10 seconds into the mission, the team realized the sonar bearing of the torpedo did not proceed toward the target. Instead, the direction became constant, and the torpedo propeller noise kept getting louder.

114

The deadly, sonar-homing, war-shot torpedo, had acquired the *Sea Fox* and was zooming at high speed directly toward us!

Simultaneously I heard the captain in the Control Room shout, "Emergency deep, flood negative!" The *negative* tank on older submarines is a pressure-proof chamber that can be flooded with seawater which gives additional negative buoyancy to the ship so that it can plunge deep–and fast. And just in time. As I turned to make my way upward toward the Control Room near the center of the sub, I felt the ship heading downward just seconds after the mission had begun.

What stays with me, even now, is the sound — the sound of that torpedo's screaming propeller, easily heard through the submarine hull, racing toward us, then over us and past the top side of our sub, roaring like a low-flying airplane, disappearing into the distance, eventually sinking.

After a few hours and a brief review by the leaders, the small task group instituted a fix and a reset. We three ships once again took our allotted positions. After all, the Navy is no different from many other operating organizations — the show must go on. Our crew braced for another attempt at shooting the old target submarine.

On the second attempt, the torpedo found its mark — not us. Our sonar crew recorded the destructive explosion of the target submarine's break-up as it crushed, while *Sea Fox* paralleled its sinking to the limits of our own depth restrictions. As the last sounds were recorded, the crew shared knowing glances. Many of us knew what a close call we just experienced.

Those final death throes might have been from us. There would have been no survivors. We all would have fed the damn fish. The truth is that over time there eventually are no human remains left. Sea creatures of all kinds scavenge and consume everything, bones and all. Many war ships have sunk over the years. These wrecks are officially considered memorial grave sites.

So, what had happened?

For WW II era submarines, torpedoes are fired using an

electro-mechanical machine called a Torpedo Data Computer or TDC. Bulky, about the size of a small closet, it displays a myriad dials, switches, and control knobs. The device takes input data, most importantly, the bearing toward the target. Then the TDC calculates the initial direction the torpedo should go. This is all done with analog technology, not by the electronic-digital methods in modern computers. Using various knobs and switches, the Weapons Officer controls this launch. Human error came in at this point.

The knob that selects the crucial bearing toward target had been adjusted with an erroneous setting. The misadjusted knob was pushed in and locked in place rather than being popped out into its normal position which caused the TDC to calculate the launch angle using relative direction from the firing ship rather than the true compass direction. The young officer, probably about my contemporary in age, had missed this subtle, but crucial detail. Through a terrible set of circumstances that erroneous direction happened to be right toward *Sea Fox*. By the time the error was realized, the Mark 37 Mod 2 acoustical-guided torpedo had acquired our ship by its on-board sonar. It was too late to stop it.

In the aftermath of hair-raising events, people normally pause to consider what consequences might have been. Had the worst occurred and we sank, there would have been a huge outpouring of grief from families of the entire crew. When I selected submarine duty while at the Academy, little did I realize at the time the ominous terror my family had felt. Gratefully, my family did not belabor the point back then. After all, the military can be a dangerous business.

And, by the way, there was a serious war going on in Vietnam, which had yet to reach its peak. Loss of the nuclear submarine *Thresher* a few years before, in April 1963, was still fresh in people's minds. As a serving Navy pilot, my dad knew his own profession had its particular history of accidents. And some of these came about by small mishaps equally as innocuous as a submarine TDC knob pushed in to create a wrong setting. Automobile accidents killed over 50,000 Americans in 1969. In truth, we are all at some level of risk.

The old fable persists about cats having nine lives. Perhaps this applies to humans as well. And for some unfortunate souls, old Number Ten could be the first one. The truth is, we will never know. Maybe it just means that nine times out of ten in the feline world, cats get lucky, too.

Catching a Lift

Lawrence Carleton

Ten a.m. There he was. The rideshare from Mylift arrived at Pilar Cervantes's apartment right on schedule. She and the driver exchanged greetings. Handing him her travel bag, she slid onto the back seat, and they were off to the airport.

As they drove, she quietly reviewed the talk she was to give during the panel discussion on The Varieties of Altruism, to be presented at her alma mater homecoming celebration. She was going to talk about her experiences at the charity where she worked.

After some miles the driver broke the silence. "Do you recognize me?"

Pilar searched her memory. "To tell the truth you do look familiar to me, but I can't place you."

At a red light he dropped his mask and turned to her with a wide, gap-toothed smile. "I'm Rodney Shoebottom. At the celebration at the Hilton last year, you gave the speech honoring me for being clean for a year."

He looked different with his hair cut short and combed. She replied, "Oh yes, that's right. You're one of the determined ones who overcame the odds. Drug free and legal, successfully worked off your probation. Now I see you're a Mylift driver. I take it things are going well for you."

"You gave an inspiring speech. I still remind myself of some of the things you said. Then after the show, my brother gave me a break. He presented me with this car—used, but in good condition. He even does the maintenance on it for free at his body shop."

"You're lucky to have such a generous brother. Yes, I had a Prius like this at one time. I didn't know they came in dark blue though. Is this the original color?"

"It's had some work. But for me, it's my sweet ride, source of my pride."

Pilar remembered that reception at the Hilton. Each of the officers of her charity gave speeches honoring specific success stories, examples of individuals who beat the odds to overcome drug dependencies and scrapes with the law. Rodney was her honoree. The event was a success. She stayed late to help clean up the ballroom. It was about two in the morning when she made her way to the valet post. The lone remaining valet couldn't find her key. Her car was gone! The valet called in the police. Pilar would file a report, but they never found the car. The on-duty valet, very apologetic, paid for her ride home. So far as anyone knew, her Prius by now had become one of the untraceable vehicles somewhere in or around Tijuana.

She recollected out loud about the reception, but caught herself and just remembered to herself the bit about her car going missing.

"Are you all right back there?" Rodney enquired. "You've gone quiet."

"Just pondering the nature of coincidences. People tend to assume they're not really random. I think sometimes a coincidence is just that: a coincidence."

"You mean like me turning out to be your driver to the airport?"

"You could say that."

Rodney announced, "Speaking of which, here's the airport now." He navigated the entrance and gracefully glided to the curb in the unloading zone, fished out her travel bag from the trunk, collected her payment, and gave her his card with handwritten instructions on how to ask for him on her return.

He drove off. She watched.

Pilar asked herself, "What could I have done? Ask to see the VIN? He's gotten to where he is because a few key people, and I'm one of them, decided to trust him. Trying to look at the vehicle id number would tell him that I don't really trust him when it counts. The similarity to my stolen car could be a coincidence. I'll just have to believe in him 'till shown otherwise—and I'm not going to go looking for otherwise."

Pilar arrived at the conference site to learn that it had been cancelled because of the mysterious pandemic now spreading rapidly. When her flight took off she was scheduled to give a talk. By the time she landed all was cancelled. Invited speakers were to tape their speeches for later broadcast. Pilar registered her talk for taping and checked in for a place to stay in a suite provided by the university while submitting to required isolation. That same isolation stood to qualify for the flight home. It also gave her time to think about Rodney's story.

Back from the conference, she collected her bag and walked to the pickup station. She fished out Rodney's card. She turned over in her mind the suspicious coincidences in Rodney's story. "The result is the same every time: I have to trust," she decided. "What I do relies on trust." She was tempted, but would not inquire further. Still, she called on her sister Pandora to meet her at the airport to drive her home.

Pilar had just said goodbye to Pandora when her phone rang. It was the Highway Patrol: "Are you Pilar Cervantes? Did you report a missing light gray 2009 Prius last December?"

Pilar's thoughts turned to Rodney Shoebottom. "I did. It's still missing. Have you found anything?"

"We think we've found it. Can you get to Temecula today?" Pilar's car had been discovered abandoned, used but usable, in a parking lot in Temecula. Keys were on the front seat.

She phoned Mylift and requested Rodney as her driver.

Lulu, Mitzi, and the 10 Gs

Anne Casey

On an ordinary night at 10:00, I'd be where any other single middle-aged American male with little time and money would be: home, barefooted and in my sweats, popping open my second Burning River IPA, and ready to watch the early news. That sometimes gave me a lead for another day's work, maybe some Joe with trouble of his own who might find my services useful. Earlier today I heard a strange story on the police scanner about a robbery at Arff and Meow Hotel. That's a dog and cat resort for some folks with a lot of money to spend on loving their pets while they're away doing something important like uncorking yet another notable wine on the French Riviera. Anyway, it was a crude break-in using a crow bar to smash a window. Police were called, an APB was already out. Something nuts, like one dog was missing. Nothing else. Just a dog. What a smash and grab! Maybe a case for me here, probably not.

Sometimes I think I may be getting too old, too lazy or jaded to do this chasing the bad guys and almighty dollar, maybe get into something a little more steady, like car sales. And then something happens, like tonight. Well. My phone rang at 9:20 p.m. A husky, yet almost innocent-sounding dame called, breathless and desperate to meet tonight. You never know. This would be a different kind of case, and I was curious.

* * *

Back in my office at East 125th Street on this cold rainy October night, I turned on the desk light, shrugged out of my

121

raincoat, swiped a paper towel across my damp hair, and sat down at the oak desk that came with the office lease when the previous tenant died. I waited. Half of me wanted her not to show so that I could go back home and finish the news, my beer, and warm up. The other half tried to imagine. What was so important that it couldn't wait until daylight? While I mused, quick, light footsteps approached.

At exactly 10:00 the brass doorknob turned, and there she was: all 5'10" of drop-dead gorgeous 35-year-old redhead, silhouetted against the frosted glass of my office door. At another time, another life, unwrapping what lay beneath the ten shiny buttons of the gold satin rain coat would claim my attention … but tonight, my private eye was riveted on the promised 10 Gs in the gold lamé purse slung carelessly over her shoulder.

* * *

"Thank you so much for agreeing to see me on short notice, on Saturday night of all times, Mr. Broadbent," she said, pushing out each word as if it were a gift.

I managed to answer, "Not at all, Miss Divine. But please, call me Rex." I struggled to remain professional in the face of this beauty.

My office steam heater clunked and whined, punctuating our conversation with an off-measure drumbeat to our words. The heater, original in the 1926 building, warmed the room slowly, and I realized that the few minutes before her arrival weren't enough to do it on a cold, rainy night. Lulu shivered noticeably despite the dark chocolate-brown lambskin gloves covering her long-fingered hands and a marine blue cashmere scarf, the color of her eyes, that was nestled against her luscious, creamy neck.

"You're cold and I don't have any coffee here now. Perhaps you'd like to go someplace more comfortable to talk, Miss Divine?"

Disturbed and shocked, she shook her head slightly, tipped it to one side, unsmiling. "Wow, you work fast! How

122

long have we known each other, five minutes?"

Embarrassed that she had read my desire but missed my plan, I also shook my head and protested. "Nah, nah, you have me all wrong. This is strictly business, and I thought it would be easier for you to discuss a difficult subject if you were in a more pleasant place." Turning, I pointed out the window and toward the east. "There's a place around the corner, on Superior, where we can get coffee, tea, or whatever you'd like. It's about a notch above a dive bar and has decent food if you're hungry."

Her relief apparent, Lulu smiled slightly. "It would help. It's been a long day, and it's not going to end soon. Where is this place exactly? I don't think I can walk very far."

"It's not quite up to Murray Hill, not far to walk in good weather, but tonight we'll take my car, parked in front. Also, it's faster to take the stairs if you don't mind. The elevator is old and slow." I grabbed my coat and car keys then turned to lock the door. She nodded agreement and we quickly descended the marble stairs, ran through the lobby and to my car. With the destination only a block away, there wasn't time for conversation. We parked and sprinted through the rain then ducked through the green leather door.

Miles Was Here was as I had described it to Lulu. Clean, not quite sleazy, and it housed a mix of patrons at the bar, high tables, pool tables, and dart boards. A neighborhood bar just south of Little Italy, Miles served a nice fresh Lake Erie Blue Perch fish fry on Fridays, other stuff on other days, jazz played occasionally.

In unspoken agreement we headed to a booth in the rear. "If you don't mind, I prefer to sit facing the door," Lulu said.

"Sure, no problem," although that was my preferred spot.

Settled opposite each other on the red leather bench seats, I scanned the menu which I could recite faster than the waitstaff could and watched her look at it without seeing, her distress apparent. I waited. People usually tell you what they're thinking if you give them a minute.

"Some people may be after me," she began.

"Oh?" Wait a beat for her ... Nothing.

"What makes you think so? I mean, what for? Have you done something, know something important?"

"No, nothing about me. Exactly. It's confusing and complicated." She sighed. "It's Mitzi." She looked down, shaken at the thought of what she'd said. Was that moisture in her eyes?

"Mitzi. Okay. Mitzi is someone important to you. What about Mitzi?" This was going to be a pulling teeth conversation in what could become a very long and boring night. I was almost starting to forget how beautiful this female was.

Rita, the waitress arrived to take our orders as I breathed a relieved sigh. Lulu wanted chamomile tea, *surprise, surprise.* I desperately wanted a double Johnny Walker neat, so of course ordered a coffee, black, and a burger plus onion rings. Lulu said she was too upset to eat, yet kept a soft eye on the clam chowder at the next table. I added a cup of chowder to my order, in case Lulu's appetite had a sudden awakening. Lulu still hadn't answered. As the drinks arrived, Lulu removed her gloves, and yes, her hands were the soft looking kind you wanted ... Lulu wrapped her hands around the tea cup and looked up at me. *Oh no, I thought. She's read my mind again. Mind. Listen. This is business.*

"So you were saying, something about Mitzi and being afraid?"

She pulled herself back to the present and met my eyes. "It doesn't make sense, except that it does."

My raised eyebrows were the question mark.

"Mitzi is the companion, guard to J. Putterby Ashenschlager III, my employer. It was by my suggestion that J.P. get her, and now she's missing."

"You work for J.P. Aschenschlager III? Wow! Wow. I can see why such a rich and famous guy might need a bodyguard. But a female?" Holding up my hands, as a disclaimer. "Not that there's anything wrong with that. Kinda unusual, maybe? She a martial arts sort?" *I had visions of hunting down a Brunhilde type female who should have easily overpowered an assailant or ten.* Now I was listening.

For the first time, Lulu had a genuine smile when she looked up at me. "Oh no! No." She was near laughter. "No, Mitzi is a companion and guard *dog* for the house and J.P. personally. When there was a minor break-in at the lab a few months ago, we increased security, added new cameras, and reconfigured the iris scan program. We did the same at the residence. But I told J.P. that I'd feel more secure for him if he had a watch dog also, one noisy when necessary, small enough to take with him when he travels."

"So Mitzi's a Chihuahua?" This conversation had suddenly taken on a déjà vu turn, if you can say that about words.

"No, Mitzi's a rare Blue Merle schnoodle. Easy to train, intelligent, loyal." Lulu reached into the little gold bag and lifted out a photo. For a second I fixed on the bag, wondering how she had fit 10 Gs into it? *Oh please. Not cryptocurrency. Please.*

"Huh. So that's a sch … noodle … Cute and small." And it was. Buttony eyes and curly coat. "Could be easy to like and lift. She wasn't by chance paying a visit to Arff and Meow today, was she?"

"How did you know?"

"Wild guess. No. I heard on the police scanner about the burglary there. Still doesn't seem reasonable. Why would anyone steal your dog unless there's a big ransom or reward? J.P.'s obviously loaded, but you haven't heard from the dognappers, right?"

"Ahm." Her full lips parted as if to clarify something, then closed. "Ahm," she began again, "yes, I did receive a phone call. The usual that you see on TV, no police, come alone, and so on. But no time or place. That's when I phoned you."

"And you're sure that they have Mitzi?"

"Yes. They put her on speaker phone barking so that I'd know she was alive, held up a picture of her."

"You're absolutely certain that it was Mitzi and not some recording?"

"I'd know that sweet high-pitched aarf anywhere. But. There's something else. Mitzi wasn't wearing her collar."

125

It was just getting interesting when Rita appeared with our food. By now, Lulu was relaxed enough to notice the chowder that I slid over to her. I looked up at Rita as she served me. On a hunch, I said, "Say, Rita, you know all the regulars and a lot of the locals who come here now and then. Seen anybody unusual or new recently, like today or yesterday?"

"You know, funny you should ask that, Rex. I was gonna tell you about them when you came in but saw that you had company and didn't wanna intrude. So, yeah, yesterday two guys, wearing loud red plaid flannel shirts and right-out-of-the-box heavy work boots came in around 8. Seemed like they thought that look would make them fit in. They hung around for about an hour or so. Cheap. Ordered steaks and left a dollar tip."

"Could you pick them out again?"

"Definitely. They were strange looking even without the lumberjack clothes. You'll know what I mean when you find them."

"Thanks, Rita."

"Sure thing, Rex. Let me know." And she turned to answer a raised hand at the bar.

Lulu had made short work of the chowder by then and was ready to talk. I was more than ready to tuck into my burger and listen. I slid the onion rings to the middle of the table to share and waited. Again.

She wiped her lips, cleared her throat, and wrapped her hands around the tea cup. Again. Seemed to be a ritual. I could have helped with those hands in another time ... instead concentrated on my food then prompted her.

"So missing Mitzi also has a missing collar. That means what? Couldn't the nappers have removed it to look for a phone number or information to contact J.P.?"

"It's not any old collar. Mitzi's collar was designed for her because of her position. It has specifically faceted diamonds. See, look." She again produced the photo and sure enough, Mitzi sported a very snazzy collar.

"Okay. So, they have the rocks that they can take to their

local fence. Why not give you a time and place to retrieve Mitzi and be done?"

"They aren't any old diamonds, Rex. Look." Pointing to the middle of the collar in the now familiar photo, Lulu said, "This is a very rare red diamond." It was (*surprise*) heart-shaped and showed several intricate facets. Flanking it were two smaller, round blue diamonds, also with extraordinary cuts, next to which followed two colorless emerald cut diamonds.

Lulu continued, "The stones are only worth about $31,000 on the open market, black market price would be anyone's guess. But that's not the point. The diamonds are faceted to create numbers."

I swallowed quickly trying to digest burger and information together. "Only $31K, you said?"

"Yes."

"And. The numbers, if anyone could read them would be what? Phone, address, offshore bank account?"

"Not exactly. And Mitzi doesn't wear her genuine collar to a spa treatment."

"So the mystery numbers are on a collar, whereabouts as yet unknown, and Mitzi got boosted, dognapped, wearing paste. That's what you're telling me? And you want me to find Mitzi and do what?"

"Essentially. Mitzi must be returned. But, I think the thieves may have realized that the collar they have is fake." A moistening of her eyes convinced me she was sincere. "I'm worried that they'll harm Mitzi unless they get the genuine one along with their ransom money."

This time I was the one who sighed. "Let's wait to hear from them again. We'll sync our phones so that I'll hear the call when you do. We'll meet up, I'll drive us to the destination." I held up my hand. "Don't protest. I actually know what I'm doing, and these people don't sound like they do."

I signaled to Rita for the check. "Let's try to get some rest tonight. It's late and hard to get a cab. I'll drive you home, which will also tell me where to pick you up later." For the first time all evening I felt in control like I should be. And too tired to consider those ten gold buttons.

* * *

By the time I had been to hell and back to drop Lulu at her place out east, it was nearly 2:00 a.m. Past time for another beer or my usual TV programs, I showered and went to bed. A restless sleep consisted of complete blank black pages like a blackboard waiting for the teacher, interspersed with dogs jumping around inside a car trunk, woods, streaks of gold in a stormy sky bisected by lightning and outcroppings of jagged red pillars. At 5:00 a.m. I was finally into a deep and dreamless state.

The alarm chirped. Six a.m. arrived much too early. *Remind me again why I chose bird sounds* I asked myself for the millionth time. *Oh, right. Because they're supposed to be uplifting,* I reminded myself again. The phone also ding-donged, not my ring tone, so I looked down. Ah ha. Lulu's phone had a call from an unknown number which I allowed her to answer as I listened. If it turned out to be a personal call, I'd hang up and climb back into the empty dream I'd been enjoying.

"I'm calling about the dog. Are you the dog lady?" a nervous male voice asked. He didn't sound all that menacing. Probably his first heist, and he was uncertain how to handle it.

"I am the owner of a lost dog. Do you have my dog?"

"Could be. Describe it."

"*She*, not *it*, is a beautiful schnoodle named Mitzi. (*Whoa, Lulu, showing some spunk now! I'm thinking.*) She's friendly, wears a collar with her name on the pink bone tag. Is that the dog you have?"

"Could be."

"Uhm, Mister ... if you have a dog that isn't Mitzi, how did you find my phone number?"

"Because, lady," sarcasm dripping from his reply, "it was on last night's news."

"Then you have Mitzi. Where and when can I pick her up?"

"Not so fast. There are some, uhn, conditions related to the return of this particular cargo."

Cargo? Oh. Lulu's not gonna like that term for her precious Mitzi.

"Please. Let's start over. What do you want, how much, and where can I meet you?"

"That's better." His hand covered the phone and I could hear indistinct voices and the name Dirk.

He wasn't the top guy, no surprise there, so who was? Did it matter?

"The TV said a reward of $15,000. We, I, want that plus a million pesos. Meet us, me, under the bridge at Detroit and West 25th at 2:00 this afternoon."

"A million pesos and the reward and you'll return Mitzi to me alive and unharmed."

"Oh. Wait. Did we say alive? She's been eating some strange berries that she found out in the woods yesterday. So … I don't know, lady. You will get her back though."

"What have you done to her?" Lulu couldn't hide her fear and anger.

"Ha. Just messin' to see if you're serious. Your pooch will be okay if you show up with the payoff. See you later or not."

"Wait. Wait! How will I know you?"

"Hah. You don't need to. You'll hear your pooch."

"Right. Right. See you at 2:00 under the bridge."

While they had their negotiation, if you could call it that, I had done a quick time calculation. On your usual fall Sunday with traffic going to the lake for clam bakes or last of the year fishing, whatnot, Lulu's home was easily an hour away. Double that plus the trip to the near west side and I'd need at least three hours to get her to the rendezvous point. Okay. Okay. As if I had anything else to do on a Sunday, like maybe place some bets on a game or two, read up on more crime stats, look for an easier job with benefits. Well, I needed the dough, and gold buttons had promised it. Dirk or whoever was gone, so I called Lulu.

Ding-dong, ding-dong, like a doorbell chime. She answered on the third ring, sounded hesitant, "Hello? Who's

129

this?"

"Who's … ?" *Be nice, Rex, I reminded me.* "Lulu, it's me, Rex. Okay. I heard all that."

"Oh, thank goodness. I was worried you might not. And that Dirk was so odd sounding. Did you hear that about *pesos*?"

"Yeah, I did. Odd, all right. But first, we need to plan."

"Whatever you say, Rex." She was starting to sound more like herself, whatever that was, kind of Marilyn Monroe breathy, if you know what I mean.

"What with the distance and back and forth, how about I pick you up at 10:30. That way we can both get a little more shut eye and you can figure out how to get pesos and the reward. We'll have time to have brunch-lunch and meet up with Dirk and his tribe."

"You're a good planner, Rex. I'm sorry that you have to keep driving me around. This is the worst time for me not to have my own car."

"No problem, really, Lu. Driving is part of my thinking time." *And it all goes on the billable hours.*

* * *

The rain had stopped in the early hours leaving behind a toss of wet leaves, the ever-present offshore breeze and cool temperatures, signals of deep autumn's approach with winter closing in. On time, I pulled into Lulu's driveway and waved to her at her front door. Why she lived so far from the city and J.P.'s operation was another mystery for another day.

In dark indigo jeans, an off-white cashmere, gardenia-colored turtleneck, black ballet flats over her fashionable trouser socks, and a short camel hair coat, Lulu was more stunning than last night, if that were possible. Hair pulled into a classic chignon said she meant business, Mister. I, however, looked like my usual not-quite-made-it self in jeans, black loafers last polished in 2019 when I bought them, blue-gray long-sleeved dress shirt, top button undone, and black leather bomber-style jacket. I practice hygiene, not fashion.

130

Underway, we decided upon a quiet Mom and Pop diner near the art museum where we could strategize. Lulu had said she had a plan for those pesky, odd pesos. Settled in a Billy and Jo's Diner, Lulu ordered half the menu, a sure sign that she felt more confident about Mitzi, while I ordered my usual simple breakfast special of eggs, bacon, juice, coffee.

"About the pesos," I began.

Lulu smirked. *Smirked!* "All taken care of." She patted the large molasses-colored Chanel bag at her side. "J.P. knows everyone. I mean everyone. So I called the local B of A foreign currency administrator at his golf club, and he arranged for the delivery to my home. One million pesos."

"Amazing," I managed. "Sort of the Uber Eats of banking."

She laughed out loud, another good indicator that we were on the right path.

"Well, the connections *are* helpful."

"And again, why pesos? A million isn't all that much if they knew what they pinched. That's a lot of trouble and jail time for only ... " I consulted my phone, "... $50,643.94. Mitzi would be considered a grand theft and more, if she had been wearing her real collar. But Dirk and company didn't know much about the collar. Maybe it was just a smash and grab dognapping," I offered.

"I'd like to think it was but the collar was missing. Somebody knew what the collar represents. More is going on here," Lulu countered. *She does think,* I noted again. *Hiding her mind probably gets her further than showing it would.*

"Off topic for a bit, Lulu. I need to know. Exactly who are you and why so involved with Aschenschlager Three? How do you know him? There's more to this story than you've told me."

Lulu took a deep breath then began. "I'm Special Assistant to J.P., as I told you. Our families go back generations together to post-war Brazil. That's a story for another time. I'm his legal counsel as well as a patent attorney specializing in development of biological agents to cure plant disease. I have only one client, J.P. My career choice was a PhD in botany for

131

which I did receive degrees from UC Davis and St. Louis University. J.P. saw potential in his companies for my field and suggested that I continue on to law school. I have a JD from Yale, passed the Ohio and various other bars, and now work for J.P. in a job that I love." She folded her hands on the table and was quiet.

"Impressive. Very, very impressive. Yale. Not University of American Samoa. But how does this all tie in to Mitzi's getting stolen?" I was glad that she got the reference and smiled before replying.

"J.P. owns a biotech lab, J.P.A. Genetics, which has only one research project, the development of a process to destroy the fungus, *Fusarium xylarioides,* that attacks Arabica coffee plants and is closely related to the fungus that destroys the Cavendish banana."

"Coffee and bananas," I mused, "are big business."

"Which makes his research worth stealing. We haven't yet obtained the final patent approval on the process."

"Fascinating as this all is, it doesn't relate to Mitzi and the collar."

"It's an exact trail, if you know how to follow the breadcrumbs."

I gave her eyebrows again to continue.

"Mitzi's collar contains numbers, remember?"

I nodded.

"These are the combination to the lab safe which contains all the formulas attempted and the patent application papers for the successful one. Whoever has the collar and can decipher the facets can access the formula and steal the research."

I shook my head. Where do we go with this? "So first order is return of Mitzi. Next we find out who wants the formula."

Lulu was amazing, as I said before. She gave me that entire history without missing a beat, meanwhile devouring a short stack with extra syrup, a mini-spinach quiche, side of sausage and tomato juice. This girl knew how to enjoy food when she was herself.

132

We finished, and I drove us down under the freeway and over to West 25th. I stopped the car near a bridge stanchion, got out to let Lulu move into the driver's seat. I'd be close enough if she needed me. She continued up half a block where, yes, two thirty-something males in lumberjack clothing stood, waiting. Mitzi's bark was loud and clear. From afar she sensed or smelled Lulu's presence. Lulu stopped the car and got out.

"I have your money, dollars and pesos," she said.

"Okay, hand it over, and the dog is yours."

Mitzi appeared, on a belt leash, no sign of her collar. It seemed like an easy transaction so I stayed hidden. Dirk and his buddy didn't seem like run-of-the-mill thugs. Lulu put her hand into her purse to take out the money.

"I'm intrigued," she said, "why pesos?"

"Why," laughed Dirk. "What else do you spend in old Meh-hee-co?"

"Ah. Pesos for your ransom and dollars for the reward when you return. That's why you stole my dog?"

"Lady, we didn't steal your dog. We were on our way up to Canada for the first annual Blue Grass Whistler and Bowl Pipe convention when we spotted her running loose on Route 20. We stopped and grabbed her so she wouldn't get hit. We went to eat and saw on the news that there was a reward for the dog we found. Your phone number was on the news, like I said last night. She didn't have a collar, and we wondered how to get her back to her owner."

Lulu put her hand in her purse to get the cash for Dirk at the same time as another car careened around the corner, narrowly missing Lulu. I ran out to grab her when the car made another pass with the passenger door open. A long, hairy arm reached out to grab Mitzi. Lulu screamed and ran toward Mitzi, connecting with the hairy arm, slamming it into the car door. The owner cursed, bumped into the driver and the car drifted off to the left. Lulu reached Mitzi before I could; Dirk and friend were in shock.

Mitzi jumped into Lulu's arms and began to lick her face. Lulu shoved her purse toward me. "Quick, give them the money. They earned it." She ran to my car, clutching Mitzi for dear life. Once there, she climbed in and locked all doors.

I dumped the cash in front of Dirk. "Don't mean to pay and run, but … thanks for taking good care of Mitzi."

"It's okay, man. We're good."

I turned around and saw that Lulu had parked nearly a block away. I ran to the car and got in the passenger seat. Lulu gunned the engine and got onto the freeway.

When we had caught our breath, she said, "Thanks, Rex. That worked."

"You're the heroine in this, Lulu. All I did was drive a little."

"I'd like to take Mitzi over to J.P.'s now. It's over in Shaker Heights, on the way to your place. I'll stay there so you don't have to take me home."

"Sure, Lulu, good idea. And. Ah, about my fee. I could bill you although my usual is cash on completion."

"Why don't I take you to dinner later and pay you then? I saw the Cattleman's steak served at Miles if you don't mind going twice?"

* * *

She picked me up, well J.P.'s driver picked me up, with Lulu in tow, and dropped us at Miles. Lulu had noticed me eyeing the bar last night and wanted a little celebratory wine herself. J.P. was pleased to offer his driver for the evening as an extra thank you for Mitzi's return. We talked through dinner, nothing important or deep, she paid me in cash, as promised, and I was home in time for the 10:00 p.m. newscast. After the past two days, I was ready for a good solid 8 hours in dream land.

At 3:00 a.m. my phone chimed. Ding-dong, ding-dong … *My phone doesn't chime.* I had forgotten to unsync with Lulu's. Ding-dong. I picked up and held my breath so as not to be heard and would hang up if it was a personal call or if Lulu hadn't accidentally phoned me.

"You have your dog back for now. Better watch her carefully. You got lucky."

In Search of the Perfect Ten

Janice Coy

"A stitch in time saves ten." My husband speaks just behind me and I jump, banging my knee against one of the wood beams that supports our kitchen table.

"What?" I say, rubbing my knee.

"A stitch in time saves ten," he repeats.

"It's a stitch in time saves nine," I correct looking over my shoulder.

"I know," he says, "I'm trying to help with your anthology submission. You said the first sentence needs to have the word or number ten in it."

I turn back to the blinking cursor on my laptop. "It does." I sigh. I've been sitting here for at least forty-five minutes, my mind as blank as the page in front of me trying to come up with a stellar first sentence that incorporates the word or number ten. That time doesn't include the days I've been ruminating on opening sentences and the story that would follow. I inhale a deep breath of the calming waves candle I lit when I first sat down.

But I can't concentrate with my husband's breath on my neck.

"Thanks," I say, "you can leave now."

"I'll just be in the kitchen getting a snack," he says.

My stomach grumbles but I ignore it. I can eat another time; the anthology deadline looms. Great artistry requires sacrifice.

My husband opens the refrigerator, and I can hear him rustling around inside.

"Don't eat the leftovers," I say my focus on the laptop screen. I've always been good at multitasking. "Those are for

136

dinner."

"Got it," he says.

He fumbles around in the refrigerator then dumps some items on the counter. Next, he slides open the silverware drawer with a rattle.

"On the tenth day of Christmas, my true love gave to me, ten lords a leaping," he mumbles in a singsongy voice.

"That's not helpful," I say.

"What? You told me just the other day you wish I would take more interest in your writing," he says.

I push back my chair; the wooden legs scrape the tile floor like a desperate grab of bike brakes on a wet tire rim. I wince, then stand and stretch, rolling my shoulders to get out the kinks. "Yes, yes I did say that. And thank you. Thank you for showing an interest, but this is not what I meant." I wander into the kitchen to see what he's planning.

He's reaching into the cupboard for the blender. Yogurt, strawberries, and a banana rest on the counter.

"Smoothie?" I ask.

He nods. "Want one?"

"Sure."

The smoothie slides down in a wash of sweetness with a hint of tart from the plain yogurt. I wish the words for my anthology submission would come as easy.

He washes while I dry. When the kitchen is wiped clean, the blender nestled in its place, I settle back at my laptop while he heads to the bank.

"Back in ten," he says.

The garage door slams behind him before I can shout a rejoinder.

Silence at last. Well, except for the ticking of the wall clock and the humming of the fish tank. I ignore the clock and consider the six, seven, eight, nine fish swimming lazy laps in the nearby aquarium, hoping my concentration will soothe me into a meditative state. I've heard that's why dental offices have fish tanks. But not even the bubbling aerator stirs an idea. It's never worked for me at the dentist, anyway.

A bird sings in our backyard, perched on a sunlit Bird of

137

Paradise plant. I ponder the orange, yellow, and purple of the flower searching, searching for the perfect opening sentence.

Ten is the loneliest number that you'll ever do ... the Beatles lyric drifts into my head.

"Aaargh!" I grab my hair at the roots. "It's one, not ten!"

I close my laptop and douse the candle. Time to take the dog for a walk. Just a short one. Strolls around the neighborhood are usually founts of story creativity.

I lock the front door behind me, and dog leash in hand, head into the inspirational outdoors. I step across a line of insects cruising beside a crack in the sidewalk cement.

The ants go marching ten by ten, hoorah, hoorah.

After Ten Years of Shaving

Cyril Roseman

Over ten years,

what a pleasant surprise

to discover an everyday ordinary event

that could be so full of significance,

about one's lifetime.

To know that there is something,

so ordinary and uneventful

that could yield so much understanding,

about the nature of life eternal.

For as many times as we do it

without thinking about its relevance,

To know at once that this simple act of ordinary existence

can be so rich and full of consequence,

once we put our minds and spirit to work

to experience it at a higher level of consciousness.

Surely there is no greater understanding,

as long as we stay focused on the ordinary,

regularly performed activity — like walking or

brushing one's teeth.

But then, if we think about how this act

Gives special meaning to our life …

If, for example, we never did this activity again,

we were not able, and this was the last time

we would do this for the rest of our life.

But then how about all the times we've shaved

without thinking about it?

Is there not some profound symbolism

in not thinking about our everyday existence?

Is it not true that we could *not* continue on

with our important (self-important?) pursuits

If we were distracted by concentrating on

unimportant trivial activities —

such as shaving?

Or is it possible to think

about event ingredients?

Lathering up (and which lather to use),

where to lather first,

picking our razor for today

(assuming we have a choice

of tools always available),

whether to start on the cheeks

(which side first) or

under the jaw, the neck, and the jowls

(or is this a special focus

if we are already dressed

and do not want to lather over our collar)

so let's clear that brush first.

How much against-the-grain?

Before, or after, these with-these-grain strokes?

Will we start facial decoration —

a mustache or goatee — today

and watch it grow over the next several weeks?

Or is it time to change razors

because this blade is dull

and causes pain, as we pull through this stubble?

What about trying a different lather,

for better results?

Or are the results how smooth we feel when done?

Is it for ourselves, or

for those who look at us

that we shave?

Do we have some special performance today,

and want to *look our best*?

Or is it to please our significant other?

What about after-shave, bracer, or lotion?

Or plain old witch hazel?

Is there an image, or style, or presence

that we wish to project to the world every day?

Have we considered

purchasing an electric razor,

and for what reason—

to be able to use during the day,

even while driving, or

to simplify the event—

no lathering or choice of razors?

Do we feel ready

to face the day—or the world—unshaven?

Would we be manifesting a special soul

if behind a beard we hide our face?

Or is it that our inner soul emerges in a beard?

Are we looking more mature,

too mature if we are under 40 years of age?

What about *old man gray* that overnight appears?

Should we paint it out and lose our wizened look?

Is shaving, or deliberately not shaving,

a simple form of vanity?

And, once we think about it profoundly,

can we ever go back to *not* thinking about it profoundly?

How good it feels

to get these ten years of shaving thoughts

out in the open,

before I move on

to other mundane events.

Strength Through Time

ShuJen Walker-Askew

Ten o'clock in the morning, I sat in my SUV, flipping through the necessary documents needed to enroll my son into kindergarten—birth certificate, shot records, and the Cox cable bill to show his place of residence.

"Finally." I twirled my dark, curly hair with my finger, recalling the day I received the approval letter guaranteeing my son, Kent, a spot at one of the best early learning schools in the county. Within seconds, I called my husband on the phone, shouting, "He got in!"

"That's great," my husband said. "One less thing to worry about."

My husband and I had been nervous about which elementary school would be best for our son to attend. Recommendations came from everywhere—his preschool teacher, speech therapist, and other parents with children who required extra help in school. They all said this school, the one I stared at through my windshield, was the one that got results. So we filled out the application and sent it off, praying for his acceptance.

Documents in hand, I exited my vehicle and floated to the front of the school, toward the door that read, *Front Office*. A newness lingered in the air bouncing me with every step—a new school, new start, new world. Like the day I started the fourth grade in the United States after living overseas the first nine years of my life.

It happened thirty years ago, but the memories felt like yesterday.

* * *

My father, sharply dressed in his blue Air Force uniform, held my hand as he guided me to the school's front office. The two-story building seemed to stretch for miles in both directions, compared to my old school on base, which consisted of one building.

"It'll be great," he said. "You'll meet new friends and learn new things. Think of this as a new experience."

It was always a *new* experience with him constantly being stationed in new places.

"But, it's the middle of the school year." I fidgeted. "I'm going to be the new kid again."

He knelt, looking me in the eyes. "I know, honey. It's going to be okay. Think of this as a chance for a new start?" My father smiled, and I couldn't help but smile back.

We went through the double doors and into an office with a high ceiling and large lobby. There was a long bench to the right and to the left, a counter separating office cubicles. An aroma of coffee and popcorn tickled my nose. A tall woman in a plaid dress approached and introduced herself as Heather.

"How may I help you?" she asked.

"I'm here to enroll my daughter, Jenny Charles, in fourth grade."

"Hi, Jenny, nice to meet you." She smiled, then handed my father a stack of enrollment forms to fill out. "You can sit on the bench over there." She pointed. "And you, Jenny, follow me. You'll be taking the English and math placement tests."

We went through another door and into a smaller room with desks. "Sit anywhere you like." She handed me a pencil and two booklets. "Take your time and try to answer all the questions."

I chose a seat next to the window overlooking the playground and field. It was recess, and the students ran around chasing each other, playing ball, and climbing the jungle gym. I couldn't help but wonder which one of them would be my friend—her with the red dress reading a book or him with the blue hat playing ball. Past buddies of mine popped up in my head, blurring my vision. I turned away and opened the English booklet. The laughter from the playground faded as I tackled the questions.

I breezed through the first few pages asking to fill in the blanks with the correct nouns, verbs, and adjectives. The reading passages came next. Though not my favorite, I tried and stumbled as three-letter words morphed into four and five clumps of alphabet mush my lips struggled to pronounce.

Laughter from the playground drew my attention. I dropped the pencil and stared out the window, wishing to play outside.

"How's it going?" my father asked.

I didn't even hear him come in.

"Fine." I picked up my pencil.

He glanced out the window, then down at me. "Why don't you sit over there?" He motioned to a seat near the front. "That way, you're not distracted. After you're done, I'll take you to the park, okay?"

I took my time completing the tests while he finished filling out the enrollment forms.

Once done, my father took my hand, and we walked out.

* * *

I stumbled over a crack in the sidewalk, jolting me back to the present, where I gripped my son's documents in one hand and air in the other. *Dad?* My head swiveled around, searching for the Air Force uniform.

Nothing.

It's just me. Just me.

I entered the office of my son's new school. Like the many schools I visited in my childhood, it had the same setup and popcorn-coffee smell. Covering the walls were bulletin boards with the school calendars and photos of students partaking in various activities. The smiles on their faces provided a welcoming feel.

"Hi there." A short woman with brown, straight hair appeared at the front counter. "I'm Rita. How may I help you?"

145

"I'm Jenny. I'm here to enroll my son, Kent, into kindergarten." I straightened my back and projected my voice, hoping to sound grownup like my father did, enrolling me. "What are the necessary steps?"

"First, I'll have to check if your son is on our incoming student's list."

"He should be. He got in through the Choice Program." I handed her his documents.

Rita glanced them over then looked him up in the computer system. "I see his name. Great. Let me get you the forms to complete the enrollment process." She handed me a stack of papers with highlighted areas that needed filling out. "You can sit over there." She pointed to a table near the entrance.

Once seated, I scanned the enrollment forms to figure out what to fill out first. There were many pages, different in color, like that of a rainbow — green, blue, pink, orange, and yellow — serving no purpose but to clash with my eyes giving me a headache. Each one required the same information at the top — name, address, and date of birth. Further down the page, they varied with questions ranging from the student's medical history to their preferred food choices.

I went up to the counter. "Rita, can I take these home to fill out? I have to pick up my son from daycare soon, and I probably won't finish in time."

Rita leaned in. "Actually, it's better to get it done now because of the program. If not, the district will assume you don't want the spot and give it to another student on the waiting list."

I wanted to argue that the rush seemed ridiculous since it was March, and the school year didn't start until August, but instead, I sucked it up and dove into the paperwork.

Halfway through, I came across the yellow page asking if my son had an Individualized Education Program (IEP). I marked *yes*, then moved on to the next section where it said to elaborate on what his special needs were. I scribbled, *speech delay.* Then came the Skills Checklist asking if he could recognize the alphabet, shapes, and colors and whether or not he could orient a book correctly, trace, and write his name. Question after question, my eyes watered, knowing my son would be judged by my answers like the school system judged me after the placement tests I took many years ago.

An argument between my father and a teacher about my education came to mind.

* * *

It happened after I took my placement tests at the new school. After a week of class, the teacher noticed I had trouble understanding the readings and assignments. She set up a parent-teacher conference with my father, the principal, and me.

The meeting took place in the principal's office — the scariest place in all the school — where the bad kids went when they got in trouble.

The teacher muttered something, and my father frowned.

"I'm not holding her back." He raised his voice. "There's nothing wrong with my daughter."

"We understand how you feel, Mr. Charles." The teacher flipped through my placement tests. "She's good in math, but her score in reading is two grade levels below, like that of a second-grader."

"Can't she catch up?"

"Possibly, maybe." The principal chimed in. "But it'll take a lot of work. We don't want to put her through that. We want her to feel comfortable."

"She can do it. I know she can." My father put his arm around my shoulder. "Isn't that right, Jenny?"

I nodded, not sure what that entailed, except that it made my father smile.

"Give her a chance," he said.

* * *

Rita came over to the table and glanced over the first few pages I filled out. "Looks great," she said. "Do you have any questions?"

"Yes, about my son's IEP." I held up the yellow paper. "According to this page, it doesn't list all the therapies he'll need."

"Your son has an IEP?"

"Yes."

"What does he need help in?"

"Speech."

"Speech, and that's it?" Rita gazed at me sideways.

"No. There are other things he—"

"Where is his IEP? I didn't see it in your documents. Did you bring it?"

"I thought the school would have it." I fidgeted in my seat. "When I applied for the program, I put down he has an IEP."

"Well, this must be a mistake." Rita glared at me. "I have to see his IEP because if he needs to be in a Special Ed class as opposed to a regular kindergarten class, then we can't help him. We don't have any Special Ed classes yet."

My heart sank.

IEP

IEP

IEP

The three-letter acronym that would plague my son his entire life punched me in the gut like the day of his initial IEP Meeting with the school district.

* * *

"Welcome, Jenny, my name is Ms. Grant, and I'll be heading your son's IEP Meeting. We're so glad you're here. It's been wonderful working with your son this past week. Before we begin, do you understand your rights to privacy concerning your son's education?"

The blank stare on my face must have screamed *no* because Ms. Grant spent the next ten minutes explaining to me what they were in regards to my son's diagnosis and his IEP plan. She then introduced me to the team of personnel who evaluated my son. The group consisted of the school nurse, speech therapist, occupational therapist, and the guest intern-in-training.

Their eyes greeted me warmly, yet I felt dread, knowing their opinions of my son's learning capabilities would determine his future.

Ms. Grant started the conversation. "Kent is great and smart. He laughs all the time. He's a happy kid."

I accepted the compliment, breathing a sigh of relief until the speech therapist opened her mouth.

"He's behind in identifying verbs. He can only name four out of the ten. Sleeping, eating, jumping, and running."

I nodded.

Better than nothing.

The school nurse pulled up a chart with numbers and a big red dot. "He's slightly overweight for his age. So I recommend morning exercises and healthier food choices during lunch. He likes bananas and oranges, right?"

I didn't respond.

"He's good at sorting and can string beads." The occupational therapist chimed in. "But he needs help putting on his socks and shoes all by himself. I hope he goes to this school. I know if he's in my class, I can work with him. I see potential."

Another chimed in with his accomplishments, then another with what he needed to improve on. Soon, the cascading voices and nodding heads gave me the shakes, like the day my father yelled at my sixth-grade teacher.

* * *

"My daughter is not stupid." My father leaned in, eyes staring at both the teacher and the principal.

"That's not what I said, Mr. Charles," the teacher said. "I'm saying she needs a lot more help and may not graduate with her sixth-grade class if she doesn't get it."

The disappointed expression on my father's face made me feel like I failed him.

149

"Well, get her more help. She's smart." He tapped the table. "My daughter can do anything and be anything she wants. Look how much she's improved so far."

"We don't have the resources here," the principal said.

"Then you better find it." My father stood. "I'm not giving up on her, and neither will you." He took me by the hand and walked out.

* * *

I stared at Rita for several moments, trying to comprehend what she said — that my son didn't belong in *her* school.

"There's no mistake." I leaned in, gritting my teeth. "This school was highly recommended for my son. He got accepted into the program. According to the district, schools must accept students with an IEP. So do whatever is needed to get my son the necessary resources for his education."

I stood, pretending my father was by my side. Gripping his imaginary hand, we walked out, together.

He didn't give up on me and neither will I with my son.

Night of Longshanks

J. Dianne Dotson

Ten plastic owls bobbed like gaudy jewels along a string in the warm night. Lanterns sent bouncing by errant puffs of breeze that, given enough time, would build into a gale as a storm swilled off the cape. Jeddy wiped her chin, sticky from melted cherry popsicle juice. Her toes wriggled in the sand, still warm despite the darkness. The wind rose a bit more, and the chimes of a mobile home tinkled.

"They say," Grandma's voice crackled, "that on a night like this in 1794, the pirate Wolfgang Longshanks sent a schooner down the cape, wind filling its sails like the chest of a banty rooster. He weren't on the ship hisself; but he told the crew to swoop in with torches and set the encampments alight right out there, right at the edge of that spit. Burned them all while they slept."

Jeddy shivered. It was a likable feeling, hearing a ghost story on a dark beach at night. She tried to imagine that this ramshackle collection of campers, tents, and more permanent mobile homes known as Pine Beach Woods Campground might once have been the site of a gruesome massacre. She'd heard of Pirate Longshanks before, but thought it was just another beach legend. And the only thing that seemed remarkable nowadays were the owl string lights, in yellow, green, and red, as they swung glowing, almost taunting her with their great plastic eyes from across the sandy alley.

"You're gettin' sleepy," said Grandma. "Let's get you to bed."

Jeddy didn't want to go in. She would have preferred to sleep under the open sky, with flickering stars awash with fast-moving clouds. She listened and could hear a buoy out in

151

the black water, beyond the moan and crash of the waves. The wind had indeed picked up now. The pines sighed and bent, and the owl lights danced.

Besides, the camper smelled of mildew and ancient coffee. Jeddy didn't like sleeping in it, and it was cramped even for a young girl like herself. A table converted to a bed in the front, with a bigger bed set up in the rear of the trailer. She had to take the bed table, with its stiff bed cushion covered by an old sheet, and she hated it. She wanted her giant daisy-patterned sleeping bag right out on the sand.

"Crabs'll gitchye," said Grandpa, wriggling his fingers at her, as if reading her thoughts.

She squeaked, indulging him, and he laughed.

Grandma pursed her lips and looked at the sky.

"Well, if the crabs don't," she said, "the rain will, here in a couple hours. I can smell it."

Jeddy sighed and planted herself in the camping chair outside the door. Grandpa brought her a beach towel, which smelled like sunscreen and damp sand and a bit of mold. She tucked it around herself, refusing to go into the camper. He spoke in a low voice to Grandma, and they both went inside, leaving the door open.

Shifting in the camp chair so that she curled up with her legs on the seat, she watched the owl lights. The wind whistled more, and she became drowsy. Then she jerked, realizing she'd at some point fallen asleep, and she felt sticky and sandy. Her tongue stuck to the roof of her mouth, and she dislodged it, disliking the taste. She looked across where the owl lights had hung at the camper across the way, and sat up straight. The lights were off.

She reasoned they had probably just been unplugged. But a quick look down at the public bathrooms, usually lit from above by a streetlamp, told her the power was out at the campground. The wind funneled from the sea and into the pines, and the only other sound was that of windchimes. Even the buoy had gone silent.

She stood up, and her feet tingled, for she had been sitting for so long they had fallen asleep. She danced where she stood, and then something caught her eye. She turned and looked far to her left, out where a little stream ran to the sea, and a pale light shone on that water. The moon had risen and sparkled on its surface. But following that little thread of water, her eyes found more light ... and it was not electronic, and it was not the moon, nor the stars. They were little flames, rising and falling, ten of them, all in a line.

She swallowed, then tried to cry out for her grandparents, but she could make no sound. Some dark and silent host marched from the sea, bearing torches.

Longshanks! she thought in a panic.

She turned to enter the camper behind her, only to find the door both shut and locked. Her lips began to quiver. Her grandparents would never have locked her out. With a small whine, she turned, and then beheld the torches advancing. She made a decision.

I will not run.

She would face this dreaded throng and its dreaded leader, Wolfgang Longshanks. For at their head marched a dark figure, taller than the others, limping, with a great hat. She could barely see its outline. The sand shuffled behind him, where the ten pirates with their ten torches followed.

But this was no ordinary fire they carried: the torches did glow, but they were muted, pale tufts of eerie light, as if seen under glass and then again underwater. They more resembled phosphorescent light than any fire. And as the pirates marched toward her, she could not discern them well. They were outlines of pirates, but not at all living flesh.

Still she stood, shuddering. For she knew they would come to her. Indeed, their leader marched right up to her, and she found herself looking up and up, and into eyes with the same pale tinge as the torches behind him, but she could not make out any other features in his face in the darkness.

"An' who might you be, lass?" a low hissing voice asked her from under that great, billowing hat.

"Just ... just Jeddy," she stammered. She looked right and left, and no one else could be seen ... no one alive, anyway.

"Just Jeddy," answered Longshanks, "do yer know who I

153

am, lass?"

Jeddy nodded. "You're the pirate, Wolfgang Longshanks!"

"Aye," his quiet, low voice answered. The wind seemed to shift his image, making him flicker as much as the torches in his horde.

"An' do ye know, Jeddy-lass," continued the pirate, "what we be doin' here, at this beachhead, on this night?"

Jeddy swallowed with a very dry mouth and considered. "This was the night, wasn't it? You lit all those fires, long ago."

"Aye," said Longshanks. "Aye," and the latter word came out like a long sigh. "Drunk upon the rum, eyes on revenge, I sent the lads down to torch them all. And so damned us all. So here we be, set to wander here always, in the dark, and marchin' along the same path, over and over, as the years roll by, until the sea takes the land, and then we'll be marchin' beneath the waves yet, for all time."

Jeddy tried to make eye contact with the pirate, but it was like looking at the stars above, and so she could not see his eyes well unless she looked a bit away from him.

"So, you're sorry for what you did?" she asked.

"Aye," said Longshanks. "But there be no repaying the debt; so, on we march, ne'er to be free again, nor to see the light of day, nor feel the softness of love, nor the feel of the wind curving us down the cape …"

Jeddy shuffled her feet in and out of the sand beneath them.

"If I come back here next year, at this exact same time, will you be here?"

"Aye," said the pirate. "Doomed forever, we will be back."

"Does anyone ever see you?" she asked.

"Nay, lass, none but ye," he answered.

"Why?"

The pirate's pale, shifting eyes looked up toward the sky.

"Maybe, lass, I sensed ye had a knowing mind, and could tell stories, and remember. Can ye do that, lass? Can ye remember us? Can ye remember me?"

"I can remember you!" said Jeddy, emphatic.

154

She could see his outline nodding.

"Then on we'll go," said Longshanks. "And maybe, lass, ye'll be here again, and see us again, and maybe not. But the wind blows off the cape, and the storm draws nigh, and a young lass needs her sleep. Off with ye, and be a good lass, and do good things."

"I will," said Jeddy, and then the pirate and his line of shadowy men with their glimmering torches walked on, never leaving any tracks with their feet. Jeddy watched them walk beyond the darkened bathroom, and then they vanished. All the lights of the campground came back on. The owl lights glimmered at her, and she could swear one of them winked.

The door to the camper opened. Grandma whispered, "Get in here, girl! Storm's a comin' soon, and who knows what else."

Jeddy took a deep breath. She wanted to say in a rush everything that she had seen. But she stopped, and looked down the way, and no pirates marched with pale torches. But Grandma followed her eyes, and watched her mouth stretch into a thin line.

"We'll be back next year," Grandma told her.

Jeddy sighed and nodded. "Good," she said. "I want to come back every year." Grandma smiled at Jeddy, and led her inside, where she yawned and stretched out over the table bed.

Grandma looked once more outside, thinking back to days long buried under sand, and of ten pale lights bobbing up from the sea ahead of a gale, years ago. "They'll come back too," she whispered. She shut the camper door.

Crunching the Numbers

Richard Lederer

Whether we know it or not, we all speak numbers, from zero through ten, and well beyond. It's as easy as one-two-three.

From time to time, I hear people say, "That didn't work. I guess we'll have to go back to ground zero." *Ground zero* is a fairly new compound in English. It refers to the point on the Earth's surface closest to a detonation. The term was first used in 1946 to refer to Hiroshima and Nagasaki, Japan, the sites of nuclear detonations in World War II. It broadened its meaning to mean any detonation site, and now any site that is a center of activity. When capitalized, as in *Ground Zero*, it refers to the former site of the Twin Towers in New York City.

People often confuse *ground zero* with the more logical phrase "I guess we'll have to go back to square one." Here the metaphor is probably rooted in the playground game four-square, which first appeared in the early 1950s. A player starts in square one and tries to move through squares two and three to square four by hitting an unreturnable ball into one of the other squares. The losing player goes back to square one.

Hidden forms of the number two occur in the words *between, betwixt, combine, zwieback,* and *twilight,* in which *tween, twixt, bi, zwie, and twi* all mean *two.* The root sense of *zwieback* is *twice baked* and of *combine, to join two things.* Twilight is literally the time of two lights, the fading sunset and the emerging light of the stars. In the old days, before the creation of artificial light brighter than a candle, the light of the stars was very bright after the sun went down.

The name of the popular rock band Three Dog Night derives from the fact that a *three-dog night* is a night so cold that it takes three dogs to keep you warm.

In the eighteenth century, the three estates of a realm were the nobility, the clergy, and the common people. In modern times, because of its watchdog responsibilities, which are crucial to a functioning democracy, the press is considered the Fourth Estate.

Now let's take five for the number five. It's easy to see that the *quint* in *quintet* and *quintuplets* means *five*. Less apparent is the *quint* in *quintessence*. The ancient Greeks held that everything in the world was composed of four elements — earth, air, fire, and water. To these the philosopher Aristotle added a new element, which the Roman philosopher Cicero dubbed *quinta essentia, fifth essence,* purer than the four earthly elements. William Shakespeare's Prince Hamlet uses the word that way when he laments, "What a piece of work is man, how noble in reason, how infinite in faculties ... And yet, to me, what is this quintessence of dust?"

As attractive an explanation as it might be, *to deep six* had nothing to do with burying a body six feet deep or by walking the plank. It's a naval idiom that means *to throw overboard*, with *six* signifying *six fathoms (thirty-six feet) deep*. The original term came from measuring the water depth under a ship using a lead-weighted sounding line. The lines were marked at two, three, five, seven, ten, thirteen, fifteen, seventeen, and twenty fathoms. If the depth was at a mark, the leadsman would call "by the mark," followed by the number. If the depth was between two marks, he would call "by the deep" followed by the estimated number. Six fathoms would be "by the deep six." By extension, *to deep six* has come to denote generally *to get rid of someone or something*.

As a barefoot boy sitting on the banks of the Mississippi River, Samuel Clemens watched stern-wheeler boats churning the muddy waters, and he heard the leadsmen sounding the depth of the river by calling out to the captains, "By the deep six ... by the mark five ... by the deep four ... by the mark three." When the river bottom was only two fathoms, or twelve feet down, he would hear the lusty cry "by the mark twain." After he left the Mississippi, and after various careers as a riverboat pilot, prospector, and printer, Sam Clemens, now a journalist, contributed an article to the *Nevada Territorial Enterprise* on February 3, 1863, and signed it with a new name — Mark Twain.

The best-known expression involving the number eight is *behind the eight ball.* In Kelly pool, up to fifteen players may participate. They draw numbers out of a bottle to determine the order of play. Any player past eight has little chance of winning. *Behind the eight ball* has been generalized to mean *any difficult, troublesome situation.*

The fact that no printed citation exists for *the whole nine yards* prior to 1967 renders dubious the nautical theory that the expression refers to the nine sails on a three-masted rigger. Nor could *the whole nine yards,* which means *the whole shootin' match, whole hog, the whole ball of wax,* and *the whole enchilada,* issue from football, in which a team must gain ten, not nine, yards to reach a first down. Equally unproven or provably wrong are dozens of other etymological explanations, including the material to make a dress, bridal veil, or Scottish kilt; the length of a machine-gun belt in World War II fighter planes; the height of a prison wall; and the volume of mined ore.

My research revealed that *the whole nine yards* referred to the revolving barrels on the backs of concrete mixing trucks. Those barrels held a volume of nine cubic yards in the early 1960s, a fact that I thought explained why I had never heard the phrase when I was growing up in the 1950s.

As you can see, my explanations are never in the abstract — and always in the concrete.

Hardee har har! But *au contraire,* hold your horses, and take a chill pill. My bad. Turns out that *the whole nine yards* popped up in an Indiana newspaper article way back in 1855! That's why Yale University librarian Fred R. Shapiro describes the expression, with its duffle bag stuffed with conjectures about its origins, as "the most prominent etymological riddle of our time."

Dec is the Latin root for *ten,* as in *decade, decimal,* and *decimate. To decimate* once described the nasty habit of the Roman commanders of slaying one out of every ten soldiers, selected by lot, in a mutinous legion. Nowadays *decimate* means *to destroy a large number of living things*, with no connection to the number ten, as in *the gypsy moth caterpillars decimated the trees in our yard*.

Clearly, the days of our English language have long been numbered, twenty-four/seven.

To Baltimore and Back

Robert Mueller

Baltimore, Maryland
June, 1916

Monday through Friday, eighteen-year-old Al Capone got
up at 6 a.m., ate breakfast at his boarding house, put on a suit
and tie, and took the No. 10 Trolley to work. He made sure to
be at his desk at Baltimore's DeAmato Construction Company
before the office opened at eight. Al learned the importance of
being on time at his last job back in Brooklyn: people got fired
for being late one too many times.

He had been working as a bookkeeper at the construction
company for almost a year. During that time, Al impressed his
boss, Peter DeAmato, with his math and bookkeeping skills,
his attention to detail, and his willingness to work late and
come in on Saturdays when needed. DeAmato liked Al and
treated him with respect.

The food at the boarding house was good, he had a bed he
didn't have to share with anyone, and he even had his own
bedroom. However, he did have to share the bathroom with
the other boarders. The residents of the boarding house were
men of various ages and occupations. After dinner, most of
them, including Al, gathered in the parlor and talked about
work and the popular sports of the day: baseball, boxing, and
horse racing. One of the boarders, Sam Olin, was a big horse
racing fan. Olin was about six years older than Al, and
worked for the Baltimore and Ohio Railroad. When Olin
talked about horse racing, which he called *The Sport of Kings*,
Al listened eagerly. "It's a great way to spend a Sunday:
you're outdoors, you study the racing forms, talk to a few

people, and make your bets. If you're lucky, you can make a few bucks. Why don't you come with me this Sunday?"

"Okay, I'll go. What'll it cost?"

"We'll sit in the grandstand. It's a lot cheaper than the box seats. It's exciting to watch a race when you have a bet on it. But remember, you don't have to bet on every race. Pick your spots and keep your bets small to start. You only press your bets up if you're ahead. If you increase your bets to make up for money you lost, you'll go broke for sure."

"Yeah I know. Don't go chasin' your bets. What time do ya wanna go?"

"Let's leave here about nine. We'll take the number 27 line out to Pimlico racetrack."

When Sam and Al arrived at the track on Sunday, they sat in the grandstand, the cheap seats. Sam let Al use his binoculars to study the racetrack and the horses, but Al was more interested in watching the wealthy people in the box seats. He envied rich people and studied the way they dressed, acted, and talked. He thought, *What would it be like to be rich, to have so much money ya could do or get anything ya wanted?*

Sam bet on more races than Al, but toward the end of the day it looked like both of them would go home losers. Standing near the betting windows, Sam said to Al, "There's only one race left, and I'm down ten bucks. There's this guy over there, Lou, who claims he's got inside dope on the races, but you gotta pay, usually a couple of bucks. You wanna go in half with me to get a tip on the last race?"

"Okay."

"Wait here, I'll be right back," said Sam as he started walking toward a thin man dressed in a worn pinstripe suit and fedora with a feather in it. He returned in a few minutes and said, "It cost two bucks so ya owe me a buck." After Al paid him, Sam said "He likes Gypsy to win in the last race. He said the jockey told him she can do. She's a six-to-one shot. I'm going to make a big enough bet on Gypsy to go home a winner."

Both men made bets on Gypsy and headed back to the

grandstand to watch the race. If Gypsy won, they would both leave money ahead; if not, they would have just enough money for car fare to get back to the boarding house. Ten horses entered the starting gate with Gypsy in the third position. The horses broke quickly with Gypsy running a close second going into the first turn. She held that position going into the back stretch but two other horses pulled up beside her, and she was third going into the final turn. By the time the horses entered the home stretch, Gypsy was a distant fourth which is where she finished. Sam torn his ticket up and said, "Shit, that nag never had a chance. I'm gonna find that god damn punk and clean his clock good." Al and Sam searched the lobby but Lou was long gone. It was a long ride back to the boarding house.

"Well, that's the way it goes sometimes, Al. Sorry we didn't come home winners."

Al said, "Yeah, me too. I got just enough money to pay this month's rent, but then I'll be broke till I get paid Friday." *Don't go chasin' your bets or you'll go home broke was good advice. Too bad we didn't take it.*

"I'm gonna be short this month, and I still owe half for last month."

The next morning at breakfast, Al didn't see Sam. When he got home from work that night, he was surprised to learn that Sam had packed his bags and skipped out during the night without paying the back rent he owed.

There was a saloon near his boarding house that Al and some of the residents of the boardinghouse liked to visit, especially on Friday (pay day) and Saturday nights. What Al especially liked about the saloon was that it had two pool tables.

Al's father taught him how to shoot pool when he was just eleven at the pool hall across from his barbershop. Al really enjoyed the game and played as often as he could. At the end of the day, his father would have Al take the newspaper from his barbershop over to Jake at the poolhall. Jake, who worked nights at the poolhall, appreciated getting the paper. If business was slow, he let Al play for free. Jake noticed that Al

162

had a talent for the game but got frustrated when he couldn't make difficult shots. "Here kid, let me show ya something. When ya don't have a clear shot at a ball, ya can still sink it by banking the cue ball. Say ya got a solid ball near the corner pocket ya need to sink, but ya don't have a straight shot at it. Ya figure out where ya have to hit the cue ball off the side cushion to hit the solid and sink it. Ya hit the cue ball hard, but not too hard." Jake set up the balls, got a pool cue, then made the shot.

"Wow, let me try that," said Al. He set the balls the way Jake had, tried the shot and missed. Jake had him set up the balls again, then showed him how to figure the correct angle to make the shot. Over time, Jake taught Al when to hit the cue ball hard, when to hit it easy, how to get back spin on the cue ball so you don't snatch, and how to play the angles. Al learned quickly, practiced often, and, with his excellent hand and eye coordination, became a very good pool player.

Al studied the pool players at the saloon near his boarding house and was confident he could beat any of them. When he played for money, he kept the bets small and let his opponent win once in a while because he knew a *friendly little game*, with money on the line, could end up in a fight.

One night back in Brooklyn, Al was challenged to a match for fifty cents a game by a stranger who was about eight years older than Al. After nearly two hours, Al was ahead by four dollars which was nearly a week's pay for the average worker. Al's mother always wanted him home by ten, so at nine forty-five, he told the stranger, who was about ten pounds heavier than Al, he had to leave. His opponent stood in front of him and said, "Not so fast. You're not goin' anywhere until I win my money back." Without hesitation, Al threw a powerful right hook to the side of his jaw. The stranger dropped to the floor and didn't move; he was knocked out cold. Al stepped over his body and made it home on time. Next day, Al was the talk of the neighborhood: he had knocked out a bigger, older man with one punch.

Having a reputation for being a tough guy was all well and good in Brooklyn, but Al wanted to put that life behind him. In Brooklyn, Al had fallen under the influence of local crime boss Johnny Torrio. His father worried that Al would become more and more involved in the rackets and end in jail or dead. He wrote to his cousin, Peter DeAmato, asking if he had a job for Al with his construction company in Baltimore. DeAmato wrote back a few weeks later saying he had a job for Al if he could come to Baltimore right away. His father put Al on a train to Baltimore the next morning. That was almost a year ago and during that time Al worked hard at being straight and respectable. No more whore houses, no more bar room or poolhalls brawls. He wanted to be known as an honest, hardworking, up and coming young businessman.

Al's boss often invited him to dinner at his home. At the dinner table, Al usually sat next to DeAmato's daughter. Her name was Isabella, but everyone called her Bella. She was Al's age, had long black hair, fair complexion, and had just graduated from high school. Al thought she was the prettiest girl he had ever seen and was quite smitten by her. It was obvious to everyone the feeling was mutual. Al knew from his last job that it was family members who got ahead in the company. Besides the construction company, DeAmato had started a savings and loan company. *If I marry Bella, I could be the head of the company someday. I'd have the big office, I'd give the orders, and everyone would call me Mr. Capone.*

He thought about asking Bella out now that his condition was better. Back in Brooklyn, Al's brother Ralph caught a case of the *clap* or gonorrhea from one of the hookers on Coney Island. He had a burning sensation when urinating, yellow discharge from the penis, and swollen testicles. His doctor told him to stop having sex until the symptoms cleared up which would take a few months. When Al had the same symptoms, from the same source, Ralph told him, "Don't waste your money on a doctor. Just wait a few months and ya'll heal up."

Al agreed with Ralph. *Why waste money on a doc. I'll just wait for it to heal up.*

On Sundays, Al enjoyed sleeping late, having coffee and a prune Danish, then reading the Sunday newspaper in the

164

parlor of his boarding house. He always started with the sports section. After studying the box scores, he read an article about a local ball player named Ruth who was a star pitcher for the Boston Red Sox. After reading the article, Al studied an ad from a local department store for men's suits. He loved dressing in the latest styles, and much of his salary was spent on clothes.

Al noticed an ad for the new 1917 Cadillac Phaeton five-passenger touring car priced at $2,080. It was the same car his boss had just purchased. When Al saw it parked in the office's parking lot, he told DeAmato it was the most beautiful car he had ever seen. "Thanks, it's the model 57, the same one the Army brass use. It's got a V8 motor, seventy horsepower, and can do sixty-five miles an hour. It was expensive, but it's worth it. You can't go wrong with a Cadillac."

Al nodded his head and thought, *Yeah, if ya got the dough.*

While reading the ad, Al heard the phone ring in the hallway. It was the only phone in the house and was mounted on the wall. He heard his landlady answer it saying, "Just a minute, I'll go get him." A moment later, she was in the parlor. "Al, it's your brother Frank on the phone. He wants to talk with you. He said it's urgent."

Al put the newspaper on a table near his chair and stared at her for a moment. She could see the worry on his face. Long distance calls were expensive and almost always bad news. Without saying a word, he got up, walked to the hallway, and picked up the receiver, held it to his ear, and talked into the mouthpiece. "Hello, this is Al."

"Al, this is Frank. Ralph and I were shooting pool with Pop last night when suddenly he starting complaining about chest pains and fell to the floor. We rushed him to the hospital, but it was too late. He's dead. The doctor said it was a heart attack."

"Geez, Frank, I can't believe it. Pop wasn't that old."

"Yeah, I know. He was only fifty-five. Ma said he had been complaining about dizzy spells, chest pains, and always feeling tired for months. She begged him to see a doctor, but he refused. 'Doctors cost a lot of money, I just need to get more rest,' he said. Al, ya better come home right away. Ma's taking it pretty hard."

"Okay, I'll get back as soon as I can. My boss was pop's cousin. I gotta let him know what happened in the morning. If I get an early enough train, I should be home by tomorrow night. I'll see ya then. Goodbye for now." Al hung up the receiver and stood in the hallway while the shock of his father's death sunk in. His dreams and plans for a new life in Baltimore were shattered, and there was nothing he could do about it. After a few minutes, he started walking back to his room and passed his landlady.

"Was it bad news, Al?"

"My pop died yesterday. It was his heart."

"Oh my god, Al. I'm so sorry. What are you going to do?"

"I gotta get back to Brooklyn as soon as I can. Is it okay to use the phone later? I want to call Union Station and see what time I can get a train for New York."

"Sure Al, go ahead and don't worry about the cost."

"Thanks, I'll call later. Right now, I just want to go back to my room for a while."

Al got back to his room, closed the door, and sat down on the edge of his bed. It was hard to believe his father, the bedrock of the family, was gone. His eyes were starting to tear up. What would his poor mother do now? She still had four young children at home. Ralph had a family of his own now, and Frank lived in Manhattan. He had to go back to Brooklyn to help his family and would probably never see Baltimore, or Bella, again. After a few minutes, Al got a handkerchief out of his dresser, dried his eyes, blew his nose, and walked down the hall way to the phone. He called and found out there was a train leaving for New York the following day at noon. That night, he went to the local saloon. He didn't want to play pool, he just wanted to get drunk.

Despite a night of heavy drinking, Al got up early Monday morning, finished packing, said goodbye to his landlady, and got to the office early. As soon as Peter DeAmato arrived, Al asked to speak with him.

"Sure Al, have a seat. What's the problem?"

"I got a call yesterday from my brother Frank, back in Brooklyn." Al paused for a moment and took a deep breath. "He told me my pop had a heart attack on Saturday. He died."

The expression on DeAmato's face quickly changed from patience to shocked disbelief. "My God, Al, I can't believe it! What are you gonna do?"

"I've gotta get back to Brooklyn right away."

"Of course," said his boss. "Your family always comes first. When do you plan on leaving?"

"There's a train leaving for New York at noon today. I've got my bags packed, they're by my desk."

DeAmato said, "How long do you think you'll be gone?"

Al said, "I don't know if I will be comin' back. My mother needs me. I don't know how she's gonna manage without Pop. She's got my three younger brothers and baby sister at home."

"I have a few things to take care of, then I'll drive you to the station."

"Ya don't have to do that, I can take the trolley."

"No, it's not a problem. Please wait by your desk. I'll be ready in a few minutes." After Al left his office, DeAmato opened the office safe, removed three hundred dollars, put the money in an envelope, and put it in his breast pocket. He walked over to Al's desk and said, "Okay, let's go. Maybe you can catch an earlier train to New York." They walked out the back door of the office to the parking lot where DeAmato had parked his new car. He told Al to put his suitcases in the back seat and sit next to him in the front.

On the drive to Union Station, DeAmato told Al, "Your father and I grew up in the same small village in Italy just south of Naples — Castellar de Stabia. We went to the same school but were in different grades because he was older than me. I was kinda small for my age and got picked on by the bigger kids, but not when your father was around. 'Peter's my cousin, you better leave him alone,' he would say, and they did. No one wanted to cross him."

Arriving at the station, DeAmato stopped his car near the

entrance and turned off the motor. Turning to Al, he said, "The construction and the savings and loan businesses are doing well, and as they grow, I need people I can trust to help run them. I know you have to get back to Brooklyn now, but you'll always have a job here if you decide to come back."

Both men got out of the car. Al got his suitcases out of the backseat and set them down on the sidewalk. The two men shook hands. Al said, "Thanks for giving me a job and for treating me like part of your family. Please tell Bella goodbye for me, and tell her I'll write as soon as I can."

"Give my deepest condolences to your dear mother and the rest of your family." Reaching into his breast pocket, DeAmato took out the envelope and pressed it into Al's hand. "This should help with the expenses."

Looking into the envelope, Al was overwhelmed by the generous gift. He gave his soon to be ex-boss a big hug, and the eyes of both men began to tear up. Finally, DeAmato said, "You better get going, you might be able to catch an earlier train."

"Thank you for everything. I promise I'll find a way to pay this back someday." He picked up his suitcases and walked toward the station. When he got to the door, he stopped and looked back. DeAmato was still standing on the sidewalk and waved. Al put his suitcases down and waved back. He pulled the heavy metal door open, picked up his suitcases, and entered the station. The door slowly closed behind him.

Al didn't want to end up like his father: work hard all your life, lead a quiet respectable life, and end up with nothing. He went back to Brooklyn and used his brain and brawn to work his way up in the crime underworld. He followed his mentor, crime boss Johnny Torrio, to Chicago. Before he was thirty, Capone was the head of the multimillion-dollar crime syndicate known as The Chicago Outfit. Although Al Capone was a cold-blooded killer, a notorious bootlegger, and the most infamous criminal in American history, the only crime he was ever convicted of was tax evasion, for which he was sentenced to eleven years in prison. While serving time in Alcatraz, he was diagnosed with syphilis which he contracted as a teen-ager. He died of its effects at the age of forty-eight.

Thrift-Store Luck

Pennel Paugh

Saturday, September 10th, Edward Davies was shoved over the railing of his 47th story mini-balcony. Though his journey was brief, Ed's moment of horror felt like hours.

Being a specialist in the latest literary fiction, Ed rarely read the news. This explained how he came to purchase a thrift-store windbreaker without knowing the design had been discontinued. The thin material was air-resistant and inlets in the front, along the hip and armpits, made the jacket conducive to flight. The pleated back and billowing arms would fill up, carrying people all over the place on windy days. In New York City alone, over a hundred people had been injured and two had died.

When Ed's coat filled up and raised him past the 52nd floor, his heart fluttered. Was this the act of a merciful God carrying him to safety?

A crosswind whisked him across the street to an even taller high rise. He reached for a nearby balcony railing. Before he could grab it, a strong updraft blasted him into the bottom of the overhanging balcony where he banged his head.

Dizzy and half conscious, Ed fell hard onto the below 58th floor piazza. He landed on a wide planting box which hung over a pointy, metal railing. His right leg broke with an audible snap and the railing crushed his ankle. Excruciating pain sent him into a faint.

Regaining consciousness, Ed reeled from indescribable pain. Nevertheless, he believed he had been saved and expected to be resting on plantings hung over a rail.

Opening his eyes, his hopes evaporated — he was falling headfirst. His coat fitted tight around his neck, blocking air from entering. How could he get the wind to fill his coat again? Like a skydiver, he opened his arms. Nevertheless, he continued to nosedive like a struck-down plane.

It was 3 a.m. A moonless sky made Ed's solitary moment even more frightening. Most light emitted close to the bottom of buildings where water taxis traversed. Noise from below was faint. Even his scream seemed to be coming from afar.

The icy wind whipped Ed's long hair into his eyes. He envisioned landing on one of the many weaving concrete greenways that connected and crisscrossed tall buildings. The system made walking possible in a city five stories under water. While his leg throbbed relentlessly and his head gave him stabbing pangs, he imagined landing would cause him such intense pain, his current injuries would be insignificant.

In a state of sheer terror, Ed's torso seized in spasms while his limbs lost all strength. Each rapid heartbeat radiated electric spikes. Then, an intense flash coursed through his chest. He gasped for air, grew dizzy, and lost consciousness.

Being limp, Ed's body righted itself. Descending feet first, his coat slowed his fall and softened impact when he smashed into a huge tree on the 20th floor greenway a block from his apartment. His jacket snagged on a large branch that, in a few seconds, cracked then broke.

Coming to rest, hanging from a lower limb, Ed's body bobbed up and down. Like a ringer in a huge bell, his legs banged out a rhythm on the metal mailbox below. This jarred a nearby couple engaged in a heated disagreement.

"See. Arguing makes bad things happen." The man sped away, leaving the stunned woman gaping up at Ed's body.

Made of material developed for life on the Martian settlement and not for hanging a person on a branch, the jacket ripped. Ed collapsed at the woman's feet with a sandbag thump; his face toward the sky, right leg bent and askew. Momentarily, jolting awake he grabbed one of her feet. "We've got to stop them! WRT is planning a coup!"

As the woman called 911, she mumbled, "Quite the contrary, my dear, arguing can bring about opportunities."

171

What's in a Name?

Five days earlier

Ed worked at a *New Yorker* competitor — the *Scizzor's Edge*. The parent company of the magazine, WRT (Wright, Rawlins and Tannhauser), owned two buildings that shared a lobby. Though his office was located in a separate building from its owners, to gain access to his office, Ed placed his left index finger on an electronic scanner at the front desk. To use an elevator that only went between the 32nd through 36th floors, he used a security card. Additionally, at his office, he scanned his right eye in a device outside the door.

Enjoying quick breaks to sit in local cafes or to catch a bit of sun, Ed regarded all the safety mechanisms a hassle. God forbid if he were to leave his elevator card at the office — something he did regularly.

At the front desk, always manned by a guard, Ed wondered what all the security was about. Waiting in line to be scanned, he asked people he guessed worked at WRT what kind of work they did. He only received cold shoulders.

This made Ed wonder all the more what the mother corporation did. Its webpage only said, *Making better tomorrows all over the world.* What did that mean?

It had to be a government contractor. Perhaps it provided arms for undeclared military actions. Ed suspected the US did that sort of thing all the time. If true, he thought they would be capable of anything. With a sarcastic tone, he hoped all the checkpoints magazine staff endured would be adequate to protect *Scizzor's Edge* from its owners.

This morning, Ed made his usual crack about the unnecessary security to the guard who checked him in. "Hey, figure out what all the fuss is about?"

The burly man of mixed heritage maintained an inscrutable expression. "We have to protect the Taliban from reading good literature."

Ed laughed heartily on the way to the elevator bank.

Entering his office, Ed sighed. This was his paradise. The tiny, cluttered room had an unhampered view of the ocean. Though staff lobbied him to only accept electronic submissions, Ed preferred hard copies. Nevertheless, authors were willing to use their carbon allotment to gain a chance to publish at the magazine. As a result, high stacks of submissions lined all four of Ed's walls. Every day, the piles grew taller.

As Chief Managing Editor, Ed was given what his staff considered the very best to read. Ironic that he wielded such power and influence over writers' careers, making some very wealthy, while he barely squeaked by each month.

Placing his beat-up leather briefcase on the floor, he shed a faded suit jacket. The cheap, thin fabric of his shirt exaggerated his long thin arms and lack of body tone. Picking up a large, filthy mug with a 3D Cheshire cat reading a magazine, Ed headed to the coffee mess down the hall.

After turning forty, Ed had grown a slight paunch. He had no hips. Rather than fight gravity, he elected to wear his pants high. Luckily, because he was short, his pants were a perfect length. To compensate for the snug fit in his groin, Ed swung his right leg out and swished his hips slightly as he strolled.

Entering the long kitchen, Ed's sweet tooth walked him straight to a box of donuts at the far end of the room. He mmmed, examined each, and chose one with cherry filling. Biting in, red sticky goo splatted down his shirt. "Shit." He grabbed a paper towel.

Senior Assistant Editor, Mike Brenan, strolled in wearing a smart handmade silk suit.

"Crap," Ed looked up briefly and gave a loud sigh, "I ruined a new tie."

"Serves you right for stealing my favorite." Mike chuckled.

Over the sink, Ed cleaned his mess.

Mike poured himself coffee, selected a pastry, and walked to the door.

Ed threw out the remainder of his donut, saying, "It's just as well, the doctor told me to watch the cholesterol."

"Got a heart problem?" Mike raised an eyebrow. "Or was it just an ounce of prevention advice?"

Ed rolled his eyes, "I hope it was the latter."

Watching Mike amble down the hall, Ed felt like a ragamuffin. *Can't beat family money. Must be nice.*

Returning to his office, Ed plopped into a frayed armchair. He crossed his legs and tossed his head back to get hair out of his eyes. Thinning at the crown, he decided to grow what he did have. It was at an annoying scraggly stage.

Scooping up a pile of mail on his desk, Ed unearthed a brand-new interoffice envelope. It had a typed label, "E. Davies." Letters from within the magazine were unheard of these days. Why bother when you could send email?

Marked *Confidential,* the top flap had been secured with a thick piece of strapping tape. "Must be *very* private. Why me?"

Using office scissors, Ed attacked the flap. It was like cutting into rock with kiddy snippers.

Holding the package out, he squinted. The document inside was thin, even for a short story. With a frustrated sigh, he turned it upside down, and cut off the envelope's bottom edge.

Stapled onto a five-page document sat a half-page typed note: "These are our preliminary psyops ideas. Our military plans are more advanced." It was signed with an unintelligible scrawl. Intrigued, Ed read on.

Page one's introduction read: "America's democracy is a failed experiment. It is nothing more than tyranny of the masses. This makes our nation weak. To put things right, we will establish a New Order."

Scoffing, Ed shook his head. "Oh, right, everyone loves a dictatorship, particularly those in charge." He scowled. Was this fiction disguised as a fascist manifesto?

The paper became more outrageous, saying corporations needed to rule without taxes, environmental requirements, or health and safety regulations. The validity of workplace and environmental damages would be denied and those making complaints would be accused of conspiracies and called good-for-nothing whiners.

"Wonderful. Company profits would reign supreme — stockholders will love it."

No surprise, the paper said, "The middle class should be allowed to sink or swim on its own, unaided by governmental programs which only steal money from the producing to give to moochers."

Following the paper's logic, Ed's blood pressure rose. He sprang up and grabbed his coffee cup, mumbling as he walked. He needed to calm down and stop taking the writing so seriously. After all the submission was just fiction, wasn't it?

Minutes later he returned calmer, continuing where he'd left off.

"Post-Revolution Results. The government would be run by an executive board of military and corporate leaders. Corporate leaders, the natural aristocracy, would be the permanent governing class."

Weird that, given all of the other problems the paper listed, number one was "the homosexual agenda to destroy the American family with fake marriages. Such acts threatened to topple western civilization."

Is this just a homophobic prank?

* * *

Ed had endured plenty of bashings in his life. Starting in grad school, he made the mistake of confessing his love to a roommate. Mat not only rejected him, he blabbed to everyone.

There's nothing like a straight *man who gets turned on by one of his own gender.*

After that, he received endless pranks, jeers and beatings. Ed slumped in his chair recalling the injuries and humiliations. By midsemester he fell into a deep depression. Then, the worst happened—he developed writer's block and couldn't finish his dissertation. He left Yale with a mere master's in English, not a PhD. His career had been shattered, his esteem—flattened, and heart—eviscerated.

* * *

175

At the end, the paper proposed overthrowing the current way of governing to "establish leadership for the nation that would do what needed to be done." The author's strategy was to launch a disinformation campaign that would attract military members and rouse unrest.

The concluding suggestion raised alarms in Ed's head. "When the time is right, we could use the high-grade explosives we just picked up and take out the bridges going into the Capital City."

To exchange ideas and make plans, the author had created an encrypted folder on WRT's intranet and gave a passcode.

"They've stolen bomb-making material?"

Ed powered up his laptop. Lower in the headlines was an unsubstantiated rumor that a truck full of high-grade explosives had gone missing in Nicaragua. To date, no one had declared responsibility. Inhaling coffee, Ed coughed and took a while to recover.

He double-checked. The envelope lacked a prior address. "Oh no! The memo is on WRT letterhead!" Only people above his boss used those. "Weird. It doesn't show who penned it."

"This isn't fiction. It's a misdelivered piece of interoffice mail!" Was there another E. Davies? He picked up the phone and dialed HR. They put him on hold. The receptionist finally returned, stating in a cold flat tone that the information was classified.

He had interceded a humdinger conspiracy. Not only that, it was being hatched right inside WRT by an executive!

He considered going to the authorities. He'd only be laughed at. Besides, if the police pursued with an inquiry, it would put his job at risk. He was a middle-aged man and this job had been hard to come by.

Ed paced. He could go to the mailroom at lunch, get a new envelope, tape it up and send the damn thing on its way.

The idea sickened him. If the paper's purpose was to justify a nefarious plot, he wasn't going to help it along. Ed jammed the manuscript in the middle of a stack of stories.

Ed's Fall

Friday, Ed went to a bar off the greenway near his place.

On his way, Ed told himself he was too old and out of shape to attract attention. The best picks his age would be settled. The younger guys wouldn't be interested if he didn't have dough. Nevertheless, as he stepped through the door, he searched the room with a smile.

The inside was crammed with men. The music and noise from the crowd almost burst his eardrums. Elbowing through a tight cluster of handsome specimens, he approached the bar to order a drink. To his delight, a twenty-something, blue-eyed blond at a nearby table smiled broadly at him. Disconcerted, Ed tripped and stumbled into the bar's footrest. Laughing, he ordered a drink for himself and sent one over to the fellow. To his delight, the man not only raised his glass, he waved Ed over.

An hour later, they entered Ed's apartment. As he turned to close the door, something heavy crashed onto his backside. The world went black. Waking to a pounding head, he tried to reach up to touch his injury, but couldn't.

His arms and legs had been tied up to a chair. A glance around the room made Ed almost crap his pants.

Like at his office, he had filled his apartment with stacks of manuscripts. Chuck, or so the bastard called himself, had thrown papers everywhere. He was in Ed's only closet, which also was full of manuscripts.

Yelling with his back to Ed, Chuck pitched out a handful of documents. Every time he threw a stack, the blanket on the floor deepened. The youth screamed, "Where is it?" Each time he was a little louder. By the time he emptied the closet, Chuck's voice was so high Ed wanted to cover his ears.

Turning, Chuck glared.

Ed's vision blurred. This wasn't really happening.

Running over, Chuck yanked Ed's head back. "You son-of-a-bitch, where is it?"

Without a doubt, Ed would not be getting a happy ending tonight. Was this the interoffice note's author?

Considering his options, Ed decided to put on his best

innocent smile. "I can't think what you mean."

Taking one look into the raging youth's eyes, Ed resolved he would not give in to this fiend. "Be good. Works of some of the very best writers in the country now carpet this floor. Calm down and tell me what this is all about."

Scoffing, Chuck's face turned red. "Cut the crap. Where is it?"

* * *

Upon first meeting Chuck, Ed's hopes had risen. After years of being alone, maybe he'd found someone with whom a relationship would stick. On the way from the bar, Ed had suggested they walk along the greenway to his place. Halfway there, he pulled the youth to him and delivered a passionate kiss. Chuck stiffened. "Keep it cool. My boss lives near here."

Heart burning, Ed yearned for a night of romance and sex. When they were finally alone in the elevator, he pounced, sticking his tongue in Chuck's ear. Then he feasted on Chuck's neck, while slipping a hand down the young man's pants.

At first Chuck froze, but then he closed his eyes and moaned. Though the elevator rose in a New York minute, by the time they arrived, Chuck was panting and his glasses were fogged.

* * *

While suffering slugs to his gut and jaw, Ed clung to the memory of their time in the elevator. *When you're good, Eddie, you're very good. No wonder the guy is crazy-mad.* Gazing at Chuck's attractive features, a tear filled Ed's eyes.

Chuck pounded on Ed's neck and face. Past the initial pain of each slug, Ed felt very little. But he knew the day after, he'd feel like hell. Question was, would he live to see tomorrow?

Phrases in the interoffice note played in Ed's head. Was Chuck a senior exec at WRT?

No. Those people weren't tough guys. Chuck was a hired thug. Judging by the youth's lack of emotional control, the torture would escalate till Ed caved.

Ed's gut turned to acid. Was there any chance he'd be dragged back to the office? Chuck probably knew the night guard. The *Scizzor's Edge* was the most likely place to find the letter.

Nah. Chuck was desperate and pulling at straws. That's why he'd conned his way into Ed's residence.

Face full of rage, Chuck jammed a hot cigarette onto Ed's neck. Though the burning of his flesh made him grit his teeth, the years of pranks, beatings and torment that had wrecked his career put Ed in a state of grim determination. He would torment Chuck in return.

Pretending it was all a sexual come-on, Ed winced. "Ouch. I love it when you're mean."

Chuck's venom grew as Ed taunted. In minutes, he cut Ed loose and pulled him to the mini-balcony, shoving Ed against the flimsy railing.

There was no question any longer. Ed was a dead man, no matter what. Very well. If dying was his fate, he would do what he could to stand in the way of WRT's plans. With this decision, peace filled his heart and mind.

Ed reached over and licked the young man's neck. "You're cute when you're naughty."

His face contorted in revulsion, Chuck lifted Ed over the balcony. The relative ease of the act was a shock. However, Ed was ready. While being lifted, Ed flung his arms under Chuck's armpits and locked wrists behind the monster's back. Bracing his feet against the outside of the railing, Ed yanked Chuck over, then let go.

Chuck reached out with grasping hands.

With a sneer, Ed kicked his murderer in the face.

Watching Chuck fall like a stone, filled Ed with satisfaction. Pride turned to terror as he faced his demise. But then his coat gave him a wonderful surprise. He was being lifted into the air. Might he live to see another day?

179

Ed's Fate

Saturday, Ed woke in a hospital bed with his leg hoisted in a contraption. To his right, sat a short-haired man chewing gum. "I'm Detective Skinner. Sorry about your injuries."

Frowning, Ed said thanks using a questioning tone.

"Might you remember the woman in the apartment of the balcony where you landed?"

"Sorry. We didn't have a chance to meet." Without mentioning being thrown, Ed described how he had flown from his building and ended up on the woman's flowerbed.

The detective opened his notepad. "The woman, Mary Gray, filed a report stating you tried to break into her 54th floor apartment."

Waving to his raised leg, Ed grimaced. "You can see I was in no shape to commit any criminal acts."

The detective nodded. "You should know she confessed when she saw you were unable to fight her off," the detective actually rolled his eyes, "in what she called an act of self-defense, she pushed you off the railing."

Ed guffawed.

"We want to know if you wish to file charges against Ms. Gray."

Not answering the question, Ed replied, "Wait. You're telling me I survived two murder attempts in one night?" With a single laugh, he asked, "Did you find the other guy's body?"

The detective's eyes widened.

Two days passed and the woman, at whose feet Ed had fallen, showed up beside his hospital bed. "Nice to see you're recovering." She grinned. "I'm Cheri. I do freelance reporting. Want to tell me more about the coup you mentioned?"

* * *

A year later, Ed pulled back the curtains to his one-level Southern California house. He no longer enjoyed views from high places. Gazing out at the canyon edging his backyard, he reflected on all that had occurred to him since his fall from the sky.

The next time he heard from Cheri, she sent him links to several newspaper articles. Thanks to Ed, the conspiracy had fallen apart. Lots of people were arrested, including an E. Davies, son of WRT's chairman of the board.

After that, countless people from the press visited Ed's bedside.

The day before Ed was discharged, an avuncular fellow showed up. "I hear you're a managing editor of a literary magazine. Think you could write your story as a screenplay?"

Ed jumped at the offer.

Moving to Hollywood had been strange and wonderful. Using the impressive advance, he found a tiny apartment nearby. His producer introduced Robert, a blue-eyed middle-aged fellow-writer. While working intensely together on Ed's script, they became a couple. In eight months, Robert asked Ed to marry him.

Robert yelled from their joint office. "Get out here. Let's celebrate."

Ed ran.

Pointing at his monitor, Robert said, "Here's the latest." The picture featuring Ed's movie was of a buff actor, mid-air, wearing a ballooned jacket in a background of skyscrapers. "You're number one across the nation and European viewers are asking to see it."

Thinking of the royalties, Ed lifted Robert from the floor in an embrace. "Without you, I couldn't have done it."

When back on the floor, Robert continued to hold tight. "Let's get a champagne brunch and bless our current story with a bit of thrift-store luck."

Heart soaring. "I'll drink to that," Ed thought of the coat that saved his life. "My treat." Ed gave Robert a passionate kiss.

One Perfect Life

Ty Piz

It was not a case of love at first sight. It was a reuniting of souls.

Ten years multiplied by three is how long it's been since they had seen one another. They grew up just a mile or two apart in the very same suburban town. When they were about twelve, their paths nearly intersected. They had crisscrossed many times before, though never stopped in the same place long enough to meet.

It was the early '70s and they were both in the same junior high school. She had long blonde hair and wore hot pants and liked the boys an awful lot. Boys were, in fact, starting to become almost as important to her as horses. Almost!

After many years of crew cuts and the unfortunate nick names, he followed the lead of his older brothers and began to rebel. He let his hair grow long, he wore corduroy bell bottoms. He started to become mildly interested in girls, but dirt bikes and things of that nature were still more important to him.

At this point, their timing was however a little off. Then, life took a tragic turn. The girl got an incurable disease that took her kidneys and turned her world upside down. She kept on living, though, despite a lot of pain and heartache. She learned early on to quit dreaming of the future and using the word *someday*. Before long her only goal was to live like there was no tomorrow.

Alone, wanting to leave all of her past behind, she rode wild horses and chased wild boys. And, like the wild horses she loved, she never let anybody get too close. She would after all be dead any day.

He always had a longing for danger, for pushing the envelope to the extremes, and for flying too close to the sun, even had a few near misses with death of his own. He, like this girl with her loss of kidneys, understood the frailty of human life. Then, seemingly out of nowhere, terrible loss and sorrow crept in and broke his heart. With his childhood dream of racing motorcycles worldwide and having a family to travel with, the three daughters, now in their twenties and on their own, his first wife suddenly moved away. His body so badly busted up from an incident on a racetrack, he absolutely needed the kind of faith that could move mountains to help him carry on again. Before long, his only goal was to live like there was no tomorrow.

With his dream of speed as his aim, he rode faster and faster motorcycles. Through all of his torment of living without his family he never quit loving his fellow human beings. In a sport that can quickly take so much away, he breathed a sigh and was reminded that God has always moved in miraculous ways through him. He has his health and his wonderful daughters.

On a rainy summer night last July, their high school reunion was held. She, still alive despite a thousand odds, not in her favor, was a published writer now, and still in love with her horses and their wingless flight. She had had her share of being loved by a few men, and she even believed she loved back a time or two. But she was alone that night, braving the mysterious unknown of a high school reunion with people she long ago had all but forgotten.

After years of professional motorbike racing, the shelves filled with trophies to show for his efforts, along with numerous championships under his belt—plus the broken bones and injuries that were part of that life—his world had changed. He was a teacher now, a loving father, and grandfather, grateful for his daughters and the shared spirit that kept them connected. He coached soccer, and although he was satisfied with where he was in life, he still loved his motorbikes and yearned for the thrill of the ride—more riding, always riding. Despite a thousand disappointments he

183

had become more in tune with his spiritual side. He listened closer to the soul within him as it continued to guide him on one adventure after another.

And so it was that he was among friends he had never forgotten that chilly July night. It was by chance, through old friends they had in common, that he and she finally met. They spoke for the first time that either one of them could recall. It was only a few minutes of conversation but the connection was extraordinary — you might even say magical.

At the end of the second night of the reunion, under stars which spread across the sky like diamonds and with a radiant moon shining overhead, they hugged for the first time and neither of them ever wanted to let go. In that magic-filled moment they remembered each other, as if they had loved at another time on the astral plane. They shared all the very same feelings and memories that could not be accounted for in this lifetime alone. They remembered how perfectly they fit together.

In the days and months that followed, the memories continued to flow. As their individual passions for riding and writing became clearer as to the importance of who each person is, their bond and love for one another grew stronger.

If you ask her, she could tell you, *someday* is in every beat of this beautiful heart. She feels it there. She knows it was worth waiting for. She trusts him with her imperfections, and because he works with students with special needs, he understands like no one ever has, that without them, she wouldn't be here. It's her imperfections that made her right for him. Ask her and she'll tell you that he alone has awakened those parts of her that were never wounded from the falls from horses, and never sick from renal failure.

He says, if they had never met, he'd still be missing her. The spiritual connection was so powerful he'd still be reaching out to the poles at the farthest ends of the earth to find her. He'd still be seeking the wisdom of Eastern philosophy to enlighten him and to prepare all aspects of him, for her. In his search for her, he would seek the inspirations of Western civilization, while channeling his deepest meditations to guide his footsteps to intersect with hers at just the right time. They relax together in a quiet moment outside the barn, earnestly viewing the Rocky Mountains.

From the tallest peaks, the icy runoff flows to the cold rivers below and through the deepest valleys which countless angels had finally crossed to complete their tasks to bring the paths of this boy and the girl together. Now in the later stages of their forties, still young at heart, no longer do two separate journeys exist, they are joined as one.

Finding Benjamin

Jeff Mason

October 10, 2012, and already winter rains moistened the chaparral, bringing forth the pungent aroma of creosote. Ben lived in the foothills of the San Gabriel mountains in a modern subdivision which looked out at the valley. He walked the familiar path from Laurel's home to his own under a darkening gray sky. The path descended between sumac and toyon then climbed a more barren slope to the street where he and his mother had lived for five years. The rain, a mist when he had started out, now fell steadily wetting his hair and threatening to soak his Florence and the Machine T-shirt.

He ran the last hundred yards to his home and stood dripping in the entry. The house was quiet. Faint pattering of raindrops on the roof was the only sound. Ben's mother wouldn't be home for another hour. She had an hour commute from her job as a hospital administrator in Riverside to their eastern Los Angeles county bedroom community. He could use this time however he wanted, and what he wanted was to dry off, listen to music, and not think about the English assignment due tomorrow.

His homework was to write a 500-word essay about someone he admired. This afternoon a vague anxiety wormed its way into his consciousness. Ben didn't know who he admired. He liked alternative music and appreciated its composers and singers. He hated rap and sports equally.

Ben couldn't decide if he admired or despised his father, Brian. He had been sure he hated him when his dad left his mother to be with Jenna, who'd been his secretary. Lately Dad was reaching out, offering to take him to ball games or go camping. Maybe he did respect his dad, a criminal defense attorney, but not enough to write about him.

The vibrating and ringing in his pocket startled him. He pulled his cell phone from his pocket. He didn't recognize the number. He thought about not answering, but curiosity got the better of him. An unfamiliar female voice on the phone said, "Hello?"

"This is Ben. Who's calling?"

"It's Maggie. I sit behind you in Mrs. Agnos's fourth period English class."

"Hi, Maggie. Are you working on the writing assignment for tomorrow?"

"Yes, that's why I'm calling. Who've you decided to write about? Maybe we can work on it together. Can you bring your laptop over to my house after dinner? I think we can figure this out and whip it out tonight."

The rapid-fire requests flustered Ben, but he said, "I guess so. I'll ask my mom when she gets home."

"Great. Write down my address."

Ben wrote as Maggie rattled off her address.

"See you around seven," she said.

Ben changed clothes, dried the front entry with old towels, then started dinner for him and his mom. He used what he found in the fridge—salad, spaghetti with bottled marinara sauce, and sweet Italian sausage. He had just added the pasta into the boiling water when his mother came into the kitchen from the garage and smiled.

"To what good fortune do I owe your making my dinner?"

"I have a homework assignment for English due tomorrow, a 500-word essay on the person I admire most. Maggie and I are going to work on it together tonight. Can you drive me over to her house after dinner?"

"Who's Maggie?"

"A girl that sits behind me in English class."

"I didn't know you had any girlfriends except Laurel."

"Laurel isn't a girlfriend, just a friend."

* * *

187

It was still raining when Ben's mother drove him down to the flats where Maggie lived. "I wish you could drive," Marie said, not hiding the tiredness in her voice after a long workday. "Next year you'll be able to drive yourself. Call me when you want to be picked up."

Maggie's house was neither new nor old, big nor small. Ben could hear some commotion inside when he rang the bell. It took a minute for the door to open, and when it did a girl he recognized welcomed him. Maggie had dark eyes and long brown hair pulled back in a ponytail. She wore a man's dress shirt loose over denim jeans.

Maggie smiled. "Come in. I'm glad you remembered to bring your laptop. I've cleared the kitchen table. We can work there. Sit next to me, so I can see what you've written."

"I haven't written anything yet," Ben said as he set up his computer. "Have you decided who you are writing about?"

"I'm going to write about Florence Welch. She's a woman in touch with herself. She has demons, needs, fears, and hopes. She is anything but perfect, a fallen goddess, who still commands belief."

"Did you know that Florence and the Machine is my favorite band?" Ben said.

"I knew you like to wear their T-shirt," Maggie said. "I figured you must know something about her."

"Can I read what you've written so far?" Ben asked.

"Yeah, but let's get you started first. Who are you going to write about?"

"I had thought of Florence, but you've already taken her."

"Well Florence idolized Stevie Nicks. You could write about her."

"She must be 100 years old. Is she even alive?"

"Why don't you Google her?"

Ben entered Stevie Nicks in the Google search box and hundreds of links popped up. He started with her Wikipedia entry. The name of her group, Fleetwood Mac, and the titles of her most popular songs didn't mean much to him. He pulled some ear buds from his pocket and plugged them into his computer. He went to YouTube and selected one of her first songs, "Rhiannon." The first few bars of the music electrified him, transformed him. The words made him imagine what it would be like to ring like a bell, and he realized he would want to love her, whoever she was.

Although he couldn't remember hearing the song, it was almost as if it were imprinted on his soul. The music, more than the words, triggered a warmth that suffused him.

Ben didn't fully understand the song's meaning, but he felt its power. "Rhiannon" triggered something primal, inarticulate, and elemental in him. He removed the earbud jack from his computer and the music flooded the kitchen.

Maggie looked up from her computer, smiled, and said, "That's Stevie Nicks."

After listening to half a dozen more songs that Stevie Nicks had written and performed for Fleetwood Mac, Ben had a sense that Stevie Nicks and Fleetwood Mac spoke directly to him.

He began compose his report and words spilled out. As he wrote he thought, *Stevie Nicks is all about loss and remembrance and especially about love.*

Maggie looked over Ben's shoulder. "You've already written 750 words according to your computer."

Ben and Maggie exchanged computers to read each other's essays. Maggie began her paper by saying that she admired Florence because she's a famous and successful recording artist who gave voice to female aspiration and the dark side of love.

"I told you that Stevie and Florence are a pair," Maggie said, "just in different generations. I like the way you write, going to the heart where all the darkness is." Maggie read out loud from Ben's computer, "Stevie Nicks is all about the beauty of love, fragility of love, and ultimately the evanescence of love."

"Thanks for suggesting Stevie Nicks," Ben said. "She and I click. I don't know why."

Maggie smiled at Ben, the kind of smile you felt, but she said, "I guess you should call your mom. I'll see you in Mrs.

Agnos's class tomorrow."

On the way home Ben couldn't stop talking about Stevie Nicks and Fleetwood Mac. Marie said, "Fleetwood Mac has always been Brian's favorite band. He played their music constantly when you were a baby."

* * *

Cool crisp air surrounded Ben when his mother dropped him off at school the next morning. Laurel was waiting for him in the breezeway where they usually met before school. "Did you finish your English assignment?" she asked.

"Sure, Maggie gave me a good idea, to write about Stevie Nicks."

Laurel fixed Ben with a hard stare. Her voice had a sharp edge when she asked, "Who's Maggie, and who's Stevie Nicks?"

"Maggie's a girl in my English class, and Stevie Nicks is a singer. She was the lead singer-songwriter for Fleetwood Mac."

"Why would you admire some long dead rocker from before you were born?"

"She's not dead, and she's still writing and performing. Besides she was idolized by Florence Welch."

"That's who you should have written about," Laurel said, turning her back and walking away.

Fourth period was Mrs. Agnos's English class. Maggie and Ben came in almost together and took their seats after placing their papers in the basket on the teacher's desk.

"Thanks for helping me last night," Ben said.

"Happy to help. Let's get together for our next paper," Maggie said as Mrs. Agnos stood and asked for the class's attention.

After school Ben and Laurel rode the bus home as they did every school day and got off at the same stop. Together they talked as they walked to Laurel's house, but Laurel seemed remote and diffident. She asked, "How do you know Maggie?"

190

"She sits behind me in English."

"What's she like?"

"I don't know. She's just a girl in my class. I was surprised when she called me and asked to work on the assignment together."

At Laurel's house they followed their usual routine of a snack and video games before Ben took the path through the arroyo. The pungent smell of the chaparral was slightly diminished today. Ben carefully avoided muddy spots on the path.

As he walked he reflected on Stevie Nicks's "Dreams." *Why did players only love you when they're playing?* He understood that rain could wash you clean, but he asked himself what he would know after the rain had washed him. Ben didn't know. He only knew he was captivated by the music and intrigued by the words.

He was near home when his phone vibrated once with a text message. He opened it even though Ben knew it wasn't from someone in his contacts list.

<Going to the mall after dinner. Want to join me? Maggie.>

Ben created a new contact using Maggie's number and stored it. He texted back that he would ask his mom when she got home.

Marie was fixing dinner when Ben got home. He asked her if he could meet a friend after dinner at the mall. She said he could if his homework was finished. It wasn't, so he texted Maggie telling her he couldn't. Almost immediately she texted him back.

< No worries. Let's plan to meet on Saturday.>

Ben responded <Okay>

At dinner Ben asked his mom about Fleetwood Mac and what their lyrics meant.

"One of the truly great bands of the '70s and '80s," she said. "But your father is the expert on Fleetwood Mac. Brian has all of their records and CDs. When you were a baby he used to listen to their music constantly."

Ben slid his peas and carrots around his plate while

keeping his head down, "Maggie wants us to meet at the mall on Saturday."

"Do you want to meet Maggie on Saturday?" Marie asked.

"I don't know. Yes, I guess."

"You're supposed to be spending the weekend with your dad, so you better ask him. He's picking you up here on Friday after school, and Larry and I are spending the weekend in Santa Barbara."

Before class began on Friday Maggie tapped Ben on the shoulder. "We should meet tomorrow at noon at the food court at the Ontario Mall. Don't be late."

Mrs. Agnos handed back their essays at the end of class. Ben was pleased and a little surprised when he saw a big A-minus on his paper and a comment which read, *Stevie Nicks, excellent choice, well-researched. Your grammar, spelling, and punctuation need a little work.*

Walking from the bus after school with Laurel, Ben casually mentioned that he planned to meet Maggie at the mall tomorrow.

Laurel kept walking looking down at the ground and said, "Why?"

"I don't know. She asked me."

"That doesn't mean you have to go."

"Why shouldn't I go?"

"Go if you want to," Laurel said from her doorway, then she closed the door in his face.

Walking through the familiar arroyo Ben thought. *She doesn't know Maggie. Why should she care?*

* * *

When he got home Ben found a note on the kitchen table: "I've taken a half-day off and left early with Larry. Your dad's picking you up at five, so be packed and ready to go." She'd scribbled "Love, Mom" at the bottom of the note.

Ben put a few clothes and a toothbrush in an overnight bag, then decided to listen to music on YouTube while he waited for his dad. The driving rhythm and bass from

Fleetwood Mac's "The Edge of Seventeen" enthralled him, but the words about some kind of white winged dove didn't make sense to him. Before the song finished he heard a car horn. He switched off the computer, grabbed his overnight bag, and hurried downstairs. His dad was waiting in the driveway in his new Mustang convertible.

Brian popped the trunk, and Ben squeezed his overnight bag in the car's miniature trunk before sliding into the front passenger seat. Ben waited for his dad to start the conversation, but nobody said anything until they'd driven a couple of miles east on Foothill Boulevard. Finally Brian said, "How's school?"

"Fine." Ben thought about it and said, "I got an A-minus on an English paper."

"That's great. What was it on?"

"We were asked to write about someone we admired. I wrote about Stevie Nicks."

Brain turned and looked at Ben for a long moment. "You did? What led you to choose her?"

"I was going to write about Florence Welch, but Maggie, this girl in my class, had already picked her. She said Florence idolized Stevie, and that I should write about Stevie. I didn't know anything about Stevie or Fleetwood Mac, but when I listened to their music I felt connected."

"Fleetwood Mac is the greatest band there ever was. When you were a baby we played their music every night for you, as a sort of lullaby. They always put you right to sleep."

Ben shifted in his seat and looked at this dad. "So I heard all these songs when I was a baby?" Ben furled his brow. "I think I understand some of them, but there are others I really don't. 'The Edge of Seventeen' is an example of one I don't understand. It doesn't seem to be about seventeen at all. Why is she singing about a white winged dove?"

"On one level 'whoo, whoo, whoo' is the sound a dove makes," Ben's dad said, "but the song is actually in memory of John Lennon, who had been assassinated. His murder was the impetus for Stevie writing the song. Stevie was seventeen when she first heard Lennon and the Beatles."

"What was Stevie searching for, and why does the night bird say, 'come away'?"

"She's searching for meaning in Lennon's senseless murder," Brian said as he put a disc in the CD player. "The night bird is death taking his voice and talent away."

Fleetwood Mac played as they drove in the late afternoon traffic all the way to Rancho Cucamonga. When they pulled into the garage, Brian turned off the ignition silencing the Mustang's rumble and the music.

"Dad, can you drop me off at the Ontario Mall tomorrow at noon."

"I suppose, but I was hoping we could play a round of golf tomorrow. What's so important about going to the mall?"

"I'm meeting Maggie there."

"Oh."

* * *

At dinner Brian couldn't stop talking about how Ben wrote a paper on Fleetwood Mac. "Do you remember hearing Fleetwood Mac as a baby. We played them every night when we put you to bed."

"Not really, Dad," Ben said. "But somehow when I heard them this week I got this feeling, warm and electric at the same time."

"You know, Brian has all of their songs and every CD they made," Jenna said smiling in Brian's direction.

* * *

Ben slept until nine Saturday morning when his dad got him up for breakfast.

"So, Ben," Jenna said, flipping pancakes from the hot griddle onto a plate, "Who's Maggie?"

He answered with a mouth half full of pancakes, "She's a girl in my English class who helped me with my writing assignment."

"Do you like her?"

194

Ben hadn't really thought about that. "Yeah, sort of," he said.

After breakfast Brian asked Ben if he wanted to go outside and catch some passes. Ben didn't want to, but he knew his dad did, so he said yes. Brian scoured the bottom of a hall closet until he found an old, nearly flat football. After inflating it they went to the backyard where he threw easy spiral passes to Ben, who returned wobbly ones.

"Have you thought about going out for any sports at school?" Brian asked.

"No," Ben said. "I'm not really into sports."

"What are you into?"

"I like to play video games, and I like music. Mom gave me an acoustic guitar, and I've taken some lessons. I'd like to get an electric guitar."

Brian smiled. "While you're at the mall I'll find my guitar and tonight you can show us what you've learned."

A little before noon they got back in the Mustang. "What are you and Maggie going to do at the mall?" Brian asked.

"I don't know. Hang out I guess. This is the first time I've met Maggie, or any girl, at a mall."

"Offer to buy her an ice cream soda," his dad said handing him a ten-dollar bill. "That should make her happy. Call me when you're ready to be picked up."

Ben found Maggie at the food court, but he was surprised to see that she had two girl friends with her. As soon as Maggie saw him she rushed over and grabbed his hand. Holding on tight, she dragged him to where her friends were standing and introduced him.

"This is Ben," Maggie said. "He and I are in the same English class. I think we'll be spending more time together."

Ben tried to extract his hand from Maggie's, but she wouldn't let it go. "Can I buy you some ice cream?" he said.

All three girls chorused yes.

They all ordered cones, and Maggie finally released his hand when he reached for his wallet to pay. She grabbed it again as the four of them strolled through the huge mall licking their ice cream cones.

195

The girls chattered, commenting on people and stores as they walked. They seemed to have opinions on everything. Ben wondered why they found strangers' clothing so interesting or how they could be so catty about people they didn't know.

They didn't address any of their comments to Ben and didn't seem to expect him to answer, which was fine with him. He was more interested in the stores they passed than their conversation. When they came to Marshall's Music Store, Ben said he wanted look at the instruments. The four of them went in, but the girls soon lost interest.

"We'll come back and get you in twenty minutes," Maggie said as they left.

That suited Ben. He walked the aisles and soon found the electric guitars. He was holding a Fender when a salesman said, "Would you like to try it." Ben followed the salesman to a rehearsal room in the back of the store. The salesman plugged the Fender and a pair of headphones into an amplifier.

Ben strummed a few cords on the guitar and adjusted the volume of the amplifier. Then he picked out the familiar and haunting opening licks of "Rhiannon." He closed his eyes he slid into the rhythm. He became one with the music, completely enveloped in the sound. He had no concept of time. When Ben opened his eyes he was surprised to see Maggie looking none too pleased and tapping her foot impatiently.

"The girls got tired of waiting for you," Maggie said pulling him toward the exit.

Ben got the salesman's attention and returned the guitar to him.

"That was really fun," Ben said as Maggie hurriedly dragged him out of the store and through the mall.

"We need to catch up with my friends."

They found the two girls talking to two boys who wore Cannibal Corpse T-shirts and low rider pants. Their conversation seemed focused on how to get high. The group, now six, resumed its procession around the mall. The discussion focused on comparing heavy metal bands.

He hated heavy metal music, and he found Cannibal Corpse's music especially distasteful. The conversation didn't interest him, and he found Maggie's tight grip on his hand uncomfortable.

At two o'clock Ben got a text. "My dad's on his way to pick me up. I gotta go." Maggie seemed reluctant to let go of his hand until he said, "I'll see you Monday," and he took off through the nearest exit.

Brian was nowhere to be seen. Ben called him, and five minutes later Brian picked Ben up where he'd dropped him off.

"How was your date?" Brian asked.

"Not sure it was a date. Okay I guess, but I saw a Fender electric guitar I really liked. They let me play it in the store. Can I show it to you?"

"Not right now. We need to get home to help Jenna. She's putting in a flower bed and you can help."

Ben spent the rest of the afternoon turning heavy clay soil, adding amendments, raking, and leveling the new garden.

While they worked, his dad told him about growing up in the San Fernando Valley. "In high school I played guitar for a garage band with my buddies. In college I played a few pickup gigs, but I had to study and didn't have time to play in a regular band. In law school I pretty much gave up playing, but I kept my amplifier and electric guitar. I'll show them to you tonight."

After dinner Brian and Ben rummaged in the garage until they found Brian's old Fender Stratocaster and amplifier.

"This was my second electric guitar," Brian said smiling wistfully. "At one point I thought our band might have a future and I would need a quality instrument. I got this one used. I know it's professional quality, and I've taken good care of it."

They moved the Mustang out of the garage and set up the amplifier. After tuning his guitar Brian played the opening cords of "Brown Sugar." Ben recognized the Rolling Stones song.

197

"Wow, Dad. I didn't know you could play like that."

"Ben, let's see what you can do with this."

He hung the guitar around Ben's neck and helped him find the chords for the opening refrain of "Brown Sugar." Ben strummed, and within a few minutes, he was playing a wobbly, but recognizable version of the song.

Ben and his dad passed the guitar back and forth each riffing off the other's playing. Ben was surprised that he could anticipate his dad's variation. They seemed natural, intuitive, and he somehow knew which chords would follow.

Ben had no idea of how much time had passed when Jenna stepped into the garage. "It's after 10. I'm going to bed. I think you should stop playing and let the neighbors get some sleep."

On Sunday morning Ben, Brian, and Jenna took a hike in the nearby foothills, and afterward they had a late brunch at home.

"Would you like my old Fender?" Brian said as they cleared the dishes.

Ben couldn't suppress his smile, "Sure. I'd love it. I'll practice every day."

At four Ben put his overnight bag in the Mustang's trunk. He and his dad loaded the amplifier and the Fender into the back seat. It was a glorious day as they drove down Foothill Boulevard toward Ben's home.

When they stopped for a red light his dad said, "I'm planning on going to a Stevie Nicks concert next month at the Hollywood Bowl. Would you like to join Jenna and me? I can get two extra tickets if you'd like to invite Maggie."

"That would be great, Dad. Yes, I'd love to go."

* * *

On Monday Ben and Laurel walked from the bus stop toward Laurel's home. Laurel seemed to be waiting for him to speak. Finally she said, "How was your weekend?"

"Really good," He noticed Laurel looking away but wasn't sure why. "I think I understand my dad much better. He's

198

really a cool guy. He gave me his electric guitar."

"That's wonderful. I know you're really into music. How was the mall on Saturday?"

"Good, I found a music store and got to practice on one of their new electric guitars."

"Did you meet Maggie?"

"Yeah, but she had two girlfriends. I wasn't all that comfortable with her or the setup."

Ben saw Laurel's half smile, "Oh, I thought you really liked Maggie."

"Why did you think that?"

"Because you've been talking about her a lot."

"No. I liked that she helped me with my paper, but I don't think I would like her as a girlfriend."

When they reached Laurel's house Ben said, "My dad is going to get tickets for a Stevie Nicks concert next month at the Hollywood Bowl. Would you like to go with me?"

It Started with Dimes

M. Lee Buompensiero

You wouldn't think ten cents could scare the stuffing out of you. It did me. Here's what happened.

The first dimes started appearing around the house, on tables, my desk, the bathroom countertop, on the floor. I even found one in the garage. Then they started appearing in the washing machine. I figured hubby left the change in his jeans pocket. Typically, I check those pockets—religiously, just in case. But he's been really good about not leaving tissues, or paper gas receipts in his pockets, or change of any kind. Although, just today I discovered a paper face mask balled around a fuzzy dryer ball. Still, it wasn't dimes.

I secretly wondered if the appliance was manufacturing them—you know, like Rumpelstiltskin's spinning wheel—except he got gold. I was up to finding gold. Gold is a good market, I hear. I'm not particular. But one doesn't normally speak of dimes and *mother lode* in the same sentence. I mean, *seriously*!

Still, I couldn't let it go. I wondered where those pesky dimes were coming from. Were they leftovers from previous jeans washings that got stuck, collecting in crevices under the rivets? Not likely. Those rivets are sealed solid—unlike my nerves that were beginning to unravel like a bad argument after a law student has abandoned his premises.

Still, you know, the odd and strange don't often just heal themselves. So it is with *dimes*. One night, after a brief normal respite or, as I like to call it, my *insanity hiatus*, I was getting ready to brush my teeth before bed and my eye caught a slight glimmer at the corner of the sink. There it was. A dime. Unassuming. Just—there.

I forced myself to think of it as normal. I picked it up and put in the coffee can we keep for stray change. I've started to call it *strange change*.

The next few days I didn't find any dimes. I figured the dime episode was closed. Life got back to normal. Out shopping, I spied a penny on the sidewalk.

Was I being devalued? I wondered. I stepped over it.

For the next few days my dime *gift* episodes were uneventful. No dimes.

Then — it was around 3 a.m., something woke me up. It was not a typical night sound — a car passing outside my bedroom window, the grandfather clock chiming, the cuckoo clock cuckooing — no — it wasn't anything *normal.* It was the distinct sound of a coin landing on the nightstand as if tossed by unseen hands. I froze. I didn't want to turn my head for fear I'd see something. I rolled over — away from the nightstand, and pulled the covers over my ears. But I couldn't shut my eyes. Eventually, after thinking my heart wouldn't stop pounding, it did. Miraculously, I dozed off.

The next morning, there it was. A bright, shiny dime resting on the top of the nightstand. Just where it was dropped. I didn't pick it up.

Now, I'm leery — when I wash clothes, when I doze off at night — fearing that dimes will start to reappear. So far, they haven't.

Maybe there's a Dime Fairy, like the Tooth Fairy. Maybe there's going to be a shortage of dimes and my Dime-Fairy Godmother was just stocking me up. Or maybe, just maybe, the dimes are a portent of some big motherlode coming my way. The Publisher's Clearing House bonanza — a thousand dollars a week for life. Now that would be worth any anxiety I might feel about miracle money being dropped into my lap by unseen hands.

I'm a realist — no, really. So I started buying *scratchers*. Ten at a time. I use a dime to scratch off the coating. I'll let you know if I win.

Life's Little Choices

Laurie Asher

Up in the sky there were ten yellow stars

If I looked hard enough I could even see Mars

From down the mountain I spotted the cars

I stashed a few lightening bugs into the jars

Should I dot or should I dash

Write a check or just use cash

I can mish or I can mash

Should I cymbal or should I crash

When I sing shall I be loud

Did you see that moving cloud

Choose cremation or linen shroud

Stay at home or fight the crowd

Should I come or should I go

Stay up high or go down low

Start to walk or get a tow

Wear a headband or a bow

Should I like or hope for love

Release a pigeon or a dove

Pray to Earth or God above

Go bare handed or wear a glove

Should I pop or should I snap

Caress the baby or let it nap

Let the parrot poop on my lap

Or fidget with that silly app

Should I Kit or should I Kat

Choose the scarf but not the hat

Do I prefer a mouse or rat

Toss a football or strike a bat

I'd rather hear a barking dog

Than a big 'ol croaking frog

I like clear skies without the smog

Eat the cow or choose the hog

Buy some shutters or keep the shade

Should I use Lysol or stick with Glade

A jacket of leather or coat of suede

Clean it myself or hire a maid

Should I volunteer or work for pay

Confront my enemies or stay away

Let Fluffy have kittens or should I spay

And stop telling people to have a nice day

Mozilla Firefox or Google Chrome

Live in my car or buy a new home

A Pink flamingo or a bearded gnome

       And should I even finish this poem

Last Day

Kelly Bargabos

I was almost ten years old the first time I started a diet. I found an entry in the small red diary that had been a Christmas gift the year before. Each blue-lined page represented one day, with bold red lines giving space for five different years of entries. On the left-hand side was the number nineteen with a blank space after it so you could write in the corresponding year. Trying to hold five years in a small four-by-five book meant there wasn't much room to write more than a sentence or two about each day. Some days received a grade of A-plus, C-minus and sometimes just a lukewarm B. I sort of remember that I got this diary technique from a Judy Blume book, but I don't remember which one. Most of the entries were random sentences you might expect from an inexperienced fourth-grade diarist. *Today in gym class we played Red Rover. Today John K. looked at me and smiled. I think he likes me. Today I realized I really like Scott. I think he's so cute, but my sister says he likes her. She's a jerk.*

Not long ago as I was thumbing through my old journals and diaries, I came across an entry in this little red book that stopped me in my tracks. On August 31, 1977, I wrote: *Today I was secretary for the stamp club. I was closer to Jesus. I started a diet.*

As funny as those first two lines seem now, I was very serious about stamps and Jesus. I still have the collection that I accumulated while in the stamp club at North Bay Elementary School because I haven't quite figured out what to do with it yet, and I do still want to be closer to Jesus, but I'm not quite as worried about it as I was then. But it was that last line I wrote that day, *I started a diet*, that shook me the most.

Considering that I've spent the last forty years either on a

204

diet, thinking about dieting, convinced I should be dieting, thinking about how much I weigh, how much I want to weigh, how much I don't want to weigh, the realization that it started at such a young age shocked and disgusted me. At first. But then I was sad. I was sad for that little girl who must have worried that she weighed too much.

Not long after I found that diary entry, I found a picture of myself around the age I must have been when I started that diet in 1977. I wasn't fat. I wasn't skinny either. Bony has never been used to describe anyone that shares my immediate lineage or last name. I come from a long line of meat and potato people and good eaters. We were healthy, but not skinny. Then again, obesity didn't run in my family either. By standards of 1977 and probably today, we may have been bigger than what is acceptable in Hollywood and fashion modeling, but definitely average-sized in America. In this picture I found, I had on orange polyester shorts that fit snug, and a blue and orange flowered top that showed a little bit of my belly. I wasn't fat.

My mother never told me I ate too much. My father has never commented on my weight. We did a lot of teasing among my brothers and sisters, but we didn't call each other fat. We just didn't. Probably because we weren't. There was a lot going on in popular culture, especially around women's bodies. Everybody was talking about the Farrah Fawcett poster with the red swimsuit. I loved *Charlie's Angels*. I loved watching TV. I loved listening to music. I loved reading *Tiger Beat*. I can tell by the other entries in my diary that I was getting a little boy crazy and I was on the verge of hitting puberty. I suppose that I was probably, for the first time really, thinking about my body in a different way. I honestly have no idea why I had internalized the idea that I needed to lose weight. I can only assume that I fell victim to the cultural mission of making us all feel like we're not okay as we are so we'll spend our money and time buying products to fix us. Somewhere along the way, I got the message that my body was not okay as it was, and the solution was to diet and lose weight.

205

* * *

As I went on through my life and my teenage years, I sought out diet plans that promised me the solution I was searching for. A new me. A new body. Smaller. Thinner. Acceptable.

In high school, I prided myself on not eating throughout the day. Even though I was an athlete and loved to run and exercise, and I maintained a normal weight until graduating at one hundred and seventeen pounds, the need to lose weight was always on my mind.

When I went to college, I gained fifteen pounds in the first few months like so many kids do. I think that's when my habit of yo-yo dieting really kicked into high gear. On one diet, we ate nothing but canned beets. I had to stifle my gag reflex to get them down. These were canned beets. They weren't roasted, there was no goat cheese. They were gross and I ate them anyway. There was a diet of only hard-boiled eggs. There was the Carbohydrate Addicts diet, Atkins, Keto, Intermittent Fasting, Weight Watchers, Fat Smash, Blood Type, Body Type, and of course, old-fashioned calorie counting.

For years, I was convinced that my body had two modes where I was either gaining or losing weight. There was no middle ground. This habitual mentality of gaining and losing created another phenomenon in my life, the *Last Day*. Though it seems embarrassingly obvious now, this mentality that I had of either starving myself with extreme restrictive eating, or drinking and eating anything and everything I want because a restrictive diet is looming, rooted in this belief that my body was not okay the way it was, resulted in so many legendary *Last Days* that went down something like this:

* * *

6:30 a.m. Empty bladder. Strip naked. Step on scale. Nothing to drink, not even a sip of water before the weigh-in. Fingers crossed

206

that I'll be happily surprised. Maybe it won't be as bad as I think. If it's above that threshold I've set for myself, that invisible line that determines whether I'm ugly or pretty, a loser or a winner, worthy or unworthy, then I'll have to make a plan. Shit. Too high. I vow to start a rigid routine tomorrow. This is it. Today will be my last day. Therefore, each meal should be worthy of the last meal a prisoner on death row, who is scheduled for a midnight execution, might request.

* * *

8:00 a.m. Breakfast. I crave whole-wheat toast with peanut butter, Greek yogurt with granola, a tofu smoothie, egg whites or plain oatmeal with fruit. Nevertheless, I must have a breakfast sandwich from McDonald's because tomorrow I won't be able to.

* * *

10:14 a.m. Something stirs inside me. I hear my name. It's the peanut butter-filled pretzels from the kitchen, reminding me that this will be my last morning snack.

* * *

1:00 p.m. Lunch. I will go out to lunch. I can't decide what to order because the truth is, I'd rather have my usual brown rice and veggies or salad from home. But if this is my last day, I must get that grilled cheese with French fries or the chicken club with chips. I won't be able to eat that tomorrow.

* * *

2:39 p.m. Where did those come from? The pile of empty mini candy bar wrappers on my desk that I don't remember eating? I don't remember walking into the receptionist's office and digging a fistful from the candy jar. I didn't even make it until 3 o'clock, my usual snack time.

* * *

5:00 p.m. Dinner. Cheese pizza? This would be my real last meal if I were ever on death row. Turkey sub with Doritos? Spaghetti? Or should I just drink my dinner? I won't be able to have any beer after tonight either. Do I pass a Byrne Dairy on my way home? I need their Chocoholic ice cream. I'll never have chocolate again.

* * *

8:15 p.m. Still full from dinner. I don't really want that ice cream but ... I won't be able to eat it tomorrow since I'll be on my diet. And ... I don't want it in my freezer, too tempting.

* * *

11:00 p.m. My stomach aches. The ice cream. I remember that I'm mildly lactose intolerant. I can't sleep. The caffeine in the chocolate is making my blood race. Why do I always do this? No more last days. *No more scale. Who cares if I lose those last twenty pounds, again? At the end of my life it won't matter how much I weigh, it will matter what I've done. When will this caffeine get out of my system? How many calories did I eat today? 300 for breakfast, 200 for pretzels, how many mini candy wrappers were there? Way over my limit. It's okay. It's okay. Tomorrow is a new day. One ... two ... three ... seventeen days till Memorial Day. I should be able to lose five pounds at least by then. Ten if I really push it. I wonder what I'll weigh in the morning?*

* * *

Almost three years ago I was married. It was a summer day in July and the fifty people we loved most in this world were all there. The ceremony was performed in a gazebo beside a lake and the reception followed with a boat cruise where we watched the sun set, ate a meal together, danced, and laughed. The day was everything I wanted it to be. I loved my dress. I loved my shoes. I did my own hair and makeup because I was determined that I didn't need to be that

208

fussy. I hired a low-cost photographer, a friend of my niece, who took pictures at weddings as a hobby.

A couple of days after the ceremony, I started looking at the pictures. *Oh shit. Oh, I thought I looked better in that dress. Oh my gosh. Why didn't I wear more of a girdle? I wore the wrong shapewear, and I have a visible belly outline in that dress. What was I thinking?*

I quickly turned on myself with anger and regret. *You dumbass, why didn't you lose twenty pounds before your wedding? Damn it, Kelly, you could have done that. You had time. Why didn't you lose that weight?*

In spite of my negative thoughts, I couldn't look away from the snapshots of my wedding day. Other thoughts fought their way to the surface. I looked happy, which most people do in their wedding photos, but I was coming off a period in my life where I had not thought of myself as happy in a very long time, mostly because I hadn't been happy for a very long time. I didn't know I was capable of that kind of happiness again, and so when I saw my face lit up and my eyes truly smiling in those low-budget pictures from that day, it jarred me out of this bad habit of mine. I became determined to not let my disappointment in how I looked in my dress and the fact that I hadn't lost weight before my wedding override the joy I saw in my own face. *Oh my, Kelly. You are happy there, and you love him, and he loves you, and look at the way you're looking at each other. Look at your dad and your mom, they're dancing, and your little nieces are flouncing around in their dresses, and every single person in your family was there, so stop it. Stop it right now.*

For so many years I've carried the weight of believing I failed because I hadn't reached my goal weight yet, and I can't possibly be okay if I haven't reached that weight. I know now that when I'm constantly thinking about my weight, or about dieting, or the fact that my pants are too tight, or my belly is showing when I sit down, when I'm constantly thinking about everything I'm not, there's no room left for what is really happening in my life. I'm not present in the moments. The moments of conversation or enjoying a meal, dancing or

209

listening to music, reading a good book or watching a show have been overshadowed with this dissatisfaction. I've missed so much.

It has taken too many years to realize that the real weight I need to lose is the heavy expectation that how my belly looks or what the scale says is more important than the love and laughter I have within me and in front of me at any moment. It is time for a new habit, a new goal, a new day.

Perhaps I'll see if I can find a blank space in that little red diary and give myself an A.

Pain Killer

E. M. Criman

The pain hits level ten, and I want everyone to feel it. I want them to know the shooting and stabbing that controls my brain, leaving me unable to think. I want them to feel the desire to vomit the anguish, the constant desire to give up, lay down, and curl up into a ball of dramatic self-pity.

Victims appear on the street. At first I want to avoid everyone I pass, hating their proximity to my hazy bubble. I find comfort in visualizing their torture and demise, wondering how it would feel to tie the nearest man to a fence and flog him skinless in the darkness of an alley's end. The pain and anger bubbles in me, overflowing, an ugliness I embrace like a second skin. The pain is a personality all its own. I am Dr. Jekyll, and Mrs. Hyde has emerged.

The release is like a heavy sigh, deflating the darkness as I expel the evil onto the dying shell of the bound male. Skin, sliced from his body, litters the pavement at his feet. As his last breath casts out into the air, my relief is replete, and Mrs. Hyde leaves without warning.

The shock of remorse and horror surfacing with my sanity forces my stomach from my throat. I jackknife toward the pavement as the contents of my body splash in a putrid mess.

I sound like a sick cat.

My surroundings are unfamiliar. I still wear my old jeans, but have stripped to my worn, pink sports bra now covered in a spray of blood extending to my waist. The denim barely escapes the sticky mess.

I hold a whip in my left hand, unclear how I came to possess it. It, too, is sprayed with blood. What have I done?

My soul is a vile, unclean thing.

The enormity of the situation begins to set in. I can't be seen here. I've created a crime scene. I strip off the sports bra and wipe down my exposed, bloody skin. I grab a discarded plastic bag from the ground and stuff it in, donning my shirt and jacket, cramming the bag into my left pocket. I am surprised to find scissors in that pocket. There's no way to know my intent. I find another plastic bag and thrust my hand in, not daring to consider the previous contents. I grab the man's forearm and cut the zip tie from his wrists. He slides down the fence into a slump, arms flopping to his sides. I try to rub the marks from his wrists through the bag, but my heart is in my throat, and my now-empty stomach roils from fear and panic.

My right pocket contains bleach and a hand towel. The preparation terrifies me, but I follow the steps I left for myself and clean the body as I can, pouring leftover bleach into my own vomit. Clothing from the dumpster helps to wipe up the mess. Disturbing and contaminating the crime scene. I'm only adding up the counts against me if I'm caught. Based on my research, I know enough to believe there's a good chance I'll get caught. Just great. May as well try to escape this mess.

I stuff the vomit covered clothing in another discarded bag and toss in the zip tie. I wipe down everything I think I may have touched. I hightail it home taking every dark street I can.

I blacked out again. I woke up on the bed with blood under my nails. That nine-tailed whip is next to me. I don't even want to know. I'm sure I left prints.

I hate my pain pills. I deal with the agony for as long as I can before giving in. I think I'm getting better. I haven't had to take them as much, but the pain isn't improving. Maybe my pain tolerance is increasing.

I spend today writing. I'm working on a crime novel, and the scenes come to me in dreamlike reality. I cringe as the words escape my fingertips to the document, worrying I might be writing some confession.

I go to the store and pay cash for latex gloves, leaving them on the table by the door. Just in case. I coil the whip into a small circle and place it into a bag, leaving that in the

212

drawer under the table.

Back pain defies sanity, but I haven't taken a pain pill in three days. I toss the bottle into the trash under the sink and lift my head high. No more pills.

The next week is the best sleep I've had for a month. I've been really tired and sometimes wake up still dressed. But no more blood. No more worries. The glove box is still closed.

I can smile.

I've lost my keys. I never lose them. In searching, I lift up the box of latex gloves, and a single pair fall out the bottom of the box onto my keys. The last pair.

I'm in so much trouble.

I make a special trip out of town for more gloves. I buy three boxes and some bleach. I pay cash. Pretty sure this makes me an accessory.

I pull up a chair to the entry table and sit there a long time before making my decision. My hand creeps toward the drawer like I'm reaching for a poisonous snake. I take a deep breath and pull on the handle.

I almost yank the drawer out trying to snatch my hand back. The coiled whip lays covered in blood, protected only by the bag it repeatedly returns to. I turn my head away but force myself to don a pair of gloves and grab the bag.

My alter ego is a disgusting pig. Wash your murder weapons, woman.

I take a scrubber to the whip, getting into the braided nooks and crannies of the murder weapon. After it's clean, I dry it off and apply leather conditioner. She must have a real talent with this thing.

I sit down to write, and my fingers fly across the keyboard, creating realistic scenes and terrifying pictures. My book can be an award-winning best-seller. Or incriminating evidence. Or both. I shudder.

I don't want to know, but I should probably find out. I buy four surveillance cameras and hide them in my apartment. One in the bedroom, the bathroom, the living area, and one facing the front door and entry table.

I test the cameras and confirm they work. I hook them up

213

to my computer for playback later. I need to lay down. Pain overwhelms me, and as I fight the urge to throw up, I lose consciousness.

I wake up to knocking. I stumble to the entry way and remember enough to stuff the box of gloves under a coat. I crack the door.

Large brown eyes stare down at me, and even in my sleep haze, I have to bite my lip to avoid the dreamy sigh. It's Nate, *Mr. Hottie Body* across the hall. If he gets any more muscles, he'll have to double up on the ones he already has. I forget for a moment the mind-altering inmate incident in my leg. All the shooting and stabbing from my pinched nerve could lead to a prison riot.

"Nate." I offer a pleasant smile. This is not the time to flirt.

"Ruth," he starts, his deep voice strumming my happy place. I struggle to avoid an eye-roll. I'm in deep trouble here, but I'm thinking of taking a tumble with Apollo from Mt. Olympus.

I silence my inner purring and wait for Nate to speak. He looks serious. And uncomfortable. I raise my eyebrows.

"Did you get a roommate?"

"Um, why?" A chill runs through my body. What did he see?

"I was hoping you could introduce us."

My libido takes a jump off a pier. "I don't know, Nate. We have different schedules."

I wonder what she looks like, I think.

"I just saw her go in," he says.

Stalker. "Sorry to disappoint you, but she's not here now. Must have been a quick stop." I need to check those cameras.

"But –"

"See you later, Nate," I say, and shut the door.

I start up the cameras and groan. Within five minutes of falling asleep, my alter ego stares into the bathroom camera applying her lipstick. She puckers at the lens and winks. She's bold, beautiful, and – blond. She has long blond hair to my auburn locks. And big baby blues. My eyes are almond-shaped and brown. And I have these really cute freckles on

214

my cheeks. Her skin is pale and flawless. Who is she?

"Hey, sweet thing," she says and grins. "I'm Annie. And before you say it, I totally exist. Guess you should have taken those pain pills." She sighs dramatically. "Well, too late. You're stuck with me now."

I sigh and reach for my bag.

"I bet right now you're reaching for your tramadol. You tossed those, remember? Anyway, I'm here to stay. I'm going out. So many victims, so little time. Oh — cute neighbor. *Ta-tah.*" She says the last word in sing-song and blows me another kiss. In the living room, she grabs a red leather jacket and a pair of latex gloves. I watch her toss the whip and some supplies into a purse before she struts out the door.

I'm so screwed.

* * *

Every morning I scrub and polish the whip, and every night I worry that we have the same fingerprints. Annie makes a show on the camera to prove who's in charge, and she's right. She's got all the power, and she knows it.

I don't understand why we look so different. I look like me, and she ... she looks *deadly.* Like she was created to lure men to their death. Like a siren. Or a black widow spider. I shiver.

Annie buys boots on my card. They're black, four-inch heels with a steel tip. I check them every morning for blood. Good thing, too. Gross.

I turn on the news, something I've been avoiding since this began two weeks ago. My stomach hits my throat when their top story is my alter ego.

I listen to the woman report the story in stoic fashion. "A serial killer is on the loose in San Diego with six confirmed victims. Sources say the skin is flayed off the bodies. The police believe the killer may be a woman. If anyone has any information on this person, please call the San Diego Crime Stoppers hotline number at 888-580-8477. Back to you, Stan."

Stan says, "A female serial killer. How often does that

happen?"

I turn the news off, sick to my stomach. I try to remember the first incident, when I woke up as it ended. I was desperate for someone to feel my pain. I felt so angry that all these people want to whine about their life, but no one understands what real pain is. They don't know the crazy it brings. In hindsight, I guess I didn't either. I just wanted others to know what it felt like.

I still don't think they do.

I wanted them to understand, to feel the way the pain encompasses first the body, and then the mind. I wanted them to feel the way the discomfort overtakes the ability to think, and how the hatred of pills makes it feel like defeat every time I have to take one.

Maybe I shouldn't have been so literal.

I go to the store and buy some melatonin and valerian root. This should keep me asleep. More specifically, it should keep *her* asleep. Just in case, I also take a zip tie from her bag and tie myself to the bedframe.

"Sleep tight, Annie." I give my alter ego a smug smile before going to sleep.

I dream of lipstick and scissors. When I wake, the bed is across the room by my desk. On the desk is the severed zip tie and my favorite sweater in tatters. On the bathroom mirror, in red lipstick, *"Don't mess with me."*

I head to my computer.

"Ruthie, honey. Haven't you learned by now? I'm the dominant here. You'll learn. Just like those pathetic, misogynistic pigs who think they're a match for me." Annie paints her nails while she talks, glancing up at me between fingers. "I'll win here, like I win with them. They think they're a match for me, like I should give them the time of day. I mean, *look* at me. I'm way out of their league. They're not good enough to lick my boots, and they act like they *own* me if they buy me one little drink." I watch Annie admire her nails and then smile up at me. "You should be *happy*, Ruthie, baby. I'm doing us a favor. I'm doing *all* women a favor. Do you have any idea how many of these losers *exist?* I mean, really.

Think about it. I'm your alter ego, and I look like *this?* You've got some unexplored issues, did you ever think of that? Not that I'm unhappy. I'm just saying. We could be a real team instead of you cleaning my whip and shoes while I have all the fun. We shouldn't be enemies, baby. We should be *allies.* Think of the fun we could have. When's the last time you had real fun? You're so worried about these idiot men and their 'poor wittle feewings,'" she says with an exaggerated pout. "Girlfriend, you worry too much. I can help you. Just let me drive for a little while, hmm? I'll show you what fun is *really* all about. Think about it. I'll even give you a little time. But no more zip ties, okay? That's for the bad boys. I can't be wasting them."

I lean back in my computer chair and sigh. Team up? Is she insane? Okay, possibly, but really?

No. No way.

I push the bed back and check the whip. It's cleaned and conditioned. Her shoes are spotless. Maybe she really means it. I check the trash under the sink. Still full. I dump it out and gratefully pull out my tramadol. Then I spend the day cleaning the apartment, trying to clear my head. I don't know what to do. There's no way I can team up with a serial killer. On the other hand, she has a point.

This time, when the tightness begins, I take the stupid pain reliever. If she's going to exist, I may as well be pain-free.

I sit down to write after a head-clearing day and find all my material comes from her. Annie has provided me with more story than I could ever come up with on my own. The problem is that she always has the same mode of operation. I mean, can't she get a little *creative?* I don't want my stories to get boring. On the other hand, if they all take place in real life, I can't exactly write about them without being in the interrogation room.

And I have my reputation to think about. I'm in good with the police precinct. Matthew gives me inside info for my crime stories and helps me keep it authentic. I don't use anything real, of course, but it's good to have a little push in the right direction.

I nod to myself. So she goes for the superiority complex. Misogyny issues. Makes sense. They make my stomach turn. Besides the pain, she has a motive. At least she picked a target I can respect her for. To an extent. I mean, if she's going to murder someone, at least it makes the world a better place, right?

What am I *thinking?* I absolutely can*not* team up with this psycho. She's a maneater, for Pete's sake! Tempting, but no.

I'll just have to come up with my own murder scenes. Something more than zip ties and back alley fences. The flaying is a nice touch, but a writer can only use it in fiction once. Maybe.

I wonder if it's really the pain that brought her out, or the stalker. That cheesedick Dean stalked me for months and, when he had me cornered, tried to make me feel like he was the almighty man and I was lowly chattel. Women across the US have had the right to own themselves since 1894. Maybe he missed the memo.

For a moment I get the warm fuzzies to my other half. It's nice of her to take my side and look out for me. It's like she's getting vengeance for me.

Oh, no, no, no. I can't be warming up to her side. She's psycho. I mean like, she's Faith, the insane vampire slayer. Of course, that would make me Buffy, which is cool, but I don't know any vampires.

I shake my head. Is she like, a female *Dexter?* Cool, but I don't want to end up alone and miserable for the rest of my life. No self-flagellation for this girl. Although, he did keep the same MO and his story ran for eight seasons.

Just stop, I tell myself. I can't be thinking of teaming up with her. I mean, she's *me*. I need to just stop. This whole thing is crazy talk, like I'm living in a Russell Nohelty novel.

Although, I mean, she does go after psycho stalker dudes. But no.

I focus back on my writing and realize I've just written an entire chapter and it's *amazing*. Maybe some of my best writing ever. And I can't use any of it.

It all sounds too familiar, like one of our nighttime

218

escapades. If I know too much and publish it, I may never see the outside of a prison cell again.

No, I need to think this through.

I wonder if we need a scapegoat. Some guy with a history who lost his woman to a stalker and wanted his revenge, then taking his own life after getting it. Yeah, but I don't think she'd quit just because we were able to wrap it up for her.

I hit my hand to my head. Great, now I'm trying to protect her. Me. It's me. Am I out of my mind?

"Girl, you got problems," I tell myself.

I really need to think this through.

It's Wednesday, and I always go to the precinct on Wednesday. I buy my detective friend lunch, plying him with food in exchange for information. Today I wonder if I'm there to turn myself in, get the scoop on what they know, or get writing information to change my book some.

"Ruth, wake up, will ya?"

"What?" I look up from my haze.

"I asked if you did something different with your makeup."

"Oh, yeah. You like it? I saw a friend of mine with it and thought I'd try it out." I thought of Annie and bit my lip. I guess she's a friend. Sort of.

"Very pretty." His eyes linger just a little too long.

"Thank you." I give him a small smile. "Matthew," I say, drawing out his name as I run my finger over the tip of my coffee cup.

"Oh, no. I know that look, and the answer is no." He holds his hands up to ward me off.

"Just a little something? You always have the best stories. Please?" I lift my eyebrows in my best pleading look.

"Why? Can't you come up with anything on your own?"

"Oh, come on, you know I'm nothing without you," I lie. I need something from him so I have a way to keep what I've written.

"That face of yours is going to get me fired," he says.

"You're the best." I give him my most innocent smile.

"Or you could go out with me."

"And ruin what we have?" I've been putting him off for months. If it didn't work out, I'd be out a great source of information. And now I don't want Annie getting her fingers into him. I like him too much for that.

His shoulders slump in defeat. "We've got a serial killer. Female, we think. We're not sure of the MO yet, but the weapon of choice seems to be a flaying whip."

"A flaying whip? That's kind of specific."

"Yeah, well, the skin is removed from the victims in pieces."

"Gross."

"Tell me about it. The killer is clean, too. I think we catalog more trash than potential evidence."

"But you do have something?" Chills start in my stomach, and my coffee curdles.

"Nah. Well, yes, but it's just a partial. Not even half a print. This one is careful. Even wipes the bodies down."

I shudder at how much they could know if Annie isn't careful.

"Ruth? What's wrong?"

"It's just unnerving to have someone like that on the street," I tell him. I should look more enthralled. I'm usually bloodthirsty for this stuff.

"I'm glad it finally gets bloody enough for you. But don't worry. These are some twisted guys. That's why we think it's a woman. Most of these men have restraining orders, Domestic Violence charges, or are just misogynistic men in general."

"So you *do* have a motive?"

"I don't know. We can't be sure yet."

A man sits at the table near us reading a newspaper when a woman shows up in a sweet, light summer dress. The pale green sets off her strawberry hair.

He could at least pretend *to stand,* I think.

"I'm sorry I'm late," she mumbles, hurrying to sit.

"Stop. *What* are you *wearing*?"

"A dress?"

"That's lingerie. I can't be seen in public with you. Go

home and change."

She sets her shoulders. "Roger, we can't reconcile with this attitude. My dress is fine."

"You look like a whore."

I roll my eyes at Matthew and give a pointed head turn to the table.

Roger looks at me. "What are you looking at? Turn your head back to your own table."

Matthew sighs and sets down his napkin. "Ma'am, is everything okay?" he asks the woman.

Roger sets his jaw. "She's fine. Mind your own business."

Matthew turns to me. "Maybe we should go."

"That's right, get out of here." Roger has his arms crossed, and I feel heat in my eyes.

Ruthie, baby, chill. We'll get him later. Annie's smooth voice soothes my temper and we leave.

"Are you wearing contacts?" Matthew asks as we leave.

"No, why?"

"I thought I saw your eyes change color."

"Hmm. Hm-mmm." I shake my head. I'll save that for later. Maybe tonight.

When I wake the next morning, there's a note on the table with a new lip color. *Try this,* it says. The red is bold, darker than hers. It's beautiful.

Thanks, Annie, baby. I think with a smile. She's a great partner. They're all going to feel that ten.

What Happened to Cindy and Frank

Bob Doublebower

The Guilded Pen, 2018

Cindy and Frank had crossed paths ten years earlier during the brief reign of Hurricane David, though neither, if asked, could recall the exact details with any certainty. For both, the subsequent pile-on of years had muddied the recollection of that and many other such encounters. Cindy had been a freshly-minted college grad enroute to her dream job as a stewardess. It's all she had ever wanted to be. She also harbored a secret plan with her boyfriend, Ramon.

Frank Grafton, at the time, was a work-a-day preacher from a small church in Clearwater, Florida, and was confounded by his lack of advancement within the church hierarchy. Enough was enough. There were other ways to bring about a job opening or two. Frank also had a plan. The hurricane had thrown them together at a shelter, a brief encounter, and they'd both come away with a slightly altered point of view.

Now we find them, ten years later …

* * *

Cindy slouched back in her lawn chair and sighed: *Ten years in this dump.* This very same thought could have come to her as easily on any crappy morning, or any late night when her thoughts were her own, but today it arrived in the full glare of the midday Florida sun. No, it wasn't that her apartment was a dump. It wasn't. It was okay, for the neighborhood. It was Jacksonville.

"Ready to re-up, soldier?" That was Kimmy. Her friend, coworker, and generally acknowledged bad influence. She sat just a few feet away and making moves to get out of her chair, the first step toward heading inside for fresh drinks. Cindy turned her head toward her, which, by some unknowable mechanism, caused her big round sunglasses to slide off her head and seat themselves, as custom would have it, on her nose.

"Kimmy, it's only noon," Cindy said, mostly to Kimmy's back. The tone was unmistakably plaintive.

Kimmy yelled back over her shoulder, "Remember, it's not day-drinking if you can see a swimming pool."

They'd met on the Jacksonville—Birmingham—Raleigh run. Cindy had landed at this regional airline after Braniff had winked out, like a star too bright for its own good. Kimmy had been newer, only two years in, but Cindy and she had endured JAX-BMH-RAL together, and now they were roommates. Funny how life turns out.

"Okay, fine. But, easy. I've gotta pick up Joey at three." And there *was* a swimming pool, not 5 feet away.

It didn't happen all that often these days, but she suddenly found herself thinking of Ramon. Poor, sweet Ramon. Idealistic Ramon. They'd met up as planned after Cindy had gotten shed of the hurricane shelter, and he found his way down to Jacksonville. 1275 Highland, #102. Back then, that seemed like heaven on earth. They'd married back in Georgia, amidst family and friends, all secrets forgiven. The county had hired Ramon as a Community Outreach worker. It was all he had ever wanted to do, but exigencies were what they were. They'd slapped him (temporarily, the memo said) in Disaster Relief.

Kimmy clanged back through the pool gate. She carried tall, dripping glasses which looked even taller against her short build. She had short red hair, too, and if you didn't know for sure that she hailed from Texas, it would have been among your top three guesses.

223

"I hear we're picking up a gate in Galveston. That's ocean-y," Kimmy said as she sat. She set Cindy's glass on a plastic table that had seen better times. Never having gotten a run to the West Coast, or Vegas, during her Braniff days, was an old ache Cindy lugged around—oh, Kimmy knew—that needed occasional balming, even if that balm was a poke in the ribs. She contended that Piedmont Air would be hard-pressed to even find the West Coast, much less reach it.

"You missed the meeting last Tuesday," Kimmy said as a follow-up.

"Yeah I know, Joey had a thing. How did it go?"

"Well, half the meeting they busted our balls about BMI. If you're a six, they want you in a five. If you're the five, they want you in a four. Same old same old."

Cindy glanced down at her hips. "So, you're saying they haven't made the jump seats smaller? Crap."

They laughed, and drank, and ragged about their jobs, and laughed some more, right up to 2:30.

* * *

Frank Grafton had dropped the dime the minute he crossed the Charlotte city limit. Half the time driving up from that Jacksonville hurricane shelter (Jee-sus, what a mess) he had thought about what that girl—whatwas'er name—had said about collateral damage, and how you never know which direction it's coming from. His old buddy at the Clearwater Sentinel back then had been all ears, what with money gone missing, and church elders shifting stories and job titles.

Frank propped his forearms on his balcony railing and looked out over his expensive view. He liked thinking about those old days, 10 years past. Sure was exciting. Lots of news hounds. Names in print. Nobody had actually gone to jail—the money had eventually gotten itself *found*—but several church honchos had decided to seek other avenues of spiritual fulfillment. The only hitch in Frank's plan was the steep falloff in First Gospel's attendance. By and by, with creditors clamoring, the Apostolics from up in Pensacola swooped in.

224

Frank turned and yelled into the condo, "Diane, you there?" (Christ, he'd had better assistants.)

Diane appeared from inside.

"Diane, where is Margaret?" Frank scowled. "She back yet? I need you to get a hold of her and get her ass over here pronto. Can you do that?"

"Yessir. She's back in today from SF. 3:20 at Douglas."

The stack of flyers on the glass table read:

Join the

- CAVALCADE of HOPE -
- Hear the Rev. Frank Grafton -
- Speak directly with an Ambassador of Hope -
- Jacksonville Civic Theater, June 17 -

"You know, Diane," Frank said, "the big summer swing through Florida kicks off next weekend, and I have to know the Ambassador count."

As the flickering light of Frank's ascension within the ranks of the Apostolics had dimmed, he began to see the brighter horizon of entrepreneurship. Who better to lead the flock to the Lord then Frank Grafton? The first three years had been small shows — community rooms, libraries — but dreaming up the Ambassador thing had changed it all. That personal touch — a sympathetic look, the holding of a hand — sold stuff every time.

Margaret barreled through the door at four on the dot. The plane had been early.

Margaret Dierdon was a hard-driving woman in her late 40s. Her appearance leaned toward the severe, and, as to the effect that had on others, she was well aware. Tall and fair, she had a fairytale air about her. She looked equal parts golden hero and evil sorceress. The State indictments that had crashed the last multilevel operation she'd worked for back in Baltimore had not so much as touched a hair on her head. She'd been with Frank now for the last four years.

"You know, chief," Margaret rarely used *Rev.* outside of official business and at rallies. "we've got it made here in the Southeast." She tossed her briefcase on that same glass table and exhaled. "People out West are hard to sell this stuff to."

"I know, Margaret. That's what I have you for. You've got to find me all those ambitious Ambassadors to hawk the tapes, the cassettes, the books. It's what keeps the ministry going. It's what enables our blessed outreach (this last with a faint smirk). So, how did San Fran look?"

Frank Grafton was having national daydreams.

This had been Margaret's third trip this year. She found some pockets of interest, mostly in California, that were now, through her efforts, loosely organized. She told Frank all this.

He nodded. "Florida good?"

"Good all except for Lauderdale. I got 12 in Jacksonville, 15 in Orlando, 20 in Clearwater — that was our biggest take last year — and 12 in Ocala. Still working on Lauderdale."

"Don't we have enough trained people?" asked Frank.

"Yeah, we got plenty in the area. Availability seems to be the bitch, though, right now. Like I said, I'm working on it."

"Yeah, Clearwater," Frank chuckled.

* * *

Kimmy surfed through the channels on their new cable TV setup. "Damn, look at all these!" she said wide-eyed. "So, Cindy, you thinking about going next Saturday?"

Cindy had batted away the plan for the better part of a week, but the time to decide had come. "Kim, that's the week I got time off so Joey and I can drive up and visit Ramon. We won't get back till Saturday morning, most likely."

The docs had Ramon bouncing between the Mt. Airy hospital and his family's home in Macon. "Good progress" they'd say. Then back to Mt. Airy when the depression returned. His assignment to Hurricane Relief had looked good at first blush. Helping people was helping people, *right*, regardless of the name on the car door. But the years dragged on, and the realities of the job began to drag him down. As more FEMA money sloshed around the city, it seemed fewer homes were getting rebuilt. Appointments with insurance adjusters kept getting postponed. Letters from distraught victims — *his* distraught victims — piled up in his inbox. He

226

became more serious, then irritable, then remote. Not the old Ramon. Toward the end he'd call in sick for four days at a time and never get out of bed.

"C'mon, it'll be a hoot. It's down at the Civic. We can catch happy hour at Jake's — it's just down the block. Then we can go see what the Hopefuls look like." Kimmy waved a flyer from her other hand.

The rain squalls that had threatened Macon later that week had prompted Cindy to drive back Friday, not Saturday. The clouds had all gathered over Northeast Florida, and the day dawned to a gray drizzle.

"Morning, sunshine. You sleep there all night?" Kimmy chirped as she walked into the kitchen. Cindy sat at the kitchen table with her arms crossed on it, and her head on them. She rolled her head to look at Kimmy. "No, been up since six." Kimmy looked back at Cindy and saw the red, puffed eyes, and new tears welling. Kimmy slid onto a chair, put her arm around Cindy's shoulders, and leaned in close.

"Oh, … no, no, no, no … don't do that," she whispered. After a bit, "How was it?"

Cindy looked at her friend, fully expecting words to appear, but none did, just tears. She put her head back on her arms and sobbed. They sat together like that for a few minutes, then Kimmy said softly, "So, how 'bout tonight? Sounds like it could be a pew-jumper, like we used to say back home. There's going to be a band, I think. Besides, you look like you could use a shot of hope … right after whatever Jake's has on special."

Cindy picked up her head and brushed her long brown hair out of her eyes. "You think?" she said with a wistful smile. "Okay, I'll get Angeline to watch Joey. Not late okay? I've got to sleep sometime."

Jake's had been hoppin', and it was a miracle they could tear themselves away. But, whatever its other merits may be, Jake's was not long on hope. So, at 7:15, they hoofed it down to the Civic, paid their 10 bucks, and walked through the door of the Rev. Frank Grafton's Cavalcade of Hope, Jacksonville edition.

227

Among the song sheets and (hopeful) Bible excerpts that sat neatly squared on each seat, Cindy also found a page with lots of fill-in boxes. She had no idea what that was for. She folded it and slipped it into her purse.

The Rev. Frank Grafton was indeed the star of the show. His gathering paunch gave him both a commanding presence, as well as a booming voice. He had the beginnings of jowls, and they moved out of synch with his head as he loudly decried the forces of Pessimism and Self-Doubt afoot in the world. "Each of you has it within you to be your best self. Hope is the answer." Those and dozens of sentences like them pelted the audience for an hour. Then the band played.

After some singing and hand waving, Frank took to the microphone again. "Reach out! Reach out, people! Reach out for the Hope that is all around you. Talk to our Ambassadors. Let them help you in your journey."

At almost that exact moment, a young woman with an earnest, friendly smile sat down next to Cindy. "Hi, my name's Ellen. I'm an Ambassador of Hope. Can we talk?" Cindy and Ellen chatted quietly, while Kimmy people-watched. Ellen asked questions in ways that were new to Cindy. The questions drew out her frustrations and shined a light on blind alleys. At one point Ellen even held her hand. *So perceptive for such a young person*, Cindy thought. She felt her burden lighten ever so much, and she admired Ellen's ability to do that.

All that, and home by 10. Cindy placed the "Realizing the Realizable" video, the two-volume *Turn Back the Darkness* bookset, the companion Hope Diary, and the handful of Frank Grafton bookmarks on her nightstand and turned in.

* * *

Frank and Margaret sat on Frank's patio a month later with a bottle of 15-year-old Scotch, showing some wear, between them.

"Is that all the new Ambassador apps we've gotten?" asked Frank. He absently stirred his drink. Margaret fanned the stack. "Yeah, about 20. Not bad for three shows."

"Anything look interesting?"

"Well, we got a bunch from the Florida State crowd. That's normal. College kids. There's two from guys fresh out of the Marines. They could be persuasive. Oh, and here's one from a stewardess in Jacksonville."

Frank perked up. He had long thought that stewardesses, with their people skills and reliability, made top-notch ambassadors. "Put that one on the call list, will ya."

And so, about a week after that, one morning as Cindy scrambled to find her keys, already late leaving the apartment, the phone rang.

"Hello, Cindy van Doren? My name is Margaret Dierden. I'm an associate of the Rev. Frank Grafton, and you submitted an application to be one of our Ambassadors of Hope, did you not?"

"Yes, yes. Thank you." Cindy had lost all interest in finding her keys. Her flight bag slid to the floor.

Margaret went on, "The Rev. Grafton was very impressed by your work history. He thinks you might be a good fit as we expand our ministry, possibly nationwide. Do you think you have that kind of commitment?"

Cindy said she was sure she did.

Margaret said, "Good, good. I'll send some additional paperwork for you to fill out. The first actual step will be your training. We've set up some weeklong sessions in a few locations that we think will be critical next year. We pay your expenses to and from, as well as while you're there. There is a modest deposit. We have one starting up in a few weeks. Ever hear of Malibu?"

Mama Jewel

Chloe Kerns Edge

When everyone was home, there were ten of us. Mama, Billy, Ar, Tank, Robin, Bertha, Emmett, Dee, Me, and Mama's friend, Charles. Dee and I were not Mama's biological children. She had taken us in.

Everyone was not home on this particular day and Mama was mad, pacing behind all seven of us with her switch, made from a tree branch, her dark brown eyes flashing, her forehead wrinkled in annoyance that she had to stop what she was doing and do the Lord's work of disciplining these children. Normally, Mama's skin is rich, chocolate brown. When she is angry, the color around her eyes and her forehead gets darker. Mama had very wide hips and a little tiny waist. Even though at least half of us were taller than she was, she was totally in command. "Ya'all shoulda been watchin' the little kids, the good Lord knows ya got nothin' betta ta do. Now be still and take whatcha got comin' and don't fuss!"

"Mama!" somebody squealed as the switch seared the back of their calves. We all took it pretty good that day for letting Robin, Bertha and Emmett get into something they were not supposed to be doing. Mama thought if the little kids got into trouble, it was everybody's fault. Many years later I heard someone at church ask Mama how she raised so many fine children and she said just that, "Every now and again I jus' line 'em all up and switch the devil out of 'em. No matter who done it."

I was in the lineup that day, and my two-year-old daughter, Heidi, was watching, horrified, as her mother got a switching with the rest of Mama's kids. Mama was scary when she was laying down the law. And it wasn't just Mama. She had the good Lord right there behind her and it was powerful. Everyone was well-behaved, and it was not so loud for a few days after that. Then it would be back to normal, everybody shouting, trying to be heard, either singing or talking. Many times, I have thought, *You either have to say something very clever or totally shocking to get any attention in this house.* Thing of it was, everyone was sharp and multi-talented, so there was always competition.

Mama was born in San Antonio, Texas, on November 5, 1923. She had a big brother, Jesse James. They were the children of Bertha Mae and Emmett Lott. When Mama was seven years old, they moved to San Diego because her Aunt Duchess bought a house here and Aunt Dutchie thought they might like it in San Diego. Mama went to Stockton Elementary, Memorial Junior High School, and she graduated from San Diego High School in 1941.

When Mama was 17, she was living with her aunt and uncle, Papa Jack and Aunt Lizzie on Clay Avenue (where the Woman's Club was). Sylvester Williams was courting her. They used to sit on the porch and look up at the big, beautiful house across the street. Sylvester was a cook in the Navy, and he had big dreams. He used to tell Jewel that he was going to buy the big house across the street, which had been built by a movie star. It is a fine house, it was grand in its day, up a lot of steps, sort of majestic, with a wide front porch and rose bushes in front.

On June 26, 1942, Jewel Arline Lott married Sylvester Andrew Williams and she became Mrs. Williams, who she still is today, at church. They bought the beautiful big house. She had six children, Sylvester, Arline, Anthony, Robin, Bertha and Emmett. I could put their middle names in here, too, if I wanted to get killed.

Sylvester was a fireman after he was a cook in the Navy, and he was gone a lot. With so many mouths to feed, he began to paint on the side, and he became an exceptionally good painter, painting homes in La Jolla and Point Loma when he was not being a fireman. I want to write this without

231

judgment, and it is very difficult because I saw over the years how many people got hurt, so I will just say that for some reason or another, Sylvester took off just after Emmett was born on January 22, 1960. The new baby was six weeks old when his dad left Jewel to figure out how to feed six kids by herself.

Now, remember, that in the '60s, in the white man's world, white women were secretaries and nurses. There were no Black people on TV, except in sports. There were no Black sitcoms, no Black women making their way in the world alone. This was a difficult time for Jewel, and she had no choice but to rely on her Lord for everything. In the long run, this has really paid off, because Mama Jewel has the kind of faith that can move mountains.

When I was eighteen years old my parents were desperate about what to do with me. After my third trip to Juvenile Hall, they had sent me to the relatives who would have me in Schwenksville, Pennsylvania, where they were sure I could not get into any trouble. I did. Then they sent me to a Jewish school in the Ojai Valley, where they had a headmaster from Auschwitz. I was expelled. It did not help any that Dr. Mandal, the director, found out I was half-German. I had radar for trouble and my parents were tired. Finally, I decided to attend the James Hall College of Beauty in Pacific Beach. My father was completely against it, which could have been expected. He wanted me to be a boy; he wanted me to be an attorney.

One day, in 1961, while I was in the bathroom at the Beauty College, they elected me the president of the school and informed me when I rejoined the group. My first assignment was to plan and produce the Christmas dance, in the near future. I had never done anything like this before. They told me to make a list of what we needed and plan a way to raise the money to pay for it. Also, I was to make calls to rent a suitable room and find a band to play.

I managed to secure the Catamaran ballroom and organize the Puerto Rican students to make these little fried sandwiches called empanadas from garbanzo beans, which we sold at lunch to make money to pay for everything. We were about six weeks away from the date when someone asked me what band was going to play. I had completely forgotten about the band. One of the girls from southeast San Diego said there was a band of brothers and sisters on her block and maybe they would be able to play. I called, set up an appointment to go hear the band, Arlene and the Pro-Teens. I found the house and climbed the long stairs up to their big front porch. As soon as I walked in the house, I was home.

The oldest brother, Sylvester, whom they called Billy, was the drummer. The first daughter, Arlene, was the singer and Anthony, whose nickname was Tank, something about football, played the saxophone. Three younger kids, Robin, Bertha, and Emmett, were hiding behind the curtains in the parlor. It was a real good band, strong and kicky, they had a lot of punch, and they knew many popular songs. I hired them. That was sixty years ago.

In the kitchen was one of the strongest people I have ever known. Their mother, Jewel Williams, has had a tremendous effect on my worldview and my life. She has taught me many things and I value her immensely.

The gig at the Catamaran went very well. Late that night, I paid the band, and everyone was satisfied. This was in 1961, almost a different world from the one we live in now. Once there was a movie about a white boy played by Steve Martin, who was taken in and raised in a Black family and it was quite funny, all the cultural difficulties which arose. I lived a story like that, only it wasn't funny. The absent husband and I have the same birthday, it was noted early on. Also, my inclusion in the Williams family happened years before the movie came out. We saw few interracial couples, and there was not a lot of racial intermingling going on.

The first time I heard anything about it was up at the corner store when Arlene was telling the storeowner that I was her sister, and he didn't believe her. "Yeah," Mama popped herself into the conversation, "that's my cracka chile." I belonged in Mama's big house. I loved it there, and after a while, I wanted to be Black, too.

After I was arrested for sales of narcotics in 1964 my father was afraid that whatever was wrong with me (it was pot) would spread to the other kids, and he did not want me around. Mama, on the other hand, was always glad to see me. I did the time, pregnant, and was released just in time to have my daughter, Heidi. My own mother, who was the light of my life, was dying and my new baby and my dying mother spent a month together staring at each other from twin beds while I cared for them both.

I got an education in the William's family. I learned to see the world from a completely different perspective from the one I had known in my childhood. Mama was strict, and she could become scary, but it was different from getting a beating at my father's hands. Mama doled out discipline without negative emotions. She believed she was doing the Lord's work, and she was grateful to be doing it. It was always clear why someone was getting a switching and although she was angry sometimes, she never attacked the character of the person she was disciplining. She was correcting a behavior and she made that clear before and after the punishment. There were times when we thought she liked it, even. By now I was twenty-one, married, with my own baby. That made no difference to Mama. "You saw the little kids messin' up and you didn't do anything about it, so this is for allaya!" And she'd lay it on. There was love in it. She loved all her kids, and I was included in that.

Mama always went to church and not just on Sunday. Back then, she attended the Apostolic Church at the corner of Hensley and L in San Diego, and she often spent Saturday afternoon cooking chicken, which would be served at church on Sunday after the long service. I had to learn how to cook soul food before I could go to church, Mama said. I had to produce a sweet potato pie (pronounced SweeTayPie) that she approved of, and this took years for me to accomplish. The other thing that happened on Saturday evening was the hair business in the kitchen, Mama with her straightening iron, doing one head of hair after another getting ready for church.

There is a scent associated with this that one never forgets — it is the combination of steam, burning hair and Dixie Peach Hair Dressing which used to come in a jar with four Black guys on the label. I cannot remember if we painted the kitchen before or after she let me go to church, but I learned how to make collard greens and black-eyed peas, cornbread, and sweet potato pie.

Mama liked volleyball and there was a volleyball net in the back yard. She encouraged us to get outside and play. James Brown's song, "I'm Black and I'm Proud," had just been released and everyone was happy about it. So the deal was, when it's your turn to serve, just before you bring your fist up, hard under the ball, you say, "I'm Black and I'm proud!" and then you slam the ball over the net. I was freaking out, wondering what am I going to say? When I got the serve, I said, "I'm white and I'm right!" The game stopped. Tank got to me first. Putting his arm around my shoulders as the others gathered around, he said, "You cain't say that! You cain't say that! You have to say I'm Black and I'm proud! You one of us! Now let's get this game going!" We played volleyball a long time that day.

Mama taught me to always dress the nicest I could when I go out and especially for church, where she always wore a beautiful hat. She taught me to wear the prettiest colors I could find and to mix them like I was a painter. Whenever I would offer to make dresses for her little girls for Easter, and I would ask what color, she'd always say, "Oh pick something nice and bright and pretty, darlin'." I used to sell fabric on the weekends for a Scottish man in Vista out of a huge Quonset hut and I could get fabric for a very good price. And then when I brought the dresses, she would say, "Oh, that's just beautiful, baby."

Through all her hard times I rarely heard Mama complain. She does not like to say things that are negative. Even when she is down and worried, she will be positive and upbeat, talkin' 'bout how things'll be all right when the mornin' come. I did hear her really upset, though, a couple times. When her granddaughter had cancer and when Arlene, who changed her name to Arbess to honor the slaves in her family, was in a coma. "You gotta go down there, baby, and talk to her. You the one who can talk her back. Just go to Mercy and say you're her sister and go talk to her." I did. I got some funny looks, like, while I'd be rubbing Arbess's feet and the nurses did not understand the familiarity, and some of the people from the church who don't know me may have wondered, too, by the looks of it. While I was talking Arbess into coming back to life I tried to hypnotize her to not eat any more hotlinks, which she loves and which are not helping her lose weight, but it did not work. She still eats hotlinks. One day, she opened her eyes, saw me, got a huge smile on her mouth, and said, "Hi, Baby, I'm ripped!" She was pretty loaded from all the medication they were giving her.

Arbess had made two CDs and her producer, Big Mike, lived in Sacramento. I called him and asked if he would send me some CDs. He did and I took them to the hospital and passed them around to her doctor and the nurses. It turned out that her main doctor had taken his wife to the Torch Club in Sacramento on their first date to see Arbess sing. Needless to say, the care at Mercy got way better, and she was released in a month.

Today, while I am writing this, everybody is well. Mama has just had a pacemaker put in and she is resting in that same big house. For years, I have been hearing Mama say, "If the Lord lets me live another day ..." That is where I got that. From Mama, who has had the same phone number for 57 years, who can make fried chicken better than anyone in the world, who has beautiful, eighty-year-old hands and who loves me, in spite of myself. She taught me that the happiest people have God in their hearts. Happy people sing and dance, they laugh deeply, and they make love. They wear bright pretty colors, and they say, "mmm, mmm, mmm." She showed me if you want to make soul food, you must get your hands into it, and that there is always enough for one more plate. "Get yourself a plate and he'p yose'f." That's Mama.

Jewel Williams will be eighty on November 5 this year, as she says, "If the Lord lets me live ..."

236

* * *

The first draft of this story was written on July 24, 2003. I was not the only adoptee in Mama's family. Dee Henderson passed in her pastor's arms and went home on July 25, 2004. Mama's beloved son, Pastor Anthony Charles Williams (Tank) returned to his Father in heaven the day after on July 26, 2004, at 4:30 p.m. Mama went home to rest on March 27, 2007. Arbess had come home from Sacramento to be with Mama in 2000 and she cared for her for seven years. Arbess was inducted into the Sacramento Blues Hall of Fame in 2008. Mama's children were singing her favorite gospel hymns to her at the time of her transition. She lives on in all of us.

Sylvester Andrew Williams, Jr. passed on Arbess's 75th birthday in May, 2021.

Finally ... the Perfect Place

Janet Hafner

Who would have imagined that I'd live in ten different places during my lifetime? Some places that I called home left deep indelible streaks on my memory while others were but a scratch. The first — what an experience. It was shortly after I was married.

My hair was full of suds and water as I hung over the kitchen sink in our tiny apartment. With the water running, I couldn't make out what my husband had said. With the faucet off, I squeezed the water from my hair, stared at my husband and asked, "What did you say, Honey?"

"The Marine Corps has issued me orders. I didn't expect orders so soon, but I'm anxious to settle into our first home." My husband's mouth curled up at the corners as if a smile wanted to appear, but he changed his mind and it disappeared.

I hope it's a nice place — a lot greener than southern California. With the towel wrapped around my head, I stretched up so I could wrap my arms around his neck, peer into those green orbs and make him talk.

"Where exactly is your presence requested, and ... when?"

"Twenty-nine Palms, my sweetie pie, *Twenty-nine Palms*," he whispered in my ear. "Two weeks. I'm due to report in two weeks."

We drove from San Diego through miles and miles of brown and tan land sprinkled with naked brush — I didn't see anything that resembled a plant or tree. An occasional palm tree doesn't qualify as a real tree.

"See those mounds. That's actually how condos are built in the desert. Everything is under the ground. It's too hot to

238

live on the surface."

I stared at the bleak scene, my stomach twisting.

"No way. You're joking, right," I objected. Almost choking on the words, I let out a hint of a sour sound to which my husband asked, "What did you say?"

"Nothing, honey." *When I married a Marine, I should've thought about moving, a lot.*

We arrived in Twenty-nine Palms with no officer housing available. We were assigned to a Quonset hut, which is a metal, half cylinder kind of structure. It was too tired to stand upright, so it stretched out lengthwise on its side. During a sandstorm, which was a common occurrence, the air inside our dome was ... hazy ... kind of like fog. I don't know how else to describe it. Particles ... millions, billions of particles danced, moved, changed position. The air was saturated. I can call to mind what it felt like to rub my fingers against my palm. It was grimy, gritty. A super-fine sand. *Why weren't we given masks? We breathed in all of that sand.*

It felt like sandpaper rubbing on my teeth. I'd wipe my tongue with my T-shirt and spit again and again. This was number one of ten duty stations we called home.

The second was not quite as bad, but it was shades of brown too. I wondered, *Will any of our future duty stations be green? I'm an eastern soul. Brown is not my color.*

Fort Sill, Oklahoma, wasn't green either. When we arrived in the middle of the night, my husband pulled off the road and we slept. We were awakened when our Volkswagen bus rocked from side to side as if we were experiencing an earthquake.

"Honey, what's going on?" My voice shook almost as much as the VW. When he pulled back the curtains, he said, "I'm eye to eye with a bison who wants to rub his giant body against our vehicle." Fear sent a shiver down my spine. We were in the middle of the largest bison herd in the US. I hoped they wouldn't mind our sharing their grazing land in the Wichita Mountains Wildlife Refuge.

"Let's see if we can sneak out of here," my husband mumbled.

We inched our way out of the park and found our next home — a structure that resembled barracks seen in WWII movies. We were on an Army artillery base. Not impressive and it wasn't long before orders were cut yet again. (That's military jargon for someone getting orders.)

"I hope there's good government housing at our next duty station. And where exactly are we headed?" I asked.

"Albuquerque."

More sand, I thought.

In Albuquerque no housing was available so we were told to find something on our own.

"This'll be fine," my husband said after checking out the last place on the list we'd been given. A sweet furnished apartment on the second floor over a business — some kind of boat shop. The surprise came when the business went into full swing in the middle of the night. What was the business you ask? A motorboat engine repair shop that didn't want to disturb customers during the day, so they revved up the engines after midnight and worked on the motors. We moved.

The fourth home we occupied was greatly improved. It was in Monterey, California, at the Naval Post Graduate School. The officers' housing area was shaded with well-established trees. Not exactly east coast style, but they were an improvement. I liked Monterey until I discovered that the beautiful beach had occupants that didn't like me.

"Ouch, something bit me," I chirped. "Ouch. I must be somebody's dinner," I laughed.

We stayed until I said three more ouches.

"Arn, look. Look at my legs." They're not mine. Something's inside pushing the outer layer of skin away from the bones. Alien-like bulges materialized and moved up my legs. I clawed at them. He slapped my hands.

"Stop it," he'd yell. I couldn't.

"Corpsman, my wife needs help," my husband shouted at the emergency room. Two corpsmen rushed over. One said, "I see you've met Monterey's finest — they gave you a real welcome."

"What are you talking about?" I couldn't stop scratching

and I could barely breathe.

Ignoring my question, the young corpsman prepared a syringe and gave me a shot. My body vibrated on the table. My legs bounced about. He left me alone. My heart didn't have its usual rhythmic silent beat. It collided against my skeleton.

I screamed, "I'm dying. My heart is going to explode. Help, help me."

I don't know the degree of terror the corpsman saw on my face as he passed our examining room, but he rushed in saying the other corpsman hadn't told me something.

"What?" I pleaded.

He explained that this happens when you get two shots of Adrenaline to move the poison more quickly so it gets out of your system. He kept telling me I wasn't going to die. I don't know if I believed him.

"A sand flea welcomed you to Monterey."

So much for visits to the beach.

Number five found us back in southern California. My husband had another Vietnam tour scheduled, but found us a house under construction that would be our future home when he retired. I planted fruit trees and right in front of the house stood a giant Sycamore. I had a tree.

My sons, Arnie, Marc, and Chris, and I spent much more time in this house than other homes, but this house was filled with sadness. Thinking about it causes me to recall two heartbreaking experiences. It was here that my husband, when he returned from Vietnam, left us, and it was here that my first-born son, Arnie, at thirty-one was diagnosed with Leiomyosarcoma, an aggressive form of cancer and where after battling for a year, he died.

While I labored to find a cure for my son, a Canadian doctor, or so he professed to be, said he had fallen in love with me and wanted to take care of me. I needed—no I wanted someone to care for me, so I fell for the charlatan who lured me to Ohio—my sixth home. Fortunately, I discovered who the man really was and escaped before he could rob me or make me disappear, or worse yet, harm me with one of the

241

seven loaded guns he kept in his office. Driving across the country I pondered how foolish I had been. The only thing I remember about that place is that it was where I almost lost my life.

The seventh house that sheltered me is where my son Chris and his wife, Sarah, lived in North Park near downtown San Diego. My two other adult sons were no longer in San Diego. I was on my own. What else could I do? I felt like a lost ship being tossed around by waves left over from a storm. They offered a safe harbor—I accepted their hospitality. In this home, I slept endless hours, regrouped, found my center, and bought a home of my own.

Number eight it was. A quaint bungalow in need of some TLC. I painted, I pruned, I tore down vintage aluminum awnings and chain link fencing. When finished, it was a fairy cottage inside and outside. I met my husband, Pai, by making a wrong turn and ending up at a dance studio where he took classes. Two years later we married, he moved in, and we rescued a marvelous Airedale, named Tessa. Life was grand. And then ...

"Wouldn't it be nice to live in the mountains where trees grow everywhere?" I asked.

"Prescott, Arizona, might be the perfect place. It's got altitude, Ponderosa Pines, and four seasons," my husband said. My ninth home materialized.

"This is the loveliest location I've ever lived in. I hope all the kids will bring the grandchildren to enjoy the mountain." We realized after a couple of years that unless there was a five- or six-day-long weekend, the trip was too long for such a short visit. Not many visitors came. A few years into the experiment as we called it, I said, "We're missing out on all the growing-up that the grandkids are doing. What do you say, we go home?" And that took us back to San Diego and the tenth home.

It's a comfortable house—nothing fancy, but just the right size. We have good neighbors, an office where I write, a pool whose water is too cold, but on very hot days, with high walls providing privacy, I can skinny-dip. Indeed, number ten is a perfect number.

Ten Marriage Proposals

Peggy Hinaekian

My friends could not believe that I had had ten marriage proposals between my first and second marriages.

"Yes, it is true," I said, "and I married the eleventh."

"Did you sleep with all of them?" they asked.

"No. Men do not appreciate easy lays. The more aloof you are the more they want to conquer you. Anyway, this was true thirty-five years ago during the 1950s and 1960s. I don't know about men nowadays. But the more things change, the more some things stay the same."

As my friends were curious to know the details of my proposals, and after much prompting, I agreed to tell them my story during a get-together in my home. This is the story I told them:

As you all know, I got married very young to my first boyfriend with whom I was hopelessly in love. It must have been puppy love because it soon dissipated, and I was looking beyond the horizon. Maybe I was just not meant for monogamy. The marriage lasted about six years during which I learned a lot about the male species.

Just before the divorce papers became final, one of his best friends called me.

"Do you want to go out for dinner tomorrow," he asked.

His name was Vako. He was a presentable fellow, not too tall, not too fat, just ordinary looking, and he had never been married. He was about six years older than me.

"But, I am not yet divorced," I told him.

"So what, you are no longer living with your husband so it would be okay. Don't worry, nobody is going to talk behind

244

your back. In any case, we are no longer in Cairo, and there is no one around to talk badly about you. This is just a dinner."

I agreed to have dinner with him. The restaurant was ordinary but the food was good and his company was amusing. I got to like him quite a bit. We talked about this and that until it was time to go home. He did not make a pass at me during the dinner, which I appreciated. We got in the car and he drove me home. Upon parting, he planted a moist kiss on my lips. I was taken aback but it felt nice. I had not been kissed by any other man except my husband.

We had a few lunches and dinners and movies and each time we got closer until finally we ended up in his apartment, and not surprisingly, we had sex. It was quite pleasurable. He was supposed to move to San Francisco in a couple of months so I did not take things seriously. It was just an adventure for me — trying another man in bed. He started to get quite romantic during the last week or so before his departure. Then, bam, during an amorous interlude, he asked me to marry him. I did not see this coming. I had in no way shown any love toward him, and he had not told me he loved me.

"I can't jump from one marriage to another so quickly," I told him. "I need some space, I would like to breathe a little."

"What are you going to breathe? You can still breathe while being married to me." We both chuckled then.

"No, Vako, this is too soon for me. You go to San Francisco, and I may follow you after a while," I told him.

I was hoping that in the meantime I would meet other fellows and expand my horizon. It would also be easier to refuse his proposal if he still insisted while being so far away. I did like Vako. I liked him a lot, but I did not love him. The sex was also good, but that was not enough. I was looking for fireworks.

He left for San Francisco and we corresponded, him always asking me what my intentions were. I finally told him that I was going to Europe to try and find a job there and that marriage was on the back burner for the time being.

"Maybe, I could come with you," he suggested.

245

I nearly panicked. That is not what I wanted. I had wanted to put more distance between us. I dislike men who try to stick to me.

"You have a good job where you are. Why on earth would you want to come to Europe?" I asked.

"To be with you, you dope," he said.

I wanted to buy some time before definitely refusing his offer, but I did not want to be my usual blunt self.

"Be patient. I'll let you know how I get along, no need for you to follow me yet."

Time passed and I became more and more distant in my letters. He finally understood my reluctance and he gave up asking me about my intentions. We remained friends.

Soon after Vako's departure, I met Rifaat, an Egyptian who was a PhD mathematics student at New York University (NYU). He was a big guy, a fun fellow, well-educated and came from a wealthy family. He wined and dined me which was fine but there were no sparks. He was a Muslim and I, a Christian. I did not see any future with him. My life would be too complicated. My parents would have flipped if I had introduced him as a husband candidate.

He came to my office one day when I was working at NYU and proposed to me right there and then, telling me he could see little Rifaats running around us. He could already visualize the children we would have even before he had taken the step to bed me. I had acted quite virginal with him and had refused any petting. As I have lived in Egypt, a Muslim country, I know that Muslim guys do not respect girls who are forward, not that I ever was. Or, girls who succumb easily. We had not even kissed and here he was dreaming of babies.

"No, Rifaat," I said. "I am not ready to get married. It is too soon after my divorce."

"I'll wait," he said staring at me with doleful brown eyes.

"Please don't do that, I am leaving for Europe in a couple of months to look for a job there."

His face fell. I could see he was sad and despondent. There was nothing more to say. I pitied the guy but there was no way I could console him. The relationship ended before it had even started. We did not remain friends.

Soon after, I went to Europe, to Geneva precisely, where I got a boring job with the United Nations. The job was tedious but the ambiance was not. There were lots and lots of men around. Conferences galore, where diplomats from all over the world attended. During the first month I was there, I met Terry, an American diplomat. He was quite an interesting fellow but not good looking. He was Jewish but not a practicing one. I always stayed away from practicing religious people — whether men or women — even if they were Christians. We hooked up. He liked to eat well so he took me to all the fancy restaurants around Geneva and in nearby France — Michelin Guide three-star restaurants. He told me that he did not like American girls because they all wanted to get married as soon as he went to bed with them. Well, he had a surprise with me. I did go to bed with him, but I did not want to get married. The sex was so-so. A week before it was time for him to return to New York, he asked me to marry him while we were in the elevator going to his car.

"I don't fancy going back to New York," I told him. "I just got here from Manhattan and I like it in Geneva. I would like to go on living in here. Manhattan overwhelms me. Too much of a rat race, no quality of life."

He looked at me aghast.

"It is the first time I have fallen in love," he said, "and it is the first time I am ever proposing to a girl."

I was speechless. I had not realized that he was in love with me. He was not an affectionate sort. It was dinner and sex, or movies and sex. I did not wish to disappoint him in his endeavor but I was adamant. Returning to New York was not in the picture at this time.

"If I had already been living in Europe for quite some time, I would have considered returning but that's not the case. I like the pace here. It suits my temperament," I told him apologetically.

He was disappointed but that was that. He returned to New York and I stayed put. We corresponded and he always

247

asked about my sex life. I evaded the question and we are still friends after so many years.

The next candidate materialized at the United Nations cafeteria. I was sitting alone at a table when a guy came around and asked me whether he could share my table.

"Be my guest," I said. "As far as I know the space is not reserved."

He turned out to be a Belgian diplomat. Good conversationalist, not bad looking but not a heartthrob. At first, I enjoyed his company. He took me skiing in winter and taught me how to ski. But then, he got too possessive and jealous. He was much older than I was and had never been married.

"When we get married, you can't do this or that," he would say.

Who the hell do you think you are, I thought and dropped him like a hot potato. I certainly did not need a control freak in my life. Actually, the way it happened was quite unexpected. While shopping one Saturday, we met for lunch. He suggested driving me home and I accepted. I noticed that he drove past my street while going home and I told him so.

"You missed my street," I said.

"I know," he said, "but I am taking you to my place."

I said nothing but when he stopped the car at a red light, I jumped out. "You can bring my stuff later on, I'll be home," I said, banging the car door real hard. He could not do anything but drive on. That evening he came over to apologize. But to no avail. I had had it.

"Thanks for bringing my stuff, but you are not the guy for me," I said. "There is one thing that I hate and that is for men to think they own me. You have the tendency to do that."

"You seem to be the type of woman who uses men and when they are no longer of any use, you discard them." He was quite upset when he came out with this statement.

"You got it wrong. *You* are trying to use me. Ciao, this conversation is over," I said and closed the door. I did not feel guilty in the least. We did not remain friends.

A week later, I met an affable Frenchman at a café in town. Geneva was full of men during my single years there. Lucky for me. I did not have to wait long to find replacements. This guy happened to be married but his wife had run away with another man. He still seemed to be in love with her. We became great friends. I told him my love stories and he told me about his wife. Ours was a platonic relationship. I could sense that he wanted to take up with me, but I was not attracted to him in the least although his company was pleasurable. He took me out quite often and we talked a lot. He gave me advice on all sorts of things, even men. Then, one day he told me his wife had divorced him and he was finally over her. He realized that he was carrying a hopeless torch. I was his confidante, I suppose. The next thing you know, during a dinner in his favorite restaurant, he proposed to me.

"I am very attracted to you," he said. "You remind me of my wife—a bitchy type of woman— which I go for, by the way. The sweet types who would do anything for a man simply don't appeal to me."

A bitchy type of woman? What was that all about?

"No, Bernard, I am not the marrying kind," I told him. I could not very well tell him that I was not attracted to him. He had not even tried to kiss me. It was a good thing because I would have turned my face away. He did not understand my revulsion toward marriage, and he tried to convince me every time we met. My decision prevailed. We parted on good terms and remained friends until eventually he remarried.

Not long after, I met Francois, another Frenchman. We worked in the same department at the United Nations. He was ten years older than me, tall, well put-together and spoke beautiful French. He had never been married, and I sensed a reticence in that direction but that was unimportant as I had no designs on him either. He amused me and I was, as he was fond of saying, his muse.

Francois taught me a lot about French literature, antiques, and classical music. He appreciated my being an artist. We had fun together going to cultural activities around town. I saw a lot of him and we often had sex. He was always eager.

249

My French improved tremendously. I started to have deep feelings toward him and even considered marrying him. He introduced me to his mother who asked us about our future. I just looked at him and waited for him to reply to her but he just changed the subject.

"You are the only woman I have introduced to my mother," he said afterwards while we were in the car driving to his place.

"Why is that?" I asked.

"Because I never considered marrying any one of them," was his reply.

Was this a proposal?

He then bought a sumptuous apartment in a posh district in Paris which he made me visit and, like a feathered cock, he went from room to room announcing which ones were for the kids. Two kids, precisely. He then looked at me.

"*Es-tu d'accord?*" he asked. (Are you in agreement?)

"Is this supposed to be a marriage proposal?" I asked.

"What else does it look like?"

"It looks like you want to have kids."

He then laughed. "You know what I mean," he said.

Yup, I got what he meant. It was indeed his marriage proposal, and I accepted because he was an excellent marriage material and I had come to love him — almost. Perhaps if time went by, I could have loved him more. But then, he was transferred to Nigeria on a post for two years. He asked me to go with him. I refused, not wanting to leave the comforts of Geneva to be in an unsettled African country. Anywhere south of the Mediterranean coastal countries did not appeal to me. We corresponded and he sometimes called. He had not given up on us getting married. He told me so in each letter and proclaimed his love toward me which he had never done in person.

But, by the end of the year, I had become tepid to his proposal, as I met a great looking British guy who came often to Geneva from London on business. He worked for Dupont. Al was separated from his wife. He had three kids. I was greatly smitten by him — for the first time since leaving my husband. I did not like that feeling too much because it made me vulnerable. However, I could see that he was smitten by me also. We had a torrid love affair. I forgot all about Francois, Nigeria, and my acceptance of Francois's marriage proposal.

Every time Al visited me, we had a wonderful time. It was a whirlwind romance.

During a candlelit dinner in a restaurant that looked like Aladdin's cave, Al took hold of my hands and proposed.

"I would like us to get married, but can you wait until my children get older?"

"How much older?" I asked.

"Well, the youngest is seven years old."

"How old should he be before we can get married?"

"At least twelve," he said. "You see, I'm very close to my children and I don't want to hurt them by marrying another woman. They know their mum and I are separated but we are not divorced and we do quite a few things together."

My jaw fell. Wait for him for five years? No sir, that would not do, but I lied and told him that I would wait. As I only saw him a couple of times a month, I decided to date other men in case I found one who was not married or was not divorced with appendages. Acting as a mother to another man's child was not in my genes. There was always Francois to fall back on when he returned from Nigeria. In the meantime, I was free and my feelings for Al were nebulous. They got to be more and more tepid during his visits. He noticed my coolness.

"You are being very casual," he remarked.

I did not offer any comments. We continued seeing each other sporadically but my heart was not in it. I did not break up with him though. He was too sexy. I could not resist being with him. He wrote to me often. Best love letters I have ever received.

During this time, I met an Italian lawyer from Milan on a ski trip. I had gone to Chamonix with a girlfriend. Martino was with a group of Italians. Well, he happened to be single but was accompanied by a girlfriend who was all over him.

251

He, on the other hand, was all over me, and I felt a little embarrassed. I do not like monopolizing someone else's merchandise, so to speak. The next evening, I was with a group dining at a chalet, when I saw Martino and his girlfriend seated at our table having an argument. Suddenly, the girlfriend jumped up, sobbing, and left the table.

I turned to the woman on my right who was in the group and asked her what the matter was. She told me that Martino had had an argument with his girlfriend about me the evening before and he had broken off with her. At this point, I had not realized that Martino had such a crush on me. I looked at him with a different eye and found him quite charming. He monopolized me during the rest of the evening. I spoke bad Italian but he spoke good French.

Martino came to visit me quite often in Geneva and we hooked up. So now I had to juggle two relationships at the same time. Al and Martino. I could not choose one over the other because I was not in love with either of them. They were just fun to be with. One positive factor about Martino was that he was unattached, free and ready — ready for marriage, that is.

"Let's get married, I am tired of these bimonthly visits," said Martino, one day while we were gazing at the moonlight, lying in bed in a luxury hotel in the Italian ski resort, Sestierre.

"Tired?" I repeated. "Is that the only reason to get married?"

"No, of course not. I adore you and want to be with you all the time."

While I was really drawn to Martino and his suave sophistication, I could not envision going to live in Milan, a city I did not really care for. I suppose you'll tell me that if I loved the guy, I would follow him to Timbuktu. Well, not me. I was not convinced the relationship would work out. I asked him for some time to ponder the situation, my job, my family, and what not.

"You don't have to work in Milan," he said. "I make good money. You can have all the household help you need. I also own a villa at the beach in Grossetto. We can have wonderful weekends there. I know you like the water."

"I'm not the type of woman who can only play house," I told him.

"Well, you can start a business, if you want to be busy, and I'll help you."

Martino was offering me an idyllic life, but I did not budge from my position. What if the relationship did not work out? We had not actually lived together. It had been a romance on weekends only. I would have lost my secure job at the United Nations and my Swiss residency papers. My head ruled my heart.

"Give me time to think about it," I said, although there was nothing to think about. My answer would always be *no*. I had no intention of jeopardizing my secure job and good life in Geneva to follow a man. His visits continued but less often and the affair trickled away after some time. He thought I had someone else and asked me about it. I denied it, of course. Martino never got married, by the way, and we are still friends. We send each other Christmas cards.

Then, lo and behold, Terry came into town again and reiterated his desire to get married. My answer was still no. One day he introduced me to a good friend of his, a physicist, a world famous one. Graham was an extremely interesting fellow and liked the arts. But he looked like a frog. I do go for looks, by the way. Not stupid and handsome, but intelligent-looking good looks. He fell for me. And during the second dinner out, he proposed. Now, I guess you'll tell me if I did not like him, why did I ever go out with him. The reason was that he was an excellent conversationalist. I enjoyed his company, specially so as we talked a lot about art. And, I liked to eat well and I was economizing on food money.

"You'll come to New York with me, we'll get married, and I shall get you a loft where you will paint all day long. You don't have to work, ever. You can't imagine how you make me feel," and on and on he went, looking at me with adoration behind his thick horn-rimmed glasses while chewing his food. I listened patiently.

253

These were words I would have liked to hear from someone I was actually in love with. But that person was nowhere in sight — not yet.

"But, you don't even know me," I said. "How can you propose to someone you have seen twice in your life?"

"I've seen enough. I want *you* and that's that. All the other women I meet fall over me and suffocate me with their attentions, but you are aloof, I like that. You are a woman to be conquered. You'll make me work hard. I know you don't love me yet, but I hope you will, soon."

I could not hurt his feelings and tell him I was not attracted to him in the least. That I just liked his company because we talked about art. The thought of being in bed with a man who looked like a toad revulsed me. I'm not one who believes in kissing a toad to reveal a prince! So, I asked that he give me more time. He had to return to New York anyway and that would provide me with the time needed to come up with an excuse not to accept his proposal. He wrote every three days and I replied once in a while. He was away for more than six months before he realized that I was not into him. He finally dropped the subject of marriage and always wrote about his impending visit to Geneva, which never materialized. Thank God. Not getting any reaction from me, he finally stopped pursuing me and we did not remain friends.

The last marriage proposal came from a man who was in the French secret service — DGSI (General Directorate for Internal Security). He was French of course. My ex-husband had met him in Paris and suggested that he look me up during his next visit to Switzerland. The French and Swiss Secret services work closely together as they have a common border. One day, a man materializes on my doorstep. He actually did that. He rang the bell. I opened the door and saw this smallish, wiry, middle-aged man grinning from ear to ear.

"Who are you?" I asked.

"Surprise," he said. "I met Charlie in Paris and he suggested I look you up. So here I am at your service."

"Charlie? Hmmm," I said. "Well, what is your name and please come in."

His name happened to be Charles. Funny thing, the two Charlies or Charles resembled each other. They were both on the short side with a dark complexion, jet black hair, and big brown bedroom eyes. They both spoke with animation and gesticulations. We chatted and then he asked me out for dinner. We went to dinner. We chatted some more. He told me about his secret service life. A dangerous one it was. He also told me that he had learned all about me by looking at my file at the Geneva headquarters for foreign persons. It is called *Contrôole de l'Habitant* which means Control of the Residents, pertaining to the foreigners. They keep a file on everyone. So, he knew my age, my provenance, how long I had been married to Charlie and everything else. I did not quite appreciate that. I do like to keep some mystery about me.

Anyway, we went out a few times. I could see he became enamored of me, but I had no such feelings toward him. He was simply not my type. He reminded me too much of my ex-husband. He had the habit of always sitting with his back to a wall in a restaurant and scrutinizing everyone. In the movies we always sat in the back row. When he walked in the street, he was aware of who was behind him at all times. He was jerky with constant movements of the eyes and body. It got on my nerves after a while. He was never relaxed and consequently I could not relax when I was with him.

He came to visit me a few times from Paris, and we went out for dinners if I had nothing better to do. I never refused a free dinner, unless of course the man in question was a total jerk. He tried some smooching sessions but I avoided them. Then one day I received a letter and the letter had an enclosure. It was a draft legal document made out in both our names with *Promesse de Mariage* (Promise of Marriage) and the birth of two fictitious children.

I flipped. I was shocked at his impertinence of taking things for granted. I wrote to him saying that I had no intention of getting married. I did not say I did not ever have the intention of getting married. I told him I was still young and liked my freedom and that I wanted to keep him as a friend. I could not possibly consider being married to such a suspicious character. I cannot bear someone being so inquisitive as to probe into my personal business behind my back.

He had high hopes and I had let him down, he said. I had not led him on, though. I had always kept him at a distance so I didn't see why he developed these affirmations. His reply was an emphatic *no* to being my friend.

"If I cannot have you as a wife, I could not possibly have you as a friend. It would hurt me too much not to be able to touch you."

Well, that was the end of Charles.

And those are my ten marriage proposals, girls. Some of these guys were quite marriageable specimens and would have made great husbands and fathers, but they were just not for me. I finally did get married, as you all know, to my second husband, Nelson, a Canadian engineer from Vancouver who had traveled extensively and had never been married. I met him in Paris while on a weekend trip. It was the second time I had fallen in love, and he was the first man who did not smother me or try to possess me. We've been married now for a very long time and have three children.

So, you see girls, life is full of choices.

Ten Life Truths

Cyril Roseman

When, looking back on my life, I realize there are ten life truths I learned by the time I was ten years old. I share them with you today.

One.
Everyone we see, hear, meet, connect with in any way, will someday die, even us. We do not know when, but we do know that no one will get out of here alive.

I discovered this truth at age 10 when my Uncle Albert, whom I genuinely loved, passed on before his 60th birthday. I began to think of my own mortality and what I should do with my own precious lifetime.

All living creatures do everything we can to avoid or postpone our own deaths. Humans go to great lengths, usually following medical advice, to avoid pain, heal better and faster, and to extend their lifetimes on this planet. As we age, our energy is focused on prolonging and improving the quality of life. Days, months, and years pass more quickly than when we were younger. Children and young adults, by comparison, often seem to act as if they were immortal, and they rarely act as if they recognize how precious their lives are.

Not only our lives are important but our pets' lives are. I saw my parents' friends, the Loebs, pay their veterinarian a fortune, about $5,000, to keep their 11-year-old dog, Brutus, alive, fighting unsuccessfully to survive. It was no better two years later when Charlie Loeb died at 63 from throat cancer, and his wife Elaine had spent at least $20,000 in medical care to save him. She failed.

This is not to say that I believed then, nor that I believe now, that all humans lack a soul that survives eternally. But it seems that people, especially seniors, focus much of their time and energy on keeping their bodies alive and healthy for as long as possible in this lifetime.

Two.

All life — animal, vegetable, mineral — is fundamentally influenced by molecular vibrations, sound, set to a rhythm that forms a regular pattern, which becomes the distinct identifier of its atomic structure.

This I learned mostly at the seashore, listening to conch shells. They reveal the vibrations and the unique sounds of seashells. I did not discover this truth conducting research on all forms of life, but rather, like all these truths, I intuitively accepted them based on my limited life experience. By the age of 10, I had spent all the sunny days of the previous four summers on the New Jersey Coast, discovering life truths and exploring the realities of life on the beach.

While I came to recognize that each creature had its own unique pattern of vibrations (often accompanied in their *mind* by a musical rhythm or life melody), I instinctively knew there was a universal similarity of life patterns among all creatures of the same species. This was especially true among us humans differentiated by sex, age, race, health, and general enlightenment. But even when differentiated, humans share a basic similarity of life patterns. Often, some individuals involved rarely accept this similarity among all people.

Three.

These vibrations are presented to the world in patterns called cycles. These cycles are set in speed, volume, and character, and are particularly observable in music.

By age 10 I knew I wanted to devote my life to studying these common patterns in people. I discovered this while listening to the music of the World War II era: Frank Sinatra, Ella Fitzgerald, the Andrew Sisters, Bing Crosby, and especially the radio songs — "Boogie-Woogie Bugle Boy," "Shoo-Shoo Baby," "I'm Making Believe," "I'll Be Seeing You," and "I'll Be Home for Christmas." My father played classical music on 45s and I listened to these as well. Often internationally recognized musicians discovered the musical cycles appealing to a large body of people over a long period of time. This of course includes the significant Renaissance composers. A corollary of this truth is that music awakens the soul of living beings. I believe this is because of its vibrational cycles.

Four.

By the age of 10 I realized that matter resembled sand on the beach; it never made sense to me that each physical object was composed of unique ingredients. The tangible world that we observe and name is comprised mostly of molecules of water and open space.

If we look at our favored car and its parts with a powerful microscope, we will see the empty space inside, among its molecules. Unfortunately, few humans carry powerful microscopes for observing this. Many persons never learn it.

Though I lacked a powerful microscope as a child, I learned this truth when I began to carefully examine sand (at the Jersey beach I visited each summer) and thought about where it came from. Though I later studied the Mendeleev table of atomic elements, as a preteen I did come to recognize protons and neutrons as the common basic building blocks of atoms. Later in life, my ideas were confirmed by my college studies of physics, microbiology, and even the philosophy of Albert Einstein. Somehow, I instinctively understood as a child that all matter was composed of either empty space, or atoms and molecules.

Five.
Our human spirits are composed of body, mind, and soul.

I learned of this truth as I was busy discovering religion and God, just before my 10th birthday. Some of us, unfortunately not enough, are blessed as I was with a mother who embedded in me the truth that God exists inside *all* humans, largely through our soul's connection to an eternal higher power.

Each of us places different values on these three elements, and some of us treat every person just like an animal, aware only of the physical body, barely recognizing mind, let alone social or spiritual existence. Some animals are aware of their minds, but often have little or no memory or sense of the future. Those of us who are aware of our souls are strongly motivated by our concepts of God, or a higher being.

Unfortunately, the bulk of humanity outside of India believe that, when our bodies die, we die. It is hard for some to recognize that the souls of previously deceased persons are still alive. Though our bodies and minds may die, our souls live on.

I knew all of this at age 10 because I was aware that my own parents did not appear to be my relatives in terms of their understanding of their souls, their origins, and their future destiny. I came to believe this because I felt strongly my soul must be linked with others like me down through the ages, and not through my parents and my family tree.

Six.
As humans, we have trouble maintaining satisfaction in life in isolation. But we often bond without maintaining a love relationship.

I discovered this truth when I realized that most of my aunts and uncles were not in love but were very much bonded with each other.

We are often bonded by friendship and common purposes

260

with others. But these connections often do not last long. Certainly not as long as the *permanent* bonds involved in mating. Sometimes we are more closely bonded in friendship to people who died many years ago. Sometimes we are even bonded to imaginary friends who are not real living people. But whatever the bonds of friendship or common purpose, these are by and large less consequential than mating. We usually form lifetime mating patterns.

This pattern of lifetime mating probably began for purposes of perpetuating the human species by creating children through sexual activity. Then these children would go through a life cycle of childhood, adolescence, adulthood, mating, and old age. This pattern of bonding or mating is often complicated by mental and spiritual yearnings for love and soulmates. Many of us cannot imagine quality mating without love.

When love and soul-mating combine with physical interaction and sexuality to produce children, we all applaud it (myself included). But we hardly ever acknowledges the low percentage of these *long-term successes*.

Often love and soul-mating interfere with long-term sexual linkage to produce and raise offspring into adulthood. Too often, marriages with children are held together only until the children are grown into adults or leave their parents' household. But even in these cases love and soul-mating is identified as absent and the reason for the breakdown of the bonding relationship.

While this does preserve bonding through the years of child rearing, once the children leave the home it is often the case that the married couple acknowledge their incompatibility and proceed to separate and divorce. The grown children at that point are not surprised when they see their parent's divorce, since they have been aware of the limitations of love in the home in which they grew up.

Unfortunately, it is often assumed that it is the lack of love that causes the divorce. The more likely reality is that the divorce is the *result, not the cause* of the absurdity of building lifetime bonds around love and soul-mating.

261

Six and 1/2.

By and large, love and soul-mating interfere with sexual linkage to produce offspring and raise these offspring into adults. This is because the desires and dreams of love often undermine the continued sexual attraction necessary to foster continuation of the human species.

This truth I learned by age 10 as I observed the few marital breakups occurring in my extended family on both my mother's and father's sides.

Bonding among those of different races, ethnicity, religious or political philosophies, are likewise considered more valued in thought rather than in reality. The more differences between *mates*, the less likely these couples will survive to continue to produce offspring raised by their parents into adulthood.

In short, humans tend to glorify love and soul bonding as the basis for successful lifetime mating. But love and soul bonding often occur outside of marriage with tragic results for all parties. For those in marriages founded on love, it is often the case that love wears thin. For those in marriages not founded on love, bonding seems to work just as well, and sometimes even better.

Seven.

Bonding over time has caused many persons to terminate their original mating—for one reason or another—and ultimately to take up bonding with another. Yet there is little evidence that the world is a better place because this set of complex familial relationships has made it so. Just because it does not solve world problems does not mean people do not embrace this pattern when it serves their personal needs to do so.

By age 10 and looking at divorced relatives in my extended families I recognized that serial marriage was often pursued by those unhappy with their first marriage, but it did not do the world any good. It did not necessarily do harm, but it did not solve problems of misguided first marriages for the world. I knew the pattern would continue to grow because people were seeking their own happiness, not the world's.

In *the old days* this did not happen often, largely because religion and social norms placed penalties on serial bonding (or marriage). But over the last century this type of inhibition has been reduced, just like inhibitions on diverse forms of sexuality. Now serial marriages and blended families — where children of one or several previous marriages of one or both marriage partners are raised as siblings in one family — are commonplace.

In today's world we tend to believe that serial marriage is a form of social problem-solving in the world. I believe at age 10 I had a better grasp of reality about the limitations of serial marriage, including those in which I myself later engaged.

Eight.

It pained me at 10 to see my older cousin Edward so often passed out drunk on the floor. People favor short-term satisfaction, and have difficulty acknowledging the degree to which substance abuse adversely affects the quality of their lives over the long term. Many humans rely on alcohol or drugs to brighten their existence, even though the scientific evidence may point to the adverse effects of such substances over time.

This problem is compounded by the fact that for most people these abused substances act as addictions — that includes tobacco, chocolate, sex, professional work, and for too many religious practices and beliefs.

Many people would not know what to do with their life energy if their habits or addictions were removed. This pattern will probably continue far into the future and for most people, they can only say "I have had a good life and, looking backward, here are the reasons (or habits) that have made my life so good. If I had it to do all over again, I wouldn't change

263

a thing." No wonder there has been so little change in the quality of life over the centuries.

At the age of 10 my only addictions seemed to be the four big S's—sun, surf, sand, and summertime. But as I grew older, like other people, I foolishly adopted other habits and addictions. For many people, including myself, this included fine dining in fine restaurants and international travel. And, as a practicing lifelong intellectual, I suspect I developed an addiction to reading books. I know some writers who have an addiction to writing.

I am now conscious of my addictions, even if I have not yet figured out how to remove them from my life. But I certainly have limited my involvement with commonly considered substance abuse, especially illicit drug use and excessive consumption of alcohol.

Nine.

Perhaps the most obvious truth I discovered at age 10 was that most of what happened in the world came from the impact of money, power, and public personality in shaping new ways of human behavior. Money talks, power controls, and celebrities influence current human behavior everywhere in the world, and it has been so since, at least, the time of Adam and Eve.

At age 10 after the death of FDR when I was following politics and the war effort zealously, I knew that it was not the fault of any one or more individuals, but it was rather in the inherent nature of *money, power,* and *personality* that bad results would be produced by those who relied on one or more of these three forces to gather their strength for opinion-shaping.

Often there is no goodness for humanity from people with money, power, and celebrity status. These classes of people—the wealthy, powerful, and well-recognized—are not ignored or criticized or chastised for the harm they are bringing to humanity. But is it too much to expect that such types of *leaders* or *opinion molders* somehow would be *corrected*?

Each of us realize that these forces do not produce positive results for the world. We do condemn them all together, or in three separate classes, and call out what they are getting wrong. However, we may occasionally refer to an individual with one or more of these traits as not being a positive influence on the world. Are these persons abusing their *birthright* by taking the world in the wrong direction?

At age 10 I knew that it was better to follow those who did *not* lead from money, power, or celebrity status. As Jesus said, "the meek shall inherit the world" and "the first shall be last and the last first." I spent much of my preteen and adolescent years seeking guidance from leaders who did not rely on money, power, or personality to influence others. It was my good fortune to learn this at an early age. And it was good fortune for me that my acceptance of this truth never left me.

Ten.

The most exotic truth I discovered at age 10 was that all beliefs and behavior toward others were not rooted in the practices or ideas of others, but rather reflect one's own beliefs and practices. In short, I discovered that any criticism I heard was founded on a mirror that one was holding up, thinking it was a magnifying glass — looking at others, but it was really a mirror of themselves, their flaws, and their character. If A has found B to be at fault for any reason, it is often really something that they have found, without looking, in themselves. Often there is more to be learned about the critic from the criticism than about the subject being criticized.

I came to this truth through a profound experience. Before my ninth birthday, on April 12, 1945, when FDR died, my dear grandfather Ike, whom I dearly loved more than anyone, flew into a violent rage and broke an umbrella across my back as I told him of FDR's passing.

"Don't you ever say that again," he shouted at me. I was being punished for simply bringing him the unvarnished truth.

As I thought about this afterward during the next year, I could not blame my Zadie, as I called him. He was extremely upset, not with me but at his own loss of his hero, and in his grief lashed out physically at me. Why did this happen? Probably I thought because he was unhappy with himself and his dedication to a man who let him down by dying. I was not being punished for what I had done or said, but rather because he wanted to punish himself for believing that FDR would never die. He could not punish himself, so he took it out on me, the messenger, bringing him bad news.

During the next year as I reflected on this situation, I realized how often children are punished for weaknesses in their parents. Often people, parents certainly included, criticize others for faults that they are experiencing in themselves.

This led me to understand the validity of this truth. All criticism is based on the mindset of the critic, not the subject of the criticism. This may even include editorial criticism of writing, although this does *not* mean that all criticism is to be ignored or is not relevant.

Since the age of 10 I have always followed the rule that *criticism is based largely on a mirror the critic is holding, not a magnifying glass*. In general, I do not trust critics to be a guide to what is wrong with others, but the criticism levied may be a guide to what is wrong with the critic.

This is a hard truth to subscribe to when we are the critics. But it is always a good idea to reflect first when we criticize — whether we are simply reflecting our own weaknesses. I hope that critics of my writings will use this idea before they criticize my work.

* * *

So, what is the BASIC TRUTH that I discovered at age 10? That *there really is only one God, and all other truths come from his role in helping us make rules to live by*. And as far as proof of this truth, I note that God gave Moses 10 Commandments. He also gave almost all humans 10 fingers and 10 toes. Were these two designed to allow humans to remember and recognize the 10 Commandments?

Maybe if God had given Moses 12 Commandments humans would have six digits on each hand and foot. And perhaps then we would respect to number 12, for the number of months of the year, and the number of tribes of Israel.

Would we celebrate the 10 years of SDWEG's Anthology, or would we wait until the 12th year to celebrate?

Sunset, Sand, and Winter Swells

Ty Piz

Ten meters out. Soft, white sand tumbles beneath the waves as they reach closer to shore, while the mighty whitecaps of the winter swell rush in. The icy salt water is then drawn back to the depths of the immense Pacific Ocean, while beneath the water's edge, the swirling sand creates ripples on the ocean's floor. My mind is awakened to its full potential with sunrise tai chi, morning yoga in solemn meditation, or quiet prayer releasing this invisible force of soul that is within us all, which breeds passion for the happiness from deep within, then showers nature's peace out to everyone. The slow turtle-like breath soothes my mind, then gently escapes as I adapt to the diverse culture of this unique land. Bowing in appreciation, my heart is delighted to be in this sensational place.

Tiny flumes of smoke linger from the coals in the fire pit that had raged with enormous flames last night. The paddle boarders, some with, some without, wetsuits, work hard to keep pace with the mighty waves. Helicopters thunder overhead while snails scurry to outrun the enormous breakers crashing in. Salt fills the air around me as I follow my routine of challenging nature. Tingling sensations dance across my exposed skin. The wetsuit feels cumbersome, and the buoyancy it creates hinders the deep dives I strive for, and I choose not to wear it. This will ultimately help me as I train for the triathlon.

While the colossal poof clouds melt in the warm rays of sunlight, I spy the sharp rocks that form a protective jetty for the intense activity of the beach sectioned off for the dogs to run and play and for the young and not-so-young toes to dip delicately in the cool liquid. Travelers quickly walk along the sturdy wooden pier. From high above they watch the world of marine life below the surface.

Beds of kelp dance atop the rolling breakers, churning with the powerful energy that began on the other side of the earth's gravitational pull. While gulls squawk and flail in the cool breeze, they seek their morning dessert. Sea lions surf the sovereignty of the curl with delight, and pelicans gracefully glide to their new perch. Along the steep jagged cliffs, moss clings tightly, holding the smallest of creatures safe within its leafy essence. Red, yellow, orange, and purple rays now crest the horizon, bringing a translucent glow of light and warmth to this fresh new day.

Ten fathoms deep, the ocean floor lies beneath me. My arms pound as I swim through the massive breakers of the Pacific Ocean. *Swoosh, swoop. Ka-whamm, gurgle gurgle.* While surfers soar down the face of these gigantic swells, my feet kick and arms paddle with fierce power to keep ahead of the mighty tumble of water crashing down upon me.

Now out beyond the powerful breakers, the beat of the ocean's heart methodically rises and slowly descends, while I swim among the surfers waiting for the next set to roll in.

Kay-ya. Kay-ya!

We hear the call as locals spot the rollers rapidly approaching. With flippers, goggles, and hand paddles strapped in place, I quickly turn and head for the calm of deep, open water. The ocean rises and the surfers disappear from my sight beyond the enormous crest. Land is a far-off memory now. All that remains is the beautiful blue sky overhead blending with the unruffled turquoise of the ocean. Time drifts on—unchecked. My mind is at peace.

* * *

Ten degrees closer to hypothermia, the sun approaches the horizon. The bright lights of the southern California pier at Sunset Cliffs shine upon the massive planks. Shivers begin to travel across my purple flesh. I step up the pace to keep my core temperature in a safe zone when long strands of seaweed wrap around my legs. I begin to rethink my choice to forego the potentially life-saving article of clothing.

I remind myself to stay calm as fright immediately tries to overwhelm my heart. I kick my legs softly and gently pull with my arms to get through this sloshy, prickly mess of weeds. The salty ocean makes me more buoyant so I can swim for longer periods of time. A glance at my wristwatch shows that I have been exposed to cold water for nearly ninety minutes. *Need to keep enough strength in reserve to make it back to shore.*

A flock of seagulls swarm, watching the fish jump high out of the water, both in search of their evening meal. A heavy sigh escapes my lips as the mirage of poof clouds float on by, and a soft mist rises from the unseen world of life below the water's surface. The large group of surfers are long gone since darkness now covers the shore. Reluctantly I decide that it's time to make the journey into the massive swells and the terrifying rip current that awaits. With sights set, my aim is between the sturdy wooden pillars supporting the vast pier and the jagged rocks of the jetty, which separate the groomed beach for the public from the cobblestones of dog beach.

A huge set of waves lifts me above the ocean's bottom of white sand. *Kick, pull, kick, pull.* As I descend the face of the enormous wave, the thrill of the ride fills me. *Whoo-hoo!* Soaring forward, my left hand reaches out for balance so I don't do a face plant into the coarse sand beneath this awesome curl. At the last instant of skimming the surface, I tuck my head — submerging into the bubbles of the thick, white water — twirling, as if I were spinning inside a washing machine. My feet land on the sandy bottom, my legs flex to launch myself upward. *Kick, pull, kick, pull,* aiming for clear sky and the next breath. *Kick, pull.* Finally, I burst through the water's outer layer and receive the warm salty air which tastes delicious.

Just as the next set of the winter swells crushes on top of my head and shoves me toward shore, the power of the rip current grabs my torso and drags me further from land. Kicking and pulling, I am lighting up the fins and paddles with all my might trying to sail along the surface of the ocean with all the strength of nature's wrath trapped within. Up, up, up. Seems like an eternity when there it is, the stars appear in the dark glistening sky.

The strong rip current has forced me toward the massive pillars of the pier. *Damn it Ty, kick, kick. Harder, man, no crashing into the pillars of logs.* With more power than the last one, the next roller lifts me above the shore, and I see the bright lights of Ocean Beach. *Come on, man, do the bodysurf thing.*

As I head over the crest and down the face of this massive wave, speed increases. My heart pounds in my chest, and my lips and throat are dry from the salty ocean water. I feel the anxiety begin to well up inside. I want to avoid crashing into the sand again. I am hoping to get a long ride but come up many yards too short of the beach. The rip current quickly sucks the sand from under my toes. I am rapidly being pulled back to the depths of the cold deep blue.

Crap, I'm so tired. Please, God, get me to the beach.
Kick, pull.

Another breaker carries me high above land, nearly to the top of the pier. *I wish I had a long surfboard to carry me to shore.* Suddenly, everything disappears as I am pulled beneath a kazillion gallons of water. The twirling bubbles swirl around me. Exhausted and frustrated and wickedly scared for my life, the steady pounding of the washing machine continues to have its way with me.

Deep underwater, I feel as if I'm screaming, when suddenly something very strong wraps around me. What can I do? Could it be seaweed, an octopus, or a human? Whatever it is squeezes even tighter around my chest, a turbulent rush of strength darts through my veins, my mind clears, my elbows strike out, and my legs swing wildly to get free. Half water, half air fills my lungs as these gigantic waves wash over me. Coughing to clear my throat I know this could be my last swim.

A set of tranquil waves comes in. *Okay!*
Kick, pull.

Swimming at full sprint, I travel parallel with the shore. Trembling, I approach the jetty. *Don't crash into the hundred yards of wicked boulders.* One stroke blends with the next. Waves lift me upward like the hand of God is carrying me. I see the dim lights of the lifeguard tower shining brilliantly. Unbelievably, this powerful force sets me down, gently onto the solid, wet sand.

I struggle to stand as my legs wobble. The sand falls away from beneath my toes. My mind is feeble, my arms shiver, and my legs ache. Turning, I gaze across the dark ocean to the vivid colors of the horizon and smile. A lone figure, mid-twenties and chiseled from granite, walks the shoreline toward me. The man has fins, goggles, and a missile-shaped flotation device strapped around his shoulders. He approaches, asks me, "Everything okay?"

Still dazed, I wipe the hair out of my eyes. "Such amazing water" is all I can summon in my reply.

He looks at me in disbelief, shakes his head, and walks up the beach toward the lifeguard tower.

Grateful to be on solid land, weak, and shivering, I realize that I need food. Off in the distance I spot the tiny home I have lived in for the past three and a half years that awaits me, parked underneath a cluster of palm trees. I stumble toward her thankful to see that she is parked right where I left her. The keys are still where I hid them under the front fender. I open the van door and quickly grab a towel and sweatshirt to dry off and warm up. My mind is working in low speed, and my hands quiver as I search for the right key to put into the ignition, then slowly move the gear shift lever to reverse and back out. Rolling forward, it's off to the burger joint located close to Catalyst Soccer where I work during the day and sleep in the parking lot at night.

I pull up to the burger joint. *Protein, carbs, and a chocolate shake!* Finally warmed up from the long exposure in the frigid January waves and from the close brush, remaining at the bottom of the ocean and becoming a part of the feeding cycle of life. I find myself thinking, *maybe it wasn't seaweed or an octopus that I fought off beneath the oceans current. That young man might have been a lifeguard that saved me!*

Less than two hours later while sitting in the van munching on salty fries, I hack and cough. Liquid spews from my nose. *Certainly did swallow a whole lot of ocean water out there*. Spit, cough, hack. More fluid pours out my lungs.

Without warning, arms collapse and chest collides with steering wheel, *whamm*. I cough, choke. My hands clinch tightly around the steering wheel. I quickly swing open the door, slide out, and crash to the asphalt floor. The terror of my potential demise sinks in, while the six-lane road just 70 feet away goes silent, and the colored lights of the restaurant blur. I struggle to move. My knees scrape along the rough black tarmac. Unable to take a breath in, I reach for the rear bumper. I throw my back against the hard steel beam. Instantly a chunk of hamburger that had been lodged in my throat is released.

Fresh cool air enters my lungs, and the *vroom vroom*, rumble of cars rushing past registers in my conscious mind. The flicker of colored lights reappears as scavenger birds strut across the dark parking lot beside me, eating scraps of food left behind.

Taking a deep breath, I stand here — gazing at the stars — listening to the thunder of a jet taking off from the Miramar Marine base just across the road. A smile comes over my heart. After years of racing motorcycles across this great country at speeds well over 170 miles per hour, I am still reveling in the good fortune to have been saved from a catastrophic incident with the endless waves of the Pacific Ocean by the young man. And now, moments ago, I am nearly taken out of the game by something as simple as a hamburger and fries. Joyfully, I find myself filled with gratitude for being in this moment.

Reality Check

Frank Primiano

In the 1980s, Bo Derek was a *ten*, at least physically, according to her publicist and movie studio. I also rated her a ten, but in a land of twelves. Like many of my male Jewish friends, I prefer a woman who is just a little more zaftig, approaching what has been called, *full-figured*, for example: Marilyn Monroe. She had Italian and Jewish seals of approval, among others. At least an eleven physically, Marilyn was, unfortunately, a four as an actor.

Some guys refer to themselves as *ass men*. Others are *leg men*. I'm a *face man*. A turned-up nose, twinkling eyes, and a ready smile get my immediate attention. And if, along with a pretty face, the person is intelligent, talented, articulate, and, as a bonus, deigns to speak to me, then she qualifies as a twelve, even with no other exceptional physical attributes. Yes, that's *cute with a great personality* of blind date fame.

But who am I to criticize *stars* on their appearance, being no great physical specimen myself? I do it by their invitation. They make their living, at least in part, on their looks. How many infants of actresses famous for a legendary decolletage have been weaned on breast milk sucked past silicone? So, to be judged relative to beauty is their choice. Regardless, I know what I like.

The first actress I saw who rated a twelve in my opinion was Grace Kelly. I became aware of her while watching a double feature at a neighborhood, second-run movie theater with my parents. *The African Queen* with Humphrey Bogart and Katherine Hepburn was shown along with *High Noon* starring Gary Cooper and Grace Kelly. I was 13 and enthralled by her.

In the car on our way home from the theater, my mother told me about Grace. She was from Philadelphia. In fact, the home in which she was brought up — in East Falls — was only a mile from our house. We lived in Germantown. Her father was a millionaire and a big man in city politics. Her home was a mansion. Ours was a three-bedroom, semidetached, row house. It wasn't lost on me, even at that age, that we lived in different worlds, economically and socially. Nevertheless, I felt a close connection to her. After all, we were practically neighbors.

Two years after Grace Kelly entered my consciousness, her mother was involved with a fair to raise money for one of her charities, Women's Medical College and Hospital, down the street from her home. Grace, who lived in New York, returned to Philadelphia and participated in her mother's event as the main attraction. I went to the fair to see her in person.

She stood on an elevated stage, in a large tent, out of the sun, selling raffle tickets. Pushing forward to the edge of the stage, I snapped the shutter on my fixed-focus, roll-film, plastic, box camera, hoping there was enough light for a picture. She was more beautiful in person than on screen, on television, or in magazines. My connection to her was now romantic.

I bought a chance for the raffle from her. She looked directly at me, reaching down to personally hand me the ticket, not unlike a priest passing out communion. And in the same manner as such a priest, she wasted no time dwelling on me. Without a pause, she moved on to the next poor schlep who was vying for her attention. In the place of altar boys, a pair of bodyguards stood on either side of her to make sure no one got grabby.

I didn't win whatever the prize was, but the picture turned out.

This occurred about the time Prince Rainier of Monaco began courting her. When I heard that news, I was in disbelief. Why couldn't she wait for me to get older and make my fortune?

But I suspected I'd probably never make enough to

compete with the riches of a prince. And Grace was ten years my senior, which wouldn't change no matter how old I became. Pursuing her would be futile.

Facing this reality, I searched for a new silver-screen twelve. I found one: Catherine Deneuve. However, she appeared long after I outgrew crushes on idealized icons. The tens and twelves who interested me by then were those whom I met in person, and with whom I developed meaningful relationships.

Give Me an Inch

Amy Wall

In terms of pleasure, on a scale of one to ten, ten being the best experience, I rate going to the doctor a one. I'm not a fan of the germ-infested waiting rooms and sitting in them for an hour even though I always arrive thirty minutes early as requested by the office staff. And although doctors try their best to nail a diagnosis, they often get it wrong, like the time my friend sought help for a stomach virus and was sent home with a course of antibiotics for a sinus infection.

I also hate the poking, prodding, and surprise vaccine boosters. Let's just say going to the doctor isn't the kind of adrenaline rush I'm chasing. Consequently, I don't go often and am fortunate, thus far; my body has cooperated, allowing me to skip a few visits over the years.

When I came back to California after living overseas for a decade, I reluctantly decided to check in with the doctor. It had been a while and I needed a doctor to assign me a clean bill of health so the insurance company couldn't claim I had pre-existing conditions.

After the predicted hour in the waiting room, I was called up by the charge nurse. What she was in charge of wasn't clear, except possibly for the interrogation that followed. She wanted to know if I'd ever taken drugs, how much alcohol I drink, and when I had my last period. I'm surprised she didn't ask about my sex life. As if that weren't enough, the interrogator asked me to step on the scale. I told her I would if she did first. She didn't laugh.

The next thing I knew I was on a scale getting my weight and height *accurately* measured. Not wanting to know what my weight was, I conveniently ignored her until I heard her say casually, "5' 7"."

"Did you say 5' 7"?" I asked.

She told me to step back on the scale and placed the metal plate on my head again to double-check. "Yep. 5' 7"," she repeated.

"But I thought I was 5' 6"."

"It shows here you are 5' 7"," she said with a slightly annoyed tone, and she continued with the interrogation, brushing it off as if it were an ordinary number.

What she didn't know was inside the head the metal plate was touching, a seed was planted. It was a seed of paranoia needing only a little imagination to flourish. Imagination is a trait I have in abundance.

It didn't happen right away. I finished the doctor's appointment. While driving home, the seed started to grow into a little sprout.

Isn't 5' 7" the required height of a supermodel? I thought.

I always wanted to be 5' 7". I had a piece of paper that claimed I was, yet I wasn't happy. What was wrong with me?

Besides being middle-aged (which meant I was too old to be a supermodel), what bothered me was being middle-aged, and yet I grew an inch. *Was that normal?* I wondered. *I was seeing a chiropractor. Perhaps his adjustment for my slight scoliosis had straightened me out a bit. But an entire inch seemed a little extreme.*

Maybe I'd spent too much time on my inversion table. When I got home, I browsed the user manual. There were no warnings saying, *Danger! You might find yourself a bit taller after extreme usage.*

As the sprout began growing into a full-sized plant, an image started flashing in my mind. It was the picture in the Guinness Book of World Records of the tallest man who ever lived. You've probably seen him. He's the guy wearing a standard, brown woolen suit about four inches too short. He's standing next to a normal-sized guy who looks like a kid in comparison, except he has a beard, so he probably isn't.

I started to picture myself on this growing journey, like the guy in the brown suit. After all, who says this would stop at 5' 7"? Maybe Giant's Disease starts slowly and then spirals into exponential growth. Maybe at my next doctor's visit I'll be 5' 8". Then after I ignore the annual appointment reminders for a few years, I'll measure myself again and I'll be six feet tall.

I could feel my heart pounding in my chest. *I don't want to be six feet tall,* I thought. *I've reached midlife and I'm used to being mostly medium-sized. Plus, I've been in one of those Big and Tall stores, and I don't like the variety of clothing. I've heard giants die early. And don't their joints hurt from all that growing? I don't want to die early with painful joints.*

The realization hit me. I had to 'fess up to my doctor about my growing an inch. Should I make an appointment for that or should I make up some other kind of ailment and casually mention that I grew a little since the last visit? It would be embarrassing to call for an appointment. I imagined it would go something like this:

"I'd like to book an appointment with my doctor."

"No problem. What is the reason for the appointment?"

"I've grown an inch and I'm in my 40s."

"Sure, I'll make the appointment right away. What time would you like to see the psychologist?"

That wasn't going to work. I thought about my other options. I could Google "growing as an adult" and see what came up. However, Dr. Google always points to cancer of some sort, and I wasn't in the mood to add *that* to my list of worries. I thought about calling the nurse's helpline but didn't want to talk to some stranger about my new and embarrassing disease.

Then it suddenly hit me. I knew exactly who to call — my friend Heather. She recently graduated from nursing school, so all the weird diseases were still fresh in her mind. She could tell me if I needed to rush to the ER.

Heather has been my friend for many years. I met her through her husband, Barry. Twenty years ago, Barry and I dated for a short time, but we went our separate ways. I attended university in San Diego, and he moved to Texas. Years later, we all ended up in San Diego, both of us now

279

married with kids. Our families became friends. It's the only time an *ex* has married someone pretty and smart, and I've been okay with it because I loved Heather from the second I met her. She was a perfect resource in this situation because she knew about my runaway imagination and would be prepared for weird questions about Giant's Disease. I called her immediately.

"Hi, Heather, this is Amy. I have a nursing question to ask you. I went to the doctor yesterday, and they measured me at 5' 7". Trouble is, I've always been 5' 6". Is it normal to grow? I'm a bit worried I have a mild version of Giant's Disease and I'm not sure if I should make another appointment." I spoke quickly while I still had the guts to admit this new development.

A brief period of silence was followed by a small snort of laughter. She kindly explained she'd never heard of anything like it before, but that it probably had to do with all of the yoga, chiropractic care, and perhaps the inversion table.

"If an inch is your only symptom, chances are it isn't anything serious," she explained.

I felt better after talking to Heather. Maybe Big and Tall stores weren't in my future. Perhaps all the good eating, exercise, and self-care helped me defy the aging process for a while. If I only knew this secret, maybe at age 18, (with quite a bit of plastic surgery) *supermodel* could have been on my resume. I gave myself a mental pat on the back for all the good work I was doing, even if it was 25 years late. After we finished our conversation, I called my chiropractor to make another appointment and went about my day.

Two days later, my phone rang. My now gazelle-like legs pranced to the phone to pick it up. It was Barry, Heather's husband. He said Heather told him about me thinking I had Giant's Disease and he had a few words to say about it. I was expecting him to ask about the healthy living I practiced for the past twenty years. He probably felt like he could do with an extra inch. He didn't ask about that.

He simply said, "Amy, you were 5' 7" twenty years ago when we dated. You've always been 5' 7"."

Tomorrow's Gift

Ken Yaros

For most Americans the tenth of October, 1960, would slip past with little notice. Richard Nixon and John Kennedy prepared for their third debate. Fidel Castro tightened his grip on Cuba. Farmers across the country were bringing in the last of their crops. But in our home, near catastrophe would unfold to become a life-changing event for this young man.

The day began innocuously. Mom took an early train from Reading, Pennsylvania, to Atlantic City, New Jersey, to visit my grandparents, who had recently retired. She would return later that night. My brother and I went to school, and Dad, a veterinarian, left for his office. At sixteen, I struggled to adjust to several new eleventh-grade teachers, not a bit interested in academics.

After classes that day, it would be my job to babysit my brother and to cook dinner for the three of us. Since Dad worked twelve-hour days, he wouldn't have time to prepare our evening meal. He preferred meat and potatoes for supper, so I broiled two large steaks, whipped up some instant mashed potatoes with lots of butter, heated a can of Spaghetti O's for my young brother, and brought out chocolate filled doughnuts for dessert, making sure Dad had an extra to take with. We ate hastily. The steaks took longer to cook than I expected. Dad had to hurry back to work.

Dad returned home later than usual that night and saw to it that my brother was put to bed. Soon after, he mentioned that he was tired and wanted to turn in early. Mom would be taking a taxi home from the train station around eleven thirty. Dad reminded me to be sure to leave the front porch light on for her.

Much later that night I heard the bathroom door close a number of times but I thought little of it.

The next morning when I woke for school, I was surprised to see my parents' bedroom door ajar, their room empty, their beds unmade. I found a note from my mother on the kitchen table, explaining they had gone out. She directed me to stay home and to keep my younger brother there as well. Mom wrote she would call later with instructions. But she never did.

They returned shortly before noon. I watched them walk slowly up the path to the house. Something appeared off. Mom's hair looked disheveled. I couldn't figure what had happened. Dad held on to Mom's waist all the way to the door. I opened it for them. For a few moments they stood in our foyer arm in arm.

"Your dad had a heart attack last night, and he doesn't want to go to the hospital right now," Mom said.

When I looked at him, his lips were bluish, and he was breathing heavy.

"Kenny," Mom said, "we were at Dr. Farber's office. Walk Dad over to the sofa. I'll pack a bag for him and maybe you can drive him to the office. He wants to take care of Tiny, Mrs. Bork's Chihuahua, before he checks in at the hospital. Talk about stubborn men. Your father takes the cake." It was then I noticed Mom's eyes looked bloodshot, like maybe she had been crying.

Dad smiled at me. "Everything will be okay," he murmured, then winked. "I promised Mrs. Bork."

I looked at him, surprised how frail he'd become. He was only forty-two years old, active, at the apex of his career. Just a week ago he and I were lassoing two-thousand-pound bulls to vaccinate them for the state. But I wasn't sure at that moment if I would be able to get him back into the car. He looked so tired.

Right before we left the house, Dr. Farber called to ask why the hell Dad wasn't at the hospital yet. Mom told him we'd have Dad there in an hour and then hung up.

After we made a brief stop at Dad's animal clinic, I drove

us to the entrance of the hospital. Dr. Farber and two orderlies brought a wheelchair, helped Dad into it, and fitted him with an oxygen mask. As they wheeled him in, he slumped. It hit me that Dad, despite his brave demeanor, might not survive.

Within the hour he was in bed in a private room in cardiac care. Mom took one look around and started complaining. She informed the nurses Dad was not going to stay there in that dirty room even one day. "If his heart doesn't kill him, the filth will!"

She was assured someone would clean it right away, but no one came. An hour later I returned to our animal hospital to pick up towels and disinfectant. Mom got on her hands and knees and wiped down the bottom of his bed, all the baseboards, and the air handler which was under the window next to his bed. In thirty minutes she had removed enough dirt to blacken three large towels. Later, Mom stopped at the nurses station and had words with the supervisor.

Every hour that afternoon Dad had his blood pressure taken, blood drawn, and an EKG. An oxygen mask remained over his nose and mouth, and an IV drip stayed attached to his wrist. Later that afternoon, Dr. Farber returned to see Dad. We plied him with questions. He said it was too soon to be sure of anything, but they would keep Dad comfortable in the meantime.

Hours turned into days. Days turned into six weeks. Much of that time Dad lay sedated. He lost over twenty pounds and all his tan. Dr. Farber concluded that Dad suffered a widow-maker's blockage and informed us that many so afflicted don't survive. Later I found out the truth of his attack, that over 25 percent of his heart muscle died that day and his heart would have to learn how to beat a new way if he was to thrive.

During his illness, some things got worse. Nearly everything that Dad had to do was now up to me. Shopping for food, returning messages, securing the clinic, fixing our cars, running Mom back and forth to the hospital, and more. All the while attending high school. For days on end it seemed he wasn't getting better. In fact, he grew weaker. As fall headed toward winter, our lives took an increasingly somber path.

Tempers wore thin. At least once a day someone wound up crying. The house was deathly quiet at night without him. If the phone rang, we would jump. Unpaid bills piled up in the kitchen. I felt guilty my cooking that night made Dad sick.

Then Mom received a special delivery letter from our health insurance company. Seems that we had a cancellable policy. Dad's heart attack had put him in a high-risk category. They gave us a 30-day notice that we were being dropped. Mom cautioned me not to tell Dad about it, but I saw she was upset.

Toward the end of his hospital stay Dad had to be helped into a wheelchair to go to the bathroom. Although he struggled to walk, we looked forward to having him home. At the same time we wondered how we would get him up our steep staircase. Dad started to do exercises in his hospital bed, and he did regain a bit of strength. Nearly every time I visited him he asked me about school. I just looked down.

Finally, Dr. Farber released him to go home. It took nearly a half hour to help Dad into our house and up the stairs. He remained home for two months while he exercised to regain his strength. Mother completely changed our diets to low fat. Within two weeks he was able to go upstairs without holding on to the banister. I remember a sunny day in early December when he sat on our porch all bundled up, and I thought how lucky we were just to have him home again. By February he had recovered enough to resume his practice two hours a day.

The Saturday before he started back to work, Mom put a one-inch notice in the weekend edition of the *Reading Eagle Times* newspaper, stating his return to practice along with his new evening office hours. Sunday morning Dad said the announcement was too small for anyone to see. Mom said, "It's fine. Tomorrow you'll know what our future will be."

I drove him to the animal clinic that Monday evening. Dad kept silent during the trip while he tapped his fingers on the armrest. Mom gave strict instructions for me to bring him home if he looked tired. To my surprise, over a dozen clients stood patiently in line waiting for us to unlock the door. When we approached, a cheer rang out. Dad teared up. I had little idea how much he was appreciated. Most of the patrons were Greek, which was funny because many neighbors insisted we had to be Greek, even though Dad denied it for years. God bless the Greek community. They helped give Dad confidence that night that the worst was truly behind him.

Dad couldn't drive until his doctor cleared him in May of 1961. As we left Dr. Farber's office, Dad asked me for the keys to the Ford wagon. It had been a long six months for all of us. I gladly handed them over. Dad turned to give me the biggest hug of my life.

As with any tragedy, there can be good things to come of it. Dad, who was a heavy smoker for twenty years, never picked up another cigarette. Mom got back into driving, which greatly helped our family. I learned what it meant to have real responsibilities. Dad, through his actions, taught me I had to fight hard for what I wanted. He never gave up. I buckled down in high school, proving I could become an honor-roll student, something I continued with until graduation. Happily, Dad went back to his profession full-time for another twenty-six years.

Tiny, who lived next door to the clinic, delivered a litter of four puppies shortly after Dad came home from the hospital. The Borks presented Dad with Penny, the runt of the litter. The cuddly and shy, long-haired, blond Chihuahua became the mascot and good will ambassador of the Animal Clinic of Reading for well over a decade.

Middle-Aged Business

Nico Waters

Someone knocked at my door at 3:10 on a spring afternoon while I was having a second lunch. I put down the sandwich, got up from my red couch, and answered the door.

"Can I help you?" I asked.

A middle-aged guy on the other side of the door greeted me with a smile. He wore a black polo with a spring-weather jacket, both branded with a red and white logo on the right side of his chest.

The guy waved, and a silver wedding band glinted in the light. "Hi, I'm Steve from Middle-Aged Business."

"Interesting company name." I kept my door slightly ajar, the way I did for solicitors or the nosy neighbor from unit 6F down the hall.

He asked, "Are you Lisa?" I nodded, then he glanced down at an iPad, which he held in front of a roundish belly. "Looks like you're forty-one." He beamed as he added, "And you're expecting."

I coughed, choking a little on the bite of food that I hadn't fully swallowed yet. "How did you know that?" Only my husband knew that I was pregnant. It was early in the process, maybe a week or so, though I had the hunger of someone farther along.

Instead of answering my question, the guy asked, "Are you taking prenatal vitamins?" His brow wrinkled with concern. "It's really important, especially with your age. You're considered high risk."

"Yeah, I know. Apparently, it's called a geriatric pregnancy. Is that what you're selling? Prenatal vitamins? And dentures?" I frowned at my bad joke. "No, seriously.

286

What are you selling? My grilled cheese is getting cold."

"We provide assistance for people. Help them navigate the uncertainties of life." He held out a business card, which seemed to appear out of nowhere. Maybe they were tucked inside his jacket sleeve like a magic trick.

I took the card and read it. Steve. Middle-Aged Business. Just like his shirt. "Shouldn't you be knocking on doors for people who are older than me? Like fifty-something?" People my age didn't need a warranty. Wasn't 41 the new 31, or something like that? "My life is going fine," I said.

Steve's voice lifted with enthusiasm. "Great. Let's keep it that way. Our preventative maintenance plan has tips and tricks to help you better anticipate life's challenges. And with the warranty, you can call on someone like me for emotional support as needed. Our customers say it gives them peace of mind."

"My mind is at peace." Or so it seemed before I opened the door.

Sure, I was pregnant at 41, which had some risks. But I was young and strong. Physically. Mentally. And I had lots of years ahead, hopefully. Crazy-life things wouldn't hit me all at once anyway. It would get spaced out over the years. I could handle it as it came. No, I didn't need a preventative maintenance package from Middle-Aged Business.

"Excuse me, but how did you find me?" I asked.

"An anonymous referral. Our business mainly runs on them. Someone who cares told us about you." He tapped his iPad. "And then number-crunchy things like algorithms, data, and statistics generate your profile."

"Was it my husband?" I prodded, still wanting to know who referred me.

Steve tilted his head but held a poker face. "The person wants to stay anonymous, and it's company policy that I honor their wishes."

"Thanks for stopping by. But you can tell my husband," I emphasized, "that I'm okay."

When Steve chuckled, I wondered if I'd guessed wrong about the anonymous person's identity after all. He said, "If you change your mind, our info is on the card. Life is tricky. It's good to have a warranty in place." The sincerity in his eyes made me pause.

I glanced down at the card again. "I'll check out the website, and I'll call you if I'm interested. Goodbye," I said as nicely as possible, then I shut the door and locked the deadbolt.

* * *

A week later, I watched Family Feud while cradling a throw pillow on my red couch. I needed cheering up after crying so much the last few days. Host Steve Harvey, the hilarious survey questions and answers helped.

The doorbell rang, and I jumped. I wasn't expecting anyone, and my husband had left for the store. I went to the peephole, looked through, and saw Steve from Middle-Aged Business. Same black jacket, polo shirt, and iPad. Hadn't I told him I'd follow up if I were interested?

Not in the mood for a soliciting repeat, I sighed. Unfortunately, it was so loud that he probably heard from the other side of the door. I opened it out of guilt.

Steve waved hello, his silver wedding band glinting in the light. With a measured smile, he said, "Hi, Lisa, it's Steve from—"

"—I remember. Sorry, I haven't had the chance to look at your website. I've been … busy." I glanced down at my slippers.

When my gaze trailed back to Steve, I recognized the seriousness and sincerity from his first impromptu visit. It resonated. Everything had resonated the last several days. My hormones were going nuts, nose-diving like a seagull toward the ocean.

A tear dropped from my eye, surprising me.

Steve opened his arms. "C'mere." When I hesitated, he said, "Come on," and waved me toward him. He respected my space and didn't move my way.

I appreciated that, but I couldn't hug him. I was a married

woman. This guy was a perfect stranger.

But it seemed like he knew what had happened to me, just like he knew I'd been pregnant the last time I'd seen him.

More tears dropped from my eyes. I couldn't control it.

I inched toward him, and he wrapped his arms around me. "There, there," he said.

He was taller than I realized, resting his chin on the top of my head. My uncles hugged me like this, and my big brother. The familiar, safe feeling gave me permission to cry more.

Steve said, "It happened to my wife about ten years ago, the first time we got pregnant. She was a few weeks along. It was hard. I'm sorry you have to go through this."

I wiped my face and slowly pulled away from him. "How come nobody talks about it? I'm finding out from people who went through the same thing, but I wouldn't know unless I told them what happened to me."

Steve slid his hands in his pockets. "I don't know why nobody talks about it."

"How did you know to come today?"

"Customer service is important in my line of business."

Was that an answer to my question? It didn't seem like it.

"Was it my husband?" I asked. "Is he the anonymous referral?"

With tight lips, Steve shrugged his shoulders. He wasn't going to spill the beans.

I recalled what he'd had said before about the plans and warranties at Middle-Aged Business, the tips and tricks to anticipate life's challenges, the emotional support. Could I have anticipated what had happened to me this past week? Maybe I hadn't wanted to. Maybe I'd wanted to ignore the what-ifs and bad statistics. I'd hoped to be the exception. But everyone did, didn't they?

Sounds blared from the television, distracting me from my thoughts. Ringing bells, loud music, and excited screams. The Johnsons won Fast Money on Family Feud. They were $20,000 richer now. And as Steve Harvey liked to put it, "They were drivin' outta here in a brand-new car."

The Johnsons were the exception. They had faced the

289

challenges of the game and won. Knowing that made me smile. Good for them.

* * *

Two years passed. My husband and I were unable to get pregnant again. I also never saw Steve.

Until I heard his voice while perusing the high-heels aisle of DSW.

I usually veered away from that area of the store. My toes had screamed like a banshee the last time I'd worn stilettos. And my left arch stung as if I'd walked on broken glass.

But today, I'd ended up in the forbidden aisle. Two twenty-somethings had caught my attention. They'd giggled at each other—youthful, joyous, animated giggles. One girl tried on a red pair of heels with a black velvet bow. The other girl strutted in a hot pink pair.

Their carefree spirits captivated me. I was like that once, ten years ago or more. I'd go shoe-shopping with girlfriends, try on sexy shoes, and talk about guys.

Now, my girlfriends and I were all married. They had kids and were busy with playdates, birthday parties, soccer games, and dance recitals. And I ... well ...

I glanced away from the twenty-somethings, scanned the row of shoes, and locked in on a pair of gold, open-toed heels. Ornate, embroidered design. Four- or five-inch heels. These things were beautiful.

I set down the box of low-heel wedge sandals I planned to buy and grabbed one of the gold shoes.

"Lisa?"

I turned to see a man at the end of the aisle. He had a kind smile and eyes and a receding hairline.

"Lisa, it's—"

"—Steve," I said, grinning back at him. I couldn't forget the man who'd comforted me two years ago. "I almost didn't recognize you without the work shirt and jacket." Today, he wore a windbreaker with no logo and a pair of jeans.

He pointed at the gold heel in my hand. "Now, *that's* a

cool shoe."

A sheepish smile crossed my face. "I really shouldn't be looking at these."

"Why not?"

"I can't wear shoes like this anymore. They hurt my feet."

"Ah. But it's okay to look, right?"

"Yeah. Sure." I turned the shoe in my hand. "I miss being able to wear shoes like these. I miss having a reason to wear shoes like these."

Steve said, "Priorities change. Life changes." That seemed like such a practical thing to say, a perfect segue to pitching Middle-Aged Business.

"I still haven't looked at your website," I admitted, feeling a bit guilty.

Steve put his hands up. "Take your time. I wasn't here to sell anything. Just wanted to say hi." He waved, the light shining against his silver wedding band, and he walked away.

I mulled over what he'd said about priorities and life, and I frowned. Maybe I didn't want things to change. Maybe I wanted life to stay the same or as close to it as possible—a combination of 43-year-old me and 25-year-old me.

I grabbed the other gold shoe, tried them on, and glanced at them in a tiny mirror attached to a bench.

"You should totally get those," one of the twenty-somethings said to me.

"Totally," the other agreed.

I didn't even realize they were paying attention. Now, I had to get the shoes, didn't I?

An hour later, I stood in front of a full-length mirror at home, wearing the gold shoes. My toes hurt, my arch burned, and I hadn't even walked a lap in my apartment.

What was wrong with me? Why did I buy these shoes?

Next thing you know, I'd be trading in my Nissan Rogue SUV for a little red corvette. Or replacing my Gap joggers for miniskirts from Forever 21.

I went to my computer and typed in the URL for Middle-Aged Business as if it would have the answer to my impulse-buy at DSW. I glimpsed the plans offered. Short-term, long-term, and lifetime plans. Plans for physical and mental health, the expected and unexpected of life. My eyes spun at the details, but I knew Steve could help explain it all.

I picked up the phone and called the main number.

A woman answered the phone. "Middle-Aged Business. Can I help you?"

Her question sent my nerves into a jumble. My breath rattled, and my knee bounced.

Did I want to sign up for a plan? It implied that I was ready for this new phase of life. But was I?

"Hello? Can I help you?"

I swallowed then said, "Hi, may I speak to Steve?"

"Steve Douglas?"

I didn't remember his last name. And I was too lazy to figure out what I did with the business card he'd given me two years ago. "I'm not sure. He came to my house a couple of times. Door-to-door sales."

"Oh, that's Steve Douglas. Unfortunately, he's no longer with the company."

Taken aback, I blinked a couple of times before speaking. "Yeah, but I saw him. At DSW. Today. He didn't say anything about leaving the company."

"Sorry to throw you off with that news." The woman sounded sincere, giving me a moment to digest the blow. "If you want, I can connect you with Earl. He's—"

"—I don't want Earl," I said as if I knew the guy. "I want to talk to Steve. It has to be Steve." I was finally ready to talk about the warranties at Middle-Aged Business, and I didn't want to do it with anyone else.

The woman sighed. "He was a tough loss for the company. Everybody loved him. Co-workers. Customers. We called him Uncle Steve."

"I get it," I said. "Totally."

* * *

A couple of years later, Steve rang the doorbell at my new house. He looked different. So did I. His hairline had receded

292

enough to be considered bald. And I had cellulite on my butt and an ice pack strapped to my knee.

He gazed down at my leg. "Lisa, what happened?"

"Oh," I said with an oh-silly-me chuckle. "I tweaked it while moving boxes."

"Was that recently, or ..."

I scratched my temple. "A couple of months ago, I think. Or maybe four." Changing the subject, I pointed at his black jacket with the red and white logo. "I see you're back at Middle-Aged Business. I called the day I saw you at DSW, and they said you weren't working with them anymore."

Steve shifted on his feet. "Yeah. They laid me off."

"Oh." The lady on the phone hadn't mentioned that part.

"Too expensive to keep me on, I guess. You can get someone half my age to do the same thing."

My throat pinched. I never used to think about that happening to me, but I had been lately. Especially when my department at work was bursting with newly hired Gen-Z'ers.

Steve said, "It all worked out in the end. They had too much turnover, so they called me back."

"Good for you," I said.

"So ... new place, huh? It's great." He stepped back to gaze at my modest Cape-Cod-style house and perennial flowers in the front yard. "Nice to get out of the apartment, right?"

"Absolutely. Plus, we needed the space."

Steve's gaze trailed away to something behind me. I turned around to see my dad walking by with his robe swinging open, no shirt, and Hanes briefs. Oops.

"Sorry about that," I said, inching the door closer to block the view of my dad. "He's the reason we got a bigger place."

Steve's gaze softened. "How's that going?"

"It's going." I folded my arms, almost hugging myself. "He started noticing memory issues several years ago. Little things. Then it got worse. My husband and I couldn't afford assisted living. Getting this place gave us more space, and we have help come once a week."

Steve glanced at the ice pack on my knee. "Don't forget to

take care of yourself, too, huh?"

I nodded. If it got worse, I'd get to the doctor. "I looked at your website a while ago."

"That's great. Did you have any questions?" He tapped something on his iPad, his silver wedding band picking up flecks of the sun.

"Yeah, I—"

Glass shattered from another room, and my dad yelled an expletive.

"Crap," I said, glancing behind me. I turned back to Steve. "Sorry, I gotta go."

* * *

Steve stopped by my place two years later. I was outside trimming overgrown leaves on a tree thanks to recent rainstorms.

I did a double take when I saw Steve. He'd lost weight. He wore a sleek fleece pullover instead of the frumpy jacket. And he'd trimmed his hair down to a low, flattering cut. He had the same kind eyes and genuine smile, though.

Waving, he walked up the driveway toward me. "How have you been, Lisa?"

"Not as good as you." I sized him up. "You had a makeover. Are they selling those at Middle-Aged Business? Or did they find the Fountain of Youth?"

He arched a brow, a crooked grin crossing his lips.

"Sign me up, Steve. My knee is killing me. My hair is grayer than ever. And I'm prediabetic."

He searched my face, his smile fading. Then, he tapped some things on his iPad. Watching his movements, I realized that something was missing. I glanced at his ring finger. The silver shiny wedding band was gone.

"Steve, what happened to your ring?"

He stopped typing and gazed down at his bare finger. Color drained from his face. "My wife and I got divorced. About eighteen months and three weeks ago. Not that I'm counting."

294

My heart broke. I set my garden tool down on the grass and opened my arms. "C'mere."

"She said I was letting myself go and that we didn't have anything in common anymore. She found someone else, I guess."

I waved Steve toward me. He inched forward, and we hugged for a bit until he sighed and let go.

He sniffed and wiped his nose. "Thanks for that," he muttered.

I patted his shoulder. "I owed you."

"Nah, you didn't owe me anything."

"A lot has happened since I first met you, huh?" I asked. "For both of us."

He nodded. "I wish I got myself in better shape when Dana and I were still together."

Since I didn't know the particulars of their situation, I said, "It's still good to be healthy. You really do look great."

"Thanks."

"How did you do it?"

"I signed up for the lifetime warranty at my company. Before that, I'd only been doing one-off monthly plans. But now I'm covered for everything. Physical health. Mental health. Finances. Preventative maintenance. Emotional support. All of it." He scratched the back of his head. "After seeing the stuff my customers go through every day, you'd think I would've gotten a warranty for myself years ago. I guess I thought I was the exception. Lesson learned."

The last several words pierced a tender spot in me, and goosebumps freckled my skin.

He said, "Things aren't perfect now, but my outlook and quality of life have improved."

I brushed my chin then glanced at his iPad. "Can you explain the lifetime warranty?"

"Sure."

I nodded toward the house. "Let's go inside. I'm pretty sure my dad has his pants on today."

Steve followed me up the driveway, and I opened the front door. Inside, my father sat in the living room wearing tuxedo pants, a mock-neck sweater, and a faraway look in his eyes.

"Hey, Dad," I announced, reminding him who I was.

The color in his cheeks and eyes brightened as he said, "Hi, Sweetheart." And before I could introduce our guest, he added, "Hi, Steve."

I turned to Steve, my dad, and back again. "Wait, how does he know ..." I gasped and led Steve toward the next room.

My hunch made sense. The timing of Steve's first visit and when Dad's memory issues began. He'd admitted that he felt so caught off-guard at the time—unprepared, angry, distraught, and afraid.

I glanced up at Steve now and whispered, "Was it my dad who reached out to you? Is he my anonymous referral?"

Steve's mouth twitched. A glimmer sparkled in his eyes, recognition and respect. "The person wants to stay anonymous, and it's company policy that I honor their wishes." He tapped a button on the iPad, and the screen came to life. "Want to go over the warranty?" he asked.

"Yes," I said. "I'm ready to sign up."

Persona

Nick Di Carlo

When I was ten years old I decided that I'd look better with my mask on.

Seeking refuge from a world suddenly unrecognizable and feeling uncomfortable in my own young, thin skin, I made my first mask from a large shimmering silver sheet of Reynolds Wrap®. I hoped that when people looked at me, they'd see their own images reflected softly back to them. I thought, *Maybe people will like me better, think I'm not an oddball, an alien, ugly – that I'm not all bad – if they look at me and see themselves.*

That happened decades ago. I guess I have to consider myself an old man now. AARP and senior discounts and earlobes that almost reach my creaky knees define me. People often address me as *sir*, and sometimes they hold doors open for me as if I'm too feeble to open them myself. But the memories remain vivid, the narcissistic wounds remain fresh. Unexpectedly, even now, I flash back to those times. Some glitch in my brain throws me back into the thick of all that mess. When that happens, as with all the flashbacks I experience, I snap the rubber band I wear on my wrist and tell myself, "I'm too damned old for this crap." Sometimes that works. When I tell people about this, they fall back on the clichéd advice to *let it go*. They tell me to get over it, it's all in the past—the past is dead. But smarter people than I agree that the past doesn't die, that it's always with us, that we are who we are because of where we've been. I can't let go of my past because the past won't let go of me.

The lens of time has sharpened the image of me sitting cross-legged on my bedroom floor, stabbing eye holes in the foil with my Lone Ranger jackknife. Slightly below those vacancies, I punctured the foil twice more, making holes to breathe through. I did not cut a slit for my mouth. I remembered my grandmother telling me once, *"Tieni gli occhi e le orecchie aperti e la bocca chiusa,"* which means *keep your eyes and ears open, and your mouth shut* — advice I always valued, but often failed to heed. Then, however, I felt no need to speak. I mean, who would listen?

The knife was dull, the mask an ill-fitting mess, but that was okay. That's how everything seemed at the time. I'd been abducted. I'd been cast into a strange land, to live among strangers — plunged into a world that did not fit my image of reality. The experience obliterated my perception of the person I believed I had been.

I felt as if the people I trusted had relegated me to the junk bin, like the stuffed toy bear, its button eyes ripped off, the Tonka truck with a missing wheel, or the doll that some small girl's bully brother tore the legs from. The world seemed a broken, senseless mess, and when my reality shattered around me, I was broken, too.

Sure — that all sounds so melodramatic now. But I was ten and just starting to feel comfortable with myself, in myself. I defined myself by my home, family, friends, my abilities and achievements — even by my nearsightedness and inability to judge a fly ball. Perhaps I was a more tender soul than other ten year olds, but the sudden shift I experienced felt seismic, cataclysmic.

* * *

One month earlier, on a September Saturday afternoon, my mother, Magdalena, dragged me out of the house and into one of those upstate New York thunderstorms where the sky looms heavy as a granite slab, the lightning-charged air smells like copper, and raindrops as big and hard as fists batter you.

She and I lived with her parents who took us in when I was little more than a year old. On that Saturday afternoon, I had been stretched out on the living room floor, watching the

Saturday shows—*My Friend Flicka, Sky King, Rin Tin Tin*—on Grandpa's DuMont television. Kitchen aromas wafted through the house as my grandfather chopped basil and oregano, sautéed onions, peppers, and garlic. I could hear the hot olive oil sizzle as Grandpa fried meatballs and sausage, and braised beef that he would add to the tomato sauce that had been simmering on the stove since dawn. I heard my grandmother's mezzo soprano softly wishing away the rain, *"Pioggia, pioggia vai via,"* while working her rolling pin back and forth over the pasta dough and cutting the dough into strips for Sunday's fettuccine that my uncles and aunts, my grandparents' friends, and I would feast upon.

"Rain, rain, go away, Grandma," I called to her.

"*Si*, Salvatore," she said. "*Si, filio mio.*"

That's when my mother came into the living room, wearing a raincoat, a transparent plastic kerchief with a red and blue flower design, and her rubber rain boots. She had put on makeup, and a bit too much perfume. She stood over me, holding my jacket like a dark cloud in front of my face. "Put this on," she said.

"Why?"

"You're coming with me."

"Where?"

"Some place. You'll find out."

"But it's raining."

"Don't make me mad. Put your coat on."

* * *

Outside, the wind tormented us—one minute a scourge, the next instant a bludgeon. With heads bowed into the wind, we pushed forward over the bridge near the mica insulator factory. A gust ripped my mother's umbrella from her hand. For a few seconds, wind currents tossed the umbrella about over the cavern below us then sent it crashing into the abyss. Still, my mother, more relentless than I'd ever seen her, dragged me onward through ankle deep puddles and small streams that flooded gutters and rushed to the storm drains.

She pulled me by my arm, up one familiar street and down another toward Armando's Market, the small neighborhood grocery where we shopped. But we didn't go to Armando's. We went to the barroom across the street.

Although I'd walked to Armando's many times, and many more times I'd passed that bar on my way to catechism or to Sunday Mass, I paid little attention to it. Except for the green neon sign in the window, I never gave it a thought. I never imagined going inside.

My mother pulled open the barroom door and nudged me forward. When I resisted, my mother pushed me through the doorway, into an alien atmosphere, tinged yellow from dusty incandescent ceiling lamps, and thick with the stench of rancid beer, stale cigarette smoke, and urinal cakes. Once inside, my glasses fogged, and in my momentary blindness my mother shoved once more, propelling me at the strange, slouch-shouldered man who sat on a bar stool, staring into his glass of beer.

"Say hello to your father," she said, before kissing him for a long time on the mouth.

* * *

In the blink of an eye, we had gone to live with the strange man—the man who had abandoned us when I was an infant. His name was Erasmo, and he looked like an anemic owl perched on that barstool, with his pale complexion, stooped shoulders, and his round, wire-rimmed eyeglasses.

The church did not allow divorce, so my parents had been legally separated for nearly a decade before they mysteriously reconciled after years of animosity and removed me from my grandparents' big, clean house. They whisked me out of the city, and carted me off to a suburban neighborhood where we rented a small, shabby house with weathered faux brick siding, a dirt driveway, and no sidewalk alongside—a house quite out of place among the neighboring pristine homes painted bright white, with gaily painted shutters and flower boxes framing the windows—homes surrounded by

300

sculptured shrubbery, fragrant gardens, and manicured lawns.

I transferred to a different school — fourth grade — where they were writing cursive and doing long division. At my old school, we still printed, and were still only adding and subtracting.

Struggling to learn long division, I listened with oversized ears I feared I'd never grow into. I stared at the workbook problems through Coke-bottle-thick glasses, feeling — and looking, I supposed — like Mr. Potato Head. My brain might as well have been a potato as I listened to the teacher drone on about divisors, dividends, quotients, and decimal points — speaking in tongues for all I knew. Other students nodded reverently, bowed their heads to their workbooks, and scribbled diligently in those books, heeding the teacher's command to show their work. I didn't have a clue how to do the work — and it showed.

Then I discovered that the back pages of my workbook had the answers to all the problems. I guess we were expected to use them only to check our solved problems. But, I figured, what good are the answers if your problems are already solved? So, unable to solve a single problem, I started sneaking peeks at the answer pages.

One day, the teacher had to leave the room. She told us which problems she wanted us to solve. She anointed Linda Fabiano as class monitor.

Perplexed by each problem on the page, and feeling powerless to solve any problem — in or out of my workbook — I repeatedly turned to the answer pages and copied the numbers into my workbook.

As soon as the teacher returned to the room, I saw Linda Fabiano's hand shoot skyward.

"Yes, Linda," the teacher said.

Linda skipped to the teacher's desk and whispered. Linda grinned at me.

"Come up here, young man," the teacher said. "And bring your workbook."

The teacher, red-faced and self-righteous, tore all the

answer pages from my workbook, ripped them to pieces, and threw the scraps into her trash bin. My face went purple, my ears burned, my heart pounded. I needed to hide, but where could I go? I stood, as if shackled, a prisoner in a strange land where strangers spoke a language I did not understand but was expected to know and punished for not knowing. If I could have been anybody else …

That night the teacher phoned and informed my mother that I was a cheater. My mother informed the strange, slouching man that I'd been caught cheating. Then the slouching stranger whom I'd seen for the first time on a stormy September Saturday as he slumped over a beer glass in the barroom's jaundiced and fetid atmosphere—the man I did not know, but was commanded to love immediately, unconditionally—finally that man stood erect and shouted, his spittle, like pin pricks, striking my face, "You're a cheater. You're disgusting." He raved on about how I never learned that from him and how my grandparents must have raised me wrong. "Get out of my sight," he said.

I turned toward the kitchen, walked to the pantry, pulled the Reynolds Wrap® box from the kitchen pantry, and I tore a large sheet of foil from it. I climbed the dark stairway to my bedroom. I opened my knife. I made my mask.

* * *

Why have I flashed back to this now? I can't cite one specific thing that triggers these episodes. Almost anything might bring one on. After so many decades, I'm amazed at which events remain fresh in memory, which wounds persist unhealed, festering. It may seem a small humiliation, standing by the teacher's desk as she, red-faced and self-righteous, tore my workbook and my ego to shreds. I guess the impact was exacerbated by accompanying events—being ripped from the security of my grandparents' home, my guilt over my unjustified anger that, allowing my abduction, my grandmother had betrayed me, my father's unrealistic demands for immediate loyalty and unconditional love after he had abandoned my mother and me when I was an infant.

* * *

By the time I was twelve, my father abandoned us for the second time. In those two years, we spent nearly every weekend night in that bar, lingering until closing time. It's where we spent Sunday evenings as well after my father made us sit and watch him bowl during the afternoons.

Before he left, my father had emptied my savings account of every penny of child support he had paid for nearly nine years. It might seem petty to say, but I figured if he couldn't extract devotion from me he'd settle for cash.

Still, I rejoiced when the slouching, owl-faced man was gone, relieved that this time, the Catholic Church be damned, a divorce made his absence final, absolute. Hallelujah and amen.

My celebration was short lived, however. After he'd gone, my mother and I moved several times. His leaving devastated my mother, a woman who'd lived her entire life on the knife edge of madness. From then on, she lived a life I would charitably call profligate, bringing home one strange man after another, each one a barroom buzzard that hungrily swooped in to feed on my mother's dead soul.

I detested those men and made no secret of it. One evening when I came home from basketball practice, I walked in on my mother and her latest companion embracing on our sofa.

The man looked up, stared at me for a few seconds, and turned to my mother, saying, "Do you see that?" He pointed at me. "Your son would kill me if he could."

Eventually, my mother left, too. I returned home from school one day to find her gone. At least she left a note explaining: "Leroy thinks he killed Ted Stone. He's running from the cops. Me too. Love, your mother."

* * *

My grandparents took me in. I finished high school, enlisted in the Army, survived two tours in Vietnam, and went to college on the GI Bill. I deluded myself into thinking I had got on with my life, doing what I should do, and being a normal, productive adult. I had grasped and appreciated the irony of being called a cheat by the man who cheated on my mother at least twice and believed that to be a sign of emotional growth.

Years later, while attending a cousin's wedding with my second wife, Margaux, I saw my mother again. I put on my best face and behaved civilly toward her, pretending, of course, that bygones were — well — gone.

During her absence, she never contacted me, and I had no idea she had returned. But when she did return from her adventures with the fugitive, she was welcomed by and had become a favorite among my younger cousins who apparently thought me heartless for bearing any animus or indifference toward the woman who'd given birth to me.

On the drive home after the reception, my wife told me that my mother had cornered her to explain why she'd behaved as she did.

"What was her excuse?" I asked.

"I want to get the words right," my wife said. She paused briefly. "Here's exactly what she told me: 'I had my reasons.'"

"Well," I said. "I am appeased."

* * *

In recent years, I've met many older adults who claimed that the appearance of long-absent or unknown fathers into their lives had been a joyous event that made them feel complete. I could only shake my head in disbelief. In the years between my infancy and dear Dad's return, I never missed him, never regretted not having a father — didn't even give it a thought, never felt disadvantaged by his absence. I thought my life was pretty darned good. It was his sudden reappearance that rendered my life empty and meaningless. Making his acquaintance convinced me to have no children of my own, effectively, I hoped, cutting off his bloodline. It was not a completely vengeful act, but a cautionary one taken out of fear that I would fail horrifyingly as a parent.

Eventually I realized that my hastily carved foil mask was not the first I'd worn. I had, after all, lived the pretense of loving the slouch-shouldered stranger — even before I left my grandparents' house. On the day I moved out, although it was only the second time I had seen my father, I knew I had to demonstrate my loyalty to him, and in my childish mind that meant signaling that I'd cut the bonds I had with my grandparents. I achieved this by manufacturing an argument with my grandmother — an act for which I still feel ashamed. So, behind the façade of the loyal and dutiful son, the adoring child, I hid my resentment for and fear of the man.

It would be pretty to say that donning masks was a childish thing that I abandoned once my father left, or even as I became an adult who did the usual adult things. Truth is, I never outgrew the practice, never discovered a permanent and persevering persona. Over and again, I assumed whatever guise I believed an occasion demanded or a person desired. It's no secret: that trick never works. You can ask my two ex-wives and all my long-gone lovers who will still ask about me, "Who was that masked man?"

In these days of my dotage, I guess I'm alert enough to admit that by my lifelong adoption of various personae I had perpetrated one fiction after another. Each morning I'd wake, stare into the mirror as I shaved, and ask, "Who do I need to be today?" (How odd I never asked, "Who do you want to be today?") When leaving the house each day I'd say, "Let's get on with the show." I returned each night exhausted, worn down by the perpetual pretense. Of course I couldn't admit that I was pretending. I considered myself adaptable, not duplicitous or insincere. I didn't realize how exhausted I was until I retired, or what a shell of a man I'd become until one day I looked in the mirror and asked the unfamiliar and blank face that stared back, "Who in hell are you?" I received no response.

Wearing masks has kept me disconnected, perpetually

305

inaccessible to and alienated from all others as well as myself. Each mask proved an ineffective barrier between me and life's dangers — real or perceived. When I hid behind masks the only barriers they created were between me and the people or things I deeply desired and truly needed.

I carried my anger for a long time, and did everything possible to repress it, to hide it, even from myself. I couldn't. These days, while I haven't forgotten, and can't quite forgive them, I'm past blaming my parents for my life. Although I could attribute my sense of brokenness to bad genes and bad parenting, I could also claim some bad decisions and bad luck as well. So, maybe now I've got this all out of my system. Maybe not. I mean, I've experienced no epiphany, no visitation from the Holy Ghost, no image of a deity staring up at me from my oatmeal bowl at breakfast. It's just been a long slog that's led me to an earlier, minor revelation: *I'm too old for this crap.*

The way I figure things, I've got a few good years before I kick the bucket, so despite my previous inability to let the past be the past, despite the flashbacks and regret, why not use the time to get things right, to live a little — unencumbered, footloose, and fancy free? Maybe I'll buy an RV, hit the open road, and find myself. Maybe I'll get married again. Folks say the third time is the charm.

The Wonders of Mother Nature

Dora Klinova

Alaska! For ten years I dreamed about the cruise to Alaska and finally it happened. Our Golden Princess was passing Tracy Arm Fjord. Holding my breath, I watched this Wonder of Mother Nature. The fjord's deep giant well, emerald colored, spoke to us, enriched with endless wisdom, kept for millennia. Its ageless spirit hovered in the air.

Spellbound, I wanted to dive in this well even though it was deadly cold and full of icebergs. To my surprise, I found myself praying to this spirit. Hungering to bring these feelings home, I asked this spirit to penetrate my mind, my soul, my every cell.

I shook my head. "Why I am doing this? What is wrong with me?"

On the ship's radio, the captain told us that people often feel here a strong current of energy. Aha! I was not alone! The ship's crew asked the passengers to express their feelings in a short poem, just one verse, and submit it to a special committee to be read in the theater before the next presentation. Here is my spontaneous admiration to Tracy Arm Fjord, a spiritual awakening place:

You look like a giant well, emerald colored and deep,
Millenia's endless wisdom you continuously keep.
I want to dive in this wisdom, though you are deadly cold.
Your ageless spirit to me is pure gold.
I will come again to Alaska, I know.
This spirit will give me strength to live, to go.
Please, penetrate my every cell, my mind, my soul;
Enrich my life and mind, accomplish my every goal.

The ship's radio invited everybody to the performing theater to hear the best poems, followed by a lecture about Alaskan Nature by Michael Modzelewski. Somebody told me that he recently appeared on the *Oprah Winfrey* show. Eager to hear how other people expressed their feelings, I went to the theater.

The poetical presentation was very short. No, they didn't read my poem.

Then Michael Modzelewski, the lecturer, started to talk. He grabbed my attention immediately when he spoke to the spiritual connection between the wilds of the Alaskan landscape and the human soul. I felt a deep connection with the speaker, his knowledge of the Alaskan wilderness and its beauty was shared with us. It was immediately clear to me that he had a kind heart and great energy for this beautiful place. After the lecture Michael was selling his book. I approached him and told him about my book. Without hesitation, he asked if we could exchange books. I was delighted and flattered.

As we signed our books to each other, a woman came closer and gave Michael something wrapped in a napkin.

He immediately gave his attention to this napkin, unfolded the flaps, and exposed a tiny object.

"What is there?" I asked.

"A hummingbird," Michael said.

"I found it on my cabin's balcony," the woman explained.

"Is it still alive? Don't let it die, please."

Can you imagine? A little exotic hummingbird appeared on the balcony of the Golden Princess cruising around cold Alaska with icebergs in the ocean. This tiny birdie should joyfully fly somewhere in California, surrounded by subtropical flowers, eucalyptus, palms and cacti, bathing in the warm rays of the sun. But here it was, in the cold north. I was astonished that it had survived this long. How, indeed! The wonders of Mother Nature are impossible to explain.

The bird was scared, exhausted, and appeared to be dying. Michael kept the napkin with the shivering birdie that huddled itself up into a fluffy ball trying to get all the warmth

308

from Michael's palms. Michael checked the bird's wings thinking they were broken.

No, the wings were okay.

Talking to the bird, Michael took it to the open deck.

"Come to the fresh air, little one, you can fly!" He said to the birdie. "Fly! You are free!"

It was windy and cold. The bird squeezed itself into Michael's palms. It didn't need cold wind; it wanted warmth and support.

"People are waiting to buy your book," I told Michael. "Please, give the bird to me, I have some healing power in my hands, I will bring it back to life."

Michael gently passed the napkin to me. Yes, definitely, this scared little Mother Nature being in the napkin was a *colibri*, a hummingbird, the smallest bird in the world, with a long beak, beautifully pearly-greenish colored. Americans do not name the hummingbirds colibri. Many of them even do not know this word. My computer also didn't know the word *colibri* and underlined it in red. Sorry, my dear computer, you must improve your knowledge in zoology.

I learned about colibri at school when I was about nine or ten years old. I was surprised to remember that colibri feeds on a flower's nectar. Its long thin beak helps the bird to reach the bottom of flowers and take a small drop of nectar without ruining the flower. Being a very sentimental romantic girl, I was amazed that other birds eat insects, but this bird drinks only nectar. For me, it was a symbol of pure love. I was born in the Ukraine and did not believe that I would ever see this kind of a bird. Now I live in Southern California. Hummingbirds are frequent guests on my patio. Each morning a colibri flutters in front of my face. Is it their way to say hello to me?

Once a couple of colibris even made a nest in my tree. The nest was about an inch in size. Two adult colibris (perhaps mama and papa) took their turns to sit on the eggs that were the size of a tiny white bean. I watched all the process as two little new colibris hatched. They stayed in the safety of my patio and I watched them grow up.

309

These thoughts hovered in my mind when I looked at the little creature in the napkin. His beak was not long enough. *Is it still a baby?* I wondered.

I whispered to colibri in the napkin: "What are you doing here, almost near the North Pole, little baby? You are completely lost. Don't be afraid, you are safe, take the warmth of all my heart."

The bird looked almost dead. Motionless, it laid in my palms with closed eyes. I talked to the bird in English. No, my English was not helpful. The bird didn't move.

"I will talk to you in Russian, my native tongue. I can do it much better than in English." I said softly to the bird. "You will absorb my Russian words."

"Моя маленькая, моя дорогая птичечка, открой глазки, пожалуйста … Пожалуйста!"

Translation: *"My little, my darling birdy, open your eyes, please … Please!"*

Amazingly the bird started to move. Indeed, the vibrations of love and support I expressed in my own language were much stronger. The soundwaves of my Russian words touched the little bird and reinvigorated him! The birdie understood my Russian much better than my halting English! It opened its left eye, as it wanted to show that it was listening to me attentively. Then it closed this eye, but opened the other one, and lifted its beak.

I asked the bird, "Maybe you are thirsty?"

There was an empty water bottle at the table, but on the bottom of it a few drops still remained. It was enough for the humming bird. I poured the drops into my palm and dipped the bird's beak into these few drops. I had no idea if some water got into its mouth, but suddenly the bird's tiny body fluttered in my palm, and I felt its heart beat. In the wink of an eye, the birdie spread its wings and flew up.

"Close immediately the door to the deck! It will die outside!" Michael shouted.

The bird flew under the fancy ceiling, trying to hide itself from the crowd of people. All passengers around worried about this little bird escaping to the outside where it would certainly die. It was clear that the bird didn't have enough strength to fly. It found a shelter somewhere above us and disappeared from our vision.

"Please, bring a ladder," Michael said. "In a couple of hours, we will be in Victoria. There are plenty of flowers there. I will bring it to the garden. We must bring the bird down."

We were intensely watching with lifted heads, a community of watchers hoping, praying that this little bird would survive.

Hope is a powerful energy, and there was a great outpouring of it among the little crowd. Then, Michael spread his palms, asking the bird to come back. I did the same, only I spoke in Russian.

Then, the impossible happened. The bird appeared, cocked his little head as if listening to us. Then, he fluttered down and landed on one of the bystanders who gave it to Michael.

I didn't see the little bird or Michael after that. We landed in Victoria, British Columbia, and went about our excursions as tourists do. I've often wondered where Michael took that precious little bird. Perhaps to Butchart Gardens.

Sometimes, when the night is still and the gentle breeze flutters the flowers on my patio, I remember that magical, wonderful spiritual place where the magnificent fjord met a tiny colibri and guided it to the safety of our ship. Where are you now, little exotic humming bird? Still in Victoria? Did you survive?

Isn't it amazing how the spirit can be calmed and renewed by the majestic grandeur of a rugged coastline, the restfulness of a lush garden, or the quickening of a tiny bird's heartbeat! Mother Nature is a wonder.

Google Is Just a Number

Gered Beeby

Ten is an order of magnitude. Science has adopted this convention for well over a hundred and fifty years. A special term labels this convention — scientific notation. Mechanics for this notation are familiar to most. For example, the number one thousand would be shown as 1×10^3 in scientific notation. Further, one thousand is called *three* orders of magnitude, or powers of ten, and the 3 in this case is also called an *exponent*.

This notation is particularly useful when expressing very large numbers, such as one billion, which becomes 1×10^9. But very small numbers are also more easily written. The prefix *nano* is familiar to many as one-billionth, such as in *nano*seconds. For us in the macroscopic world these are very short intervals in time. Scientific notation provides an easy way of showing these fractional quantities that are much less than unity — they take on *negative* orders of magnitude. In other words these numbers utilize negative exponents. One-billionth then looks like this: 1×10^{-9}. Such a subtle change, a simple minus sign, yet the magnitude differences between these two numbers are profound.

A number system based on ten, however, is not necessarily fundamental otherwise. Let's face it: most humans are equipped with ten digits on their two hands. And most philosophers agreed this fact established the base-ten number system used in most if not all of the civilized world. For that matter numbers in themselves are abstractions. Numerals and associated manipulations using a host of elaborate computations provide a means of expressing abstract ideas, particularly in science.

But what if there are no abstract ideas to express?

312

In 1947 Ukrainian-born physicist George Gamow published *One Two Three ... Infinity*. His book explored ideas about science and mathematics with a popular twist. Using a light touch, yet informative and even humorous at times, Gamow was the Carl Sagan of his day. The title refers to counting systems used by some remote tribes. Here, people had no need to express large quantities. In effect, their counting consisted of saying, "One, two, three—many."

So eventually we may ask, "How large is large?"

Of course, there is no upper limit to quantity or to imagination itself for that matter. But in 1920 mathematician Edward Kasner needed a name for the quantity expressed as numeral 1 followed by 100 zeros. Kasner, a professor at Columbia University, knew that in academic formality such a number would be called, "10 *duotrigintillion*." Oh, please! He wanted a fanciful label that would be more appealing to children for their own explorations into mathematics. So Kasner asked one of his nephews, nine-year old Milton Sirotta, during a walk in New Jersey's Palisades Woods near Manhattan. Young Milton dubbed the new word "googol."

Over the years spelling transformed into the Google we know today. And clearly this was the preferred name for the famous multibillion-dollar corporation. Google reflects a number about as close to infinity as most need to get. But even so, the scientific notation is relatively simple and looks like this: 1×10^{100}. Imagine however, trying to write this number out in conventional notation. Using this font size with commas spacing every third zero, the number would run almost four lines of text.

Science illustrates some tangible examples of size.

In the late nineteenth century the speed of light (aka: electromagnetic propagation) was known to be fast, but not infinitely fast. The first accurate measure of this speed was conducted by Albert A. Michelson while a professor at the US Naval Academy, Annapolis, Maryland, in 1879. Results revealed the speed to be 186,282 miles per second or about 670 million miles per hour. For this and many other achievements Michelson received the Nobel Prize in Physics; the first

American to do so. Further, in astronomy, a *light-year* is that distance traversed by light in one year or about 5.87 *trillion* miles. Scientific notation expresses this as 5.87×10^{12} miles. This is a gigantic distance, but not even close to a Google of miles.

Another large number comes from chemistry. Amedeo Avogadro was a nineteenth century Italian scientist who postulated the amount of atoms or other particles in a chemically reactive *mole* of a substance as being consistent for all elements. Frankly, chemistry is not everyone's favorite subject, certainly not mine. But another chemist taking after Avogadro's work calculated that amount. Officially, it is defined as the number of carbon atoms in 12 grams of carbon-12 and is known as Avogadro's Number. Once again scientists must grapple with another immense number: approximately 6.0221×10^{23} particles.

Here are more scientific values. The mass of the Earth has been estimated at 5.972×10^{24} kilograms, where a kilogram is about 2.2 pounds. Extending our discussion into astrophysics far beyond this planet, the current age of the known universe is some 14 billion years. This devolves from the popular *big bang* theory of creation. Recall the tiny unit of duration discussed earlier called a *nano*second. By computation the universe's age comes out to be only 4.41504×10^{17} *nano*seconds. Again, a Google of *nano*seconds is all but beyond comprehension.

Perhaps these mind-boggling quantities are way too much, but consider one last tidbit from cosmology. All matter is composed of atoms, which in turn consists of subatomic particles like protons, electrons, and neutrons. The size of the entire universe may never be known, but there are estimates. One of these starts with a subatomic proton or electron or neutron, then takes a series of order of magnitude step increases, getting ever larger by a power of ten with each step. That series ends with step 80. This infers that all points of matter in the known universe (i.e., all creation) can be guestimated by one number in scientific notation: 1×10^{80} particles. As shown in the previous examples, this amount is way less than a Google of particles — of any kind.

Where does all this end?

Human imagination has no limits. Nothing can quantify degrees of a person's aspiration or hope. There are no guideposts or boundaries for defining how harmony and caring integrate themselves into someone's individual qualities. When the Google Corporation selected its name, much of its purpose was to suggest an infinite search capability. Within the world of computer networking this objective may even have relevance. But facts and enumeration alone cannot define a universe. These alone cannot tell us what is important.

After all, Google is just a number.

Deca-Deca

Laurie Asher

Can you spare ten minutes while I share my day with you?

I awoke as always, at precisely 6:10 a.m., not requiring an alarm. I heard the cicadas clicking their legs in sync below and the birds harmonizing above. The sounds of nature always got me ready for a full and productive day. I took my ten-minute shower and thought about how I should start. The usual? A ten-minute meditation? Turn on the news? I chose Ten News Live. As I ate breakfast—Raisin Bran, which is currently number ten in the Top Ten list of cereals in America—I stared at the TV. There were ten shootings in Chicago (they are making progress), ten missing children around the country, and ten burglaries right here in my own county. This, of course, was Channel 10 and I thought—*if it bleeds, it leads*. I clicked it off.

After my tenth cup of coffee (just kidding), I got in my car and drove away from my home at 1010 Ten Oaks.

As I entered Main Street, a woman wearing an orange vest held a sign that said *Slow to 10 Miles an Hour, Accident Ahead*. Sure enough, there was a ten-car pileup looming in front of me. We all detoured around the smashed-up vehicles and were on our way. Guess how long that diversion took?

My first stop was the Post Office. Waiting in line, I looked up to study the photos on the Ten Most Wanted List, grateful that none were friends or relatives (this time). Then off to the cleaners. The woman at the counter said, "Ten items at $3.50 apiece. That will be $35.00, please." I handed her three tens and five ones.

She looked up at me, grinning, and said,

316

"Congratulations, you are our 10th customer of the day and it is our tenth anniversary. We offer you ten free garments to be cleaned at your leisure."

Wow. Good start after the traffic jam. Next, I visited the bank. It was already crowded.

There were nine people ahead of me. No worries, I was patient, and ten minutes later I smiled at the teller and she smiled back with a toothy grin. I could count her exposed teeth. Six on the top, five on the bottom. Somehow, I felt let down and disappointed, but was unsure why.

Following the bank, the market was my next destination. Luckily, it was just next door, less than ten yards away, so I didn't even have to find a new parking place, although my space had a sign that read *Ten-Minute Parking Only*.

I needed just a few items, milk, eggs, iced tea, fruit, veggies, my favorite soup, dog cookies, human cookies, a gallon of spring water, ice cream and a bottle of my supplement, Co-Q-10. I counted my items. There were eleven, and I went directly to the Ten Items or Less line, passing all the overflowing carts along the way. Oh, come on, you've done it!

The woman behind me had only one item, so I invited her to go ahead of me.

Her reply was, "Are you sure?" I waited about ten seconds, turned, and said, "Well, not really I guess," and I turned back around.

Why do people ask this question? Of course I'm sure, or why would I have offered to assist her in the first place? So I took a deep breath, turned back around, and with my most dazzling smile, said, "Yes, of course," and gestured for her to move ahead, rolling my eyes when she was out of range. No good deed ... and all that.

I walked through the parking lot and, looking down, there was a shiny dime which I pocketed. I suddenly noticed a trend with the number ten, and wondered what the connection might be, if any. But I thought it had to be coincidental.

I looked at my cell phone to check the time. It was ten

minutes to ten. I also noted the date. It was October 10. Okay, that was weird. Was this some form of a supernatural experience?

At the end of all my errands, I had one more visit. I don't even know why I did it, but I had purchased a Groupon to see a psychic. Her name was Madame Zelda over on 10th Street.

See? There it is again. I thought maybe she could help me figure out if there was any connection to all these tens.

When I walked through the beaded curtains into Mme. Z's parlor, I decided not to mention anything about the strange happenings of the day so far. She led me to an elaborate deep walnut decagon-shaped table, I counted ten candles burning in a circle in the middle.

She said, "For the Groupon price, we can only talk about ten short issues — you name them."

This sounded phony baloney already. *I'm* supposed to name them. She's the psychic!

So, I give her a what's-up look. "No, I answered, I'll let you decide what you think is important for me to know."

Here was her declaration: Silence, and a mouth rounded in an O.

I wanted to add a one in front of it. I got up to leave and laid down a ten-dollar bill, the cost of the Groupon, no tip. "Have a wonderful day," I said and walked the ten yards back to my car.

When I got home, I logged on to the internet searching for unusual connections to the number ten. Here is what I found ten seconds later.

The Power of Ten is a real thing, but it is very complex, algorithms and so forth.

I could go on for at least ten pages explaining integers, etc., but instead, I'm going to lie down and take a ten-minute catnap. I'm exhausted, but here's a conundrum: Why don't cats have *ten* lives? *So* close. I think they got robbed.

Santa's Helper

Frank Primiano

Big Ed paced the living room, yelling, "If I've told you once, I've told you ten thousand times, there is no Santa Claus. So don't expect any presents. That's the way it is and I can't do anything about it."

His son, Eddie, crouched in the corner, behind the far end of the tattered couch, crying. The kid hid there when his parents screamed and shouted, usually at each other.

"But, Daddy," Eddie said between sobs, "my friend Carl said Santa is gonna bring him a football and a bicycle. There must be a Santa if *he's* gonna get presents."

"Well, have Carl tell whoever brings his toys that you want some, too. And while that person's at it, he can bring some money here as well. We got barely enough for rent and food … and other essentials."

The name *Big Ed* was appropriate only relative to Eddie. Big Ed was all of five-foot-six, and a skeletal 130 pounds. In fewer than a dozen years, Eddie would tower above his father even if the boy went on a Mahatma Gandhian diet. As it was, the healthy six-year-old was as normal as could be expected living in an environment dominated by two volatile, though well-meaning, free-spirited personalities who had no commercializable talents.

Mollie, Eddie's mother, spoke. "When Daddy gets a steady job, there'll be enough for a bunch of toys, and new clothes, and you won't need to wait till Christmas for them." She was a shapely woman, substantially larger than her husband. Probably attractive in her youth, she now exhibited the erosion caused by a life deprived of the niceties that a living wage with benefits could provide.

319

Big Ed gave Mollie a sidewise glance, frowning. "Don't you have some place to be 'bout now before that old hag, Annie, grabs your corner? Those last-minute shoppers won't wait for you."

"I'm leaving soon's I bundle up some. It's cold standing out there. Where's my sign and my scarf? If I can score some green, maybe we can celebrate a little."

Big Ed said, "I have just enough to get us happy and maybe ferget where we've wound up. C'mon, Eddie. Stop cryin'. We got an errand to run."

* * *

After trudging twenty minutes through gray slush, Eddie and his dad came to a building that displayed a sign proclaiming, "Collection Center — Donate Toys and Clothes, Merry Christmas and Happy 1969." A truck was backed to the loading dock. Two workers carried into the building a large, open-topped carton with a variety of toys protruding from it. These men sported elf outfits: red leotards, sweatshirts, gloves, and pointy, floppy elf hats, all trimmed in white faux fur. A wide, shiny, black patent leather belt restrained their paunches. Each had a white beard. One guy's was home-grown; the other's, fake.

Eddie's eyes widened. Several workers, dressed in the same outfits, roamed inside, behind the large front window. Others stood on the sidewalk by the front door, holding bells they rang occasionally. Every so often, a car pulled up with a window rolled down, and someone handed them a package or an unwrapped toy.

Big Ed and his trailing son reached the building and were greeted by one of the costumed men. Patches of gray whiskers on his face tried hard to resemble a beard. His middle was wasp-like, a strong indication he could benefit from a good meal.

Although aware of what his parents said about there being no Santa, and overlooking the lack of a big belly and long white beard, Eddie, nevertheless, asked, "Are you Santa

Claus?"

The man chuckled. "No, I'm one a' his helpers."

Eddie wrinkled his brow. Before he could pose his next question, Big Ed motioned the fellow aside and said, "Hey, Pal, can you and your friends do me a favor … in the spirit of Christmas? Watch my kid for five minutes. I gotta go 'round the corner to see a guy."

The man studied Big Ed, then looked at Eddie who stared at all the activity, and all the toys. "Yeah, I guess so. But no more'n five minutes."

"Thanks," Big Ed said, smiling. To Eddie he said, "Stay here with this man. I'll be right back," and hustled away.

The impromptu babysitter called to him, "Say 'Hello' for me."

The man turned to Eddie. "Come here, Buddy. Stay away from the curb so you don't get bumped into the street." To the people passing on the sidewalk, he repeated at regular intervals, "Merry Christmas. Merry Christmas. Drop yer toys off here … Make a child happy."

Eddie tugged on the hem of the man's sweatshirt to get his attention. "What does Santa's helper do?" he asked.

"Oh, I mostly collect toys for poor youngsters."

"Do you have any extras? I'm not getting any for Christmas."

"How d'ya know?"

"My mom and dad told me I wasn't."

"Why? Were you bad?"

"No. We don't have money for toys, only for 'ssentials, like food and rent."

"Really? None for a toy for you, just for food and rent … and," the man looked toward the corner, "*essentials*?"

"Or for a Christmas tree," Eddie added.

"Are you poor?"

"I don't think so. Mommy never said we are."

"And your dad came here to see a guy. Hmmm." The man studied Eddie for a long moment. "Tell me, Kid, where d'ya live?"

"On Cedar Lane, in a building … We live down the steps."

"D'you know the address?"

"Yes. Mommy made me remember it." Beaming with pride, he recited the numbers. "Why do you want my address?"

"Oh … to make sure Santa knows where you live."

Reminded of his previous confusion, Eddie said, "Mommy and Daddy said there is no Santa. So how can you tell him anything?"

"That's what they said? Well, let's us keep two secrets."

"Okay."

"One: don't tell anyone you gave me your address."

"Okay."

"And if you keep that first secret, then here's number two: there really is a Santa Claus, and if he doesn't visit you in person, he'll send a helper instead."

"Oh, goodie."

"Y'know, I think that's what your parents meant: Santa wouldn't be coming by because one of his helpers'll be there in his place."

The boy scowled and looked at the man. He asked, "Do you think so?"

"I'm pretty sure."

A smile lit the boy's face.

"Now remember our secrets and don't tell anybody."

Big Ed approached as the boy said, "Okay."

"Ready to go, Son?" his father asked.

"Yep," was the boy's answer. To the skinny man, he said, "Goodbye," still smiling.

Big Ed thanked the guy. "No problem," Santa's helper said. "My pleasure."

As they walked toward home, Big Ed said, "Your mood has certainly improved. What did you two talk about?"

"Not much. Just that he's Santa's helper and he collects toys and helps Santa."

"Damn. He filled your head about Santa Claus and toys. Don't get your hopes up that you'll get any delivered to you."

The boy went silent. His gloom returned. After walking half a block, he asked, "What did you do when you went to

322

see the man around the corner?"

"Nothin'. I just had to pick up somethin' … for your mom."

"What is it?"

"Oh, somethin' she uses when she bakes."

* * *

Several hours later, Mollie came home carrying her sign, a small shopping bag of food, and an evergreen branch. "How'd ya do, Hon?" Big Ed asked.

"Not bad," she said, patting the bag. "People were generous for a change."

Mollie carried this burden to the kitchen table. Returning to the living room, she slipped out of her coat and flopped onto the couch. First one shoe came off, then the other, followed by a massage of each foot. "Ahh" escaped her lips.

Putting away the few groceries his wife brought home, Big Ed removed a half-gallon jug of American vintage Chardonnay from the bag, unscrewed the top, and poured a glass for Mollie and one for himself. A small bottle of 7UP also came from the bag. Big Ed poured half of it into an ice-filled glass for Eddie.

Mollie remained seated, sipping her wine, her head against the back of the couch. At last, walking to the kitchen, she placed the cut end of the fragrant branch in a half-gallon milk carton partly filled with water and propped it in Eddie's hiding place in the corner of the living room. It extended well above the arm of the couch. She tore several old newspaper pages into strips and draped them on the makeshift tree.

Eddie stood with his mother admiring her handiwork. She bent and gave him a kiss and a hug before saying, "Merry Christmas, Darling. But time's a-wastin'. I need t'get cookin'."

"Right y'be," Big Ed said. "A holiday feast to go with our holiday tree."

With her men sitting on kitchen chairs and drinking as they watched, Mollie, between sips from her glass, and the stirring of a pot on the stove, mixed two batches of cookie

323

dough. One was for cookies for Eddie; the other, for her and her husband. She joined the pair of onlookers at the kitchen table while the cookies baked. The room filled with the wonderful aroma of melting chocolate. Big Ed poured another round of drinks.

The baked cookies were placed on a pair of plates to cool. Mollie slid one batch in front of Eddie. "After dinner, you can have a couple. We'll save the rest for the holidays."

Before she could fill a large jar from the second plate, Big Ed snagged a pair and began munching on one, still warm. He held the other up for Mollie to bite.

Turning to Eddie, he pointed to the plate in front of the boy. "Remember, *those* are *your* cookies. You can eat all of them, eventually. But the ones in the jar are for adults … your mother and me. You are never to eat the adult cookies, no matter how hungry you are. Don't even touch them. That's why we keep the jar on top of the cabinet. And don't try to climb up to reach it. You might fall and hurt yourself. Understand?"

The boy nodded, content to anticipate the flavor and texture of those he'd eat after dinner.

Although this was a special occasion, the meal remained the usual: boiled franks and beans, and a couple slices of buttered bread. The cookies, however, made it festive. Eddie polished off his treats with two bites each, and washed them down with milk. Big Ed and Mollie started in on theirs in earnest, sloshing them down with the wine. By the time the dishes were done, a third of the adult cookies were gone, and less than a quarter of the wine remained in the bottle.

A half hour after dinner, the two adults crashed in their bed under Morpheus's spell. Eddie was left on his own to find sleep. In his jammies, he searched for it on the living room couch instead of his bed. He was too excited — encouraged by Santa's helper — to abandon his vigil for Santa's, or his helper's, arrival. In time, though, Eddie, too, succumbed to the Sandman's wiles and drifted off.

The next thing of which he became aware was a scratching at the front door. Initially frightened, he decided, at last, to investigate. Unlocking and opening the door just a crack, Eddie looked right into a beam of light that momentarily blinded him. When his eyes adjusted, he could see Santa's helper clutching two pieces of metal stuck in the lock. He had a flashlight wedged under his arm. The man extended an index finger and held it to his lips.

"Shhh," he said, "be really quiet. Where're yer parents?"

Eddie whispered, "In bed, asleep."

"Can I come in? I have toys I've collected in this bag."

"I guess so. Is there anything in there for me?

"Maybe one toy, if you're a good boy and help me."

Eyeing the straining bag, Eddie said, "That must be heavy."

"It sure is." The intruder continued in a hushed voice. "But I have to drag it around with me whenever I go out late at night during the holidays so people know I'm Santa's helper. I tell anyone I run into that I'm leaving presents for kids at their front door."

This seemed like a good idea to Eddie. He said, "What do you want me to do to help you?"

"First of all, promise not to tell anyone that you recognized me from this afternoon. Say I said I'm Santa's helper and that's all, and you never saw me before. Okay?"

"I promise."

"Now, d'ya know where your dad keeps what he bought today 'round the corner from where we were?"

"He didn't buy anything. He just picked something up for Mom for when she bakes."

"Then maybe it's in the kitchen. Let's go see. But be real quiet."

Eddie led Santa's helper through the living room and along the hall by the light from the man's flashlight. The beam swept the kitchen, finding the table and chairs, cupboard above the sink, a cabinet, drawers. Nothing of value was out in the open.

Before the man could begin his search in earnest, Eddie whispered, "My friend told me he leaves cookies and milk for Santa when he comes with presents. Would you like a glass of

325

milk and a cookie? They're fresh. My mom baked them tonight. I had two of mine. They were real good."

"Yer parents let you eat cookies yer mother baked? Then they can't be what I'm looking for."

"Do you want one?"

Distracted, the man said, "Sure, Kid. Just don't get in my way."

"You're grown up so you can have an adult one. You'll have to get it. They're in that jar on top of the cabinet. I can't reach it. Can you?"

Santa's helper grunted as he stretched for the container. He said, "If it'll get you out of my hair for a few minutes, here's the whole thing," and handed it to the boy.

Eddie unscrewed the top. "I guess I'm not touching the cookies if I only hold the jar."

"Huh?" the uninvited visitor said, taking a cookie. He put it between his teeth, steadying it with his lips, not biting, and paid no further attention to the boy. His concentration was on the containers marked flour, sugar, and shortening. Finding that they held only what their labels indicated, he zeroed in on his next target, the refrigerator. The light that came on when the door was opened filled the room. Nosing around in the freezer compartment, the man absentmindedly bit the cookie and chewed, holding the unbitten piece between his lips, keeping his hands free.

With the refrigerator door open, Eddie grabbed the bottle of milk. He climbed onto a chair, took a glass from the cupboard, climbed down, and filled it. Meanwhile, the man finished the cookie with one more bite.

"Mmmm. That's pretty good. Can I have 'nother?"

* * *

Christmas morning. A bleary-eyed Mollie, always the first to wake, walked unsteadily from the bathroom, through the living room, toward the kitchen. She stopped, hopping onto one bare foot and muttering expletives under her breath, when she stepped on a strip of model train track. She looked

326

at the floor. It was covered with a train set, Lincoln logs, red and black checkers scattered around, a cap pistol, and various other toys, along with several pieces of silverware, a few china plates, a gold lighter, a wristwatch, and some jewelry. An empty jar, and a nearly empty glass of milk stood on the coffee table. Eddie, clutching a small, stuffed tiger, snored on the couch.

Mollie was puzzled. She carefully returned to the bedroom and dragged the semicomatose Big Ed from the bed. In the living room, after a wobbly visit to the toilet, he surveyed the scene with Mollie before waking the boy.

"What is all this?" Big Ed asked.

Eddie yawned, rubbed his eyes, then, realizing where he was, sprang to life. "Look what Santa's helper brought me."

"What d'ya mean, 'Santa's helper'?"

"That's who he said he was."

"You let someone in here last night?"

"Yes. He was Santa's helper. And he had a bag full of presents. He said one was for me."

"And you let him in?"

"Yep."

Big Ed looked at Mollie who stood mute, wringing her hands, and surveying the room, taking mental inventory of their meager possessions.

"So, where'd all this other stuff come from?"

"Well, I offered him milk and your adult cookies, and he ate them. He acted like he was really hungry. And the more he ate, the happier he seemed to be ... he had a hard time keepin' his gigglin' quiet so he wouldn't wake you."

"But how'd you get all these ... toys and things?"

"Oh, the more cookies I let him have, the more he wanted. But I stopped him. I didn't think he should eat all your cookies since you like them so much. So, he started trading me toys for cookies. He'd pull one from his bag and give it to me if I let him take a cookie. Finally, he couldn't eat any more, or drink more milk. He said, 'I'll give you the whole bagful for the rest of the cookies.'

"I thought, Mom, you can always make more cookies, but

327

I might not have another chance to get more toys. So, I said okay. He emptied his bag on the floor and put the rest of the cookies in his pockets. He said, 'Merry Christmas, Kid,' and couldn't stop laughing when he bumped into the front door on his went out."

The two parents were dumbfounded. They looked at each other, at the floor, and then at the boy.

Eddie said, "You must be wrong. There has to be a Santa Claus if he has helpers."

Despite endless questioning, Eddie shed no more light on the event than what he had in the first telling. Not only his innate sense of honor — after all, he had promised — but also the effective bribes of Christmas toys, kept his lips sealed. At least until his parents admitted that Santa does exist, and that he sends his helpers out on Christmas Eve to burgle the homes of little boys and girls.

The Nudge

Patrick Ross

Our mark emerges about ten yards ahead. "That's him," Jimmy says under his breath.

I agree. The guy's about forty and dressed like a boss. His suit is a work of art, perfectly tailored with a light sheen that shouts class and money. His crisp white shirt is a blank canvas for a teal silk tie. *Maybe I could buy an outfit this nice after we roll the guy. Looking that good will up my con game. Better marks, bigger bucks.*

A quick glance confirms we're not in anyone's line of sight. Jimmy and I have run this hustle at least a dozen times now, and we've never been spotted. Our bench is tucked away behind hedges along one of the park's less used paths. We ignore the joggers and dog walkers, who rarely have much cash on them. Our prime bounty are office workers like this guy escaping, ever so briefly, hermetically sealed torture. Occasionally one of our victims has more than a hundred dollars on them, especially if they're over thirty and don't pay for everything with their damned smartphones.

When the dude's a few paces away, Jimmy stands. "Excuse me, sir, do you have the time? We're supposed to meet someone, and I think she's late."

Now it's my turn to use The Nudge. There's a reason I call my gift that. When I connect with someone mentally, all I can really do is push them to do something they're already inclined to. For the longest time I only used it to get laid, hitting nightclubs near closing time and targeting women projecting desperation. Now The Nudge doesn't always work out great once I lure one back to my apartment. I don't just detect and manipulate another person's desires. If they're

329

aligned with my own, ours become one. Too often when drilling a woman I sense her desire to come, and just like that I blow my wad. This will be easier. I'm not trying to bang the guy, just roll him.

The man stops in front of us and tilts his head. He's easily over six feet, broad-shouldered with defined pecs. I stand as well, looking up into his steel-gray eyes. I allow my mind to clear. The park and the man shift to a blur, like the clouded vision you get when you're drunk and trying like hell to stay awake. As I begin to read him I realize he hasn't looked at a watch or pulled out his phone. I sense now he has no desire to give Jimmy the time. He has another desire, just out of reach. I feel its intensity like heat from a too-close radiator. His emotional state becomes a covered pot on the verge of boiling. I want to use The Nudge on Jimmy, to find whatever part of him has doubts and push that to make him back down. It's too late. I'm locked in with the mark. Already feeling disconnected from myself, I force my right hand up and place it on Jimmy's left arm. He ignores my signal to stop.

"I'm sorry," Jimmy continues. "You just looked like … "

"Never mind," I hear myself say. "I just remembered I've got the time." I manage to remove my hand from Jimmy's arm and pull a phone from a side pocket of my pants.

The man turns his head and I feel the motion in my neck. What is left of my own vision sees the early afternoon sun form a halo around his close-cropped hair. "Kinda wondered about that," he says in a slow baritone.

I sense the motion Jimmy has done so many times. He's reaching for his jacket. *Nooo!* I try to scream. But our mark's calmness paralyzes me. Intoxicates me. I've never felt a connection this strong before. I see Jimmy reveal a pistol resting in his jacket's interior pocket. See it through the eyes of the man I'm now completely tethered with.

"So, this will be simple," Jimmy says. "All we want is your cash. You leave with your wallet, and everyone's happy."

This is where I'm supposed to step in. Once Jimmy shows our mark his gun, desperation to survive takes over. We meet that desire. Jimmy takes his cash but leaves all the crap that's a pain in the ass to replace. Credit cards. Driver's license. Family photos. I use The Nudge to remind our victim he's going to live, and it's for the best if he just leaves the park and doesn't involve the cops. I sense no fear in this man, however. I should say I sense no fear in me.

The boiling pot's lid flies off. It's clear what I'm experiencing. Joy. No, more than that. Anticipation. And confidence. I'm a man who does what he wants when he wants. I like it. I've never felt so powerful, so in control. I barely register that the one in control isn't really me.

My muscles coil, like a sprinter ready to pounce. Then my left arm moves. But these actions aren't mine. They're his. He/I pull back his/my suit jacket. The fabric is smooth and soft, as I already know it is. I see Jimmy spot, secured in a shoulder holster, my own gun.

"Hey buddy, it's all good," Jimmy says. "Forget about it." I can barely hear him, like he's whispering in a faraway tunnel. Now a right hand in motion. A pull on a narrow leather strap. A snap as it detaches. The comfortable feel of a pistol grip's ridges. Warmth envelopes me, a blanket of longing. *I'll take out the armed guy first, then* his pal. Wait. His pal is me.

The stranger's desire is too powerful for me to stop him. I move quickly. I nudge.

The man's confusion shakes me as the gun goes off. Then a blast of physical pain tosses me from his mind, like a spent shell from a shotgun. I see him once more through my own eyes. A crimson patch forms on his left abdomen as he falls backward. The crack of his skull hitting the pavement combines with the crunch of decaying fall leaves.

* * *

A chill wind nearly whips off my favorite baseball cap as the ancient T-Bird's speedometer needle moves to the right.

"Dude, slow down," I tell Jimmy. "This stretch is crawling with cops." I know that for a fact. A little over a year ago my mental gift got me out of a pickle with the cop who pulled me over. After reading his mental combination of exhaustion and a desire to get his ass home and pop open a cold beer, I used The Nudge to end our encounter with a warning. How different from today when I used my gift to kill a man.

Jimmy turns, sweat beading on his forehead despite the cold. "What happened?" He's talking so fast it comes out as one word.

"Obviously, he fired the gun before he pulled it on us," I say. Jimmy doesn't need to know that my nudge caused him to fire off a round while the gun wasn't fully out of his holster. Or that I'm still high from the thrill of taking his life. I sit in silence, trying to better understand what happened. Yes, it's true that the desires of who I connect with blend with my own. But I've never lost complete control like that before, in a sense become the other person. Could it be because I wanted to?

Flashing lights, alternating blue and red, fill the oversized rearview mirror.

"Shit!" Jimmy says. He moves over to the right lane, then the shoulder. We stop on the side of the road as traffic whips past. The police car stops thirty feet behind us. It takes forever before a uniformed cop steps out.

"You think he knows?"

"Don't be an idiot," I say. "He pulled you over because you were driving like a madman." Doubt fills my mind. I'm right about why we were stopped. But we ran out of that park. Were there eyewitnesses? Were descriptions of us blasted out to every cop in a fifty-mile radius? I prep our story. We watched a man take his own life. That's not a crime.

When the cop is about a dozen feet away I start reading him. He's pissed. And he's scared. What the hell? Do we seem like a threat? Two young white guys joy riding in a vintage convertible? Then, just like our mark an hour or so ago, I see us through the cop's eyes.

He/I slow, senses alert. A rush of excitement. *These two punks will give me an excuse. Body camera off? Check.* Then the familiar feel of narrow leather stretched over a handgun's grip.

What is left of me inside this cop's mind knows I should stop this. Stop him. And yet once again I savor the rush of anticipation. I need another fix.

Sleepless in San Diego

Lara Yamada

"Did you hear about the man who submitted ten puns for a local pun contest?"

The room remained silent in a collective and polite pause.

Dr. Rose shuffled his papers together and when the stack was in perfect alignment under his thumb, he placed it inside a leather folio and clipped it shut. It was a familiar routine, and it gave him exactly the right amount of time to hold his class in suspense.

"He went to the mailbox a month later," he continued. "And inside was a letter from the newspaper announcing the results. He had submitted ten puns with the hopes that at least one would make it, but unfortunately," Dr. Rose lifted his voice and drew out his last words with clear enunciation, *"no pun in ten did."*

His students responded with mild expressions of amusement and disdain.

"That was a good one," he admonished. He turned from the podium, walked out the stage exit door, and escaped from the bright overhead lights of the classroom and into the bliss of a dim corridor.

He exhaled and closed his eyes. An intense pressure throbbed behind his left eye and he blinked hard against black dots and distorted auras.

He was not well.

Dr. Gunnar Rose was the son of a wealthy family in La Jolla, one of Stanford's most gifted graduates, and a fellow at the American Association for the Advancement of Science. For a man in his late thirties, he had an abundance of ambition but a severe shortage of energy. He could barely maintain his

334

current knowledge and regurgitate the same curriculum on three hours of sleep a night, let alone finish theoretical advances in physics.

Gunnar eyed the handicap parking spots on the labored walk to his sedan. He suffered his way across the hot concrete, squinting at the white lines framing empty spots that hadn't been free when he arrived this morning.

As he walked, he tugged at the falling waistband of his pants, fingering the cold clasp of his belt. Ten years ago, he'd had the muscular physique of a casual athlete. The shirts that used to cling in an attractive fit over his muscles now hung loose, but he refused to buy smaller sizes.

Gunnar waited in his car until the ocular migraine passed. He took a residential drive home, winding his way higher up Soledad Mountain Road behind work trucks and tourists on their way to Mount Soledad.

His parents had gifted him his childhood home when they moved to Del Mar for a quieter residence, and although he tried to resist the ingratitude, the stunning overlook of red-roofed white villas against the brilliant blue coast and softer blue sky no longer impressed him.

Inside the quiet house, the air was flat. The vanishing windows of the open living room were covered with dark curtains, and the marble kitchen's curved island was covered with work papers. The opulent home with full views of the breaking surf hadn't been enjoyed for a long time.

Inside his bedroom, the smallest of the six bedrooms in the house, he yanked off his jacket and threw it against the headboard. His shirt was damp with sweat, and in those drops of water and ammonia, he wished he could shed off the sickness that kept him awake at night. The bed, like everything else in his house, was useless.

He was beyond frustrated. The months-long intense exercise program his therapist recommended when he slid below six hours of sleep hadn't helped. She'd banned caffeine, eating after 7 p.m. in case his problem was heartburn, and had him tested for every kind of cancer and heart disease. He used to think he was running on fumes when he got five hours of sleep, but on three, he didn't know how to survive. She wouldn't say it directly, but it felt like he was on an imminent course to an early demise.

The neurologist who had studied him over a three-day sleep study was more than happy to share information. As he'd positioned nodes on Gunnar's hair with sticky putty, he explained that the study of sleep was still new and that they didn't understand why the body needed eight hours of sleep. Only the symptoms of the sleep-deprived were well known, up to hallucinations and organ failure on the extreme end.

"Not that we'll let that happen to you," the neurologist told him. "We'd give you some tranquilizers well before that point." He'd given Gunnar a friendly pat on the shoulder, handed him the bundle of wires going from the power pack all the way to the nodes across his skull, and reminded him to push the call button if he had to get up in the night.

"I'll be watching you on the monitor. Get some rest."

The sleep study had confirmed what the therapist already knew. The word *insomnia* was tossed around, a cheap and common word, almost as often as its counter, *sleep*.

Sleep should be effortless. Anything universal, life-critical, and basically free shouldn't be this difficult. And yet, here he was. He let his face drop to his hands and gave in to exhausted sobs.

* * *

"Gunnar," the therapist's voice drew him back. Last night had been restless, as usual. He broke eye contact with the window and glanced at her trim black jacket. There were six silver buttons and a neat pocket below the collar. He was certain she had a new outfit every time they met, and he'd seen her at least a hundred times over the past two years.

"Tell me what's on your mind," she persisted. She was his diary. It was to her that his thoughts were revealed. The constant flow of information felt intimate, but it also felt vulnerable, because the exchange wasn't two-way.

He rolled a smooth, white pen between his palms and

336

tried to calculate how much he'd paid in therapy fees. Twenty grand? Twenty-five grand?

If it worked, it wouldn't matter. He'd happily pay her a hundred grand.

He answered her with abrupt clarity. "This will be my last session." His elbow had been resting on the wooden arm of the chair, and whether it was from him or the collective efforts of dozens of other anxious clients, the chair laminate had been rubbed off to the point the chair was a hazard.

She lifted her brown eyebrows in surprise. "Excuse me?"

When he didn't elaborate, she straightened in her chair and deepened her frown.

"Are you moving? Are you unsatisfied with the counseling?"

He pursed his lips together and held back an irritable comment. It wasn't his fault, but it wasn't hers either.

The therapist stared at him. "If that's how you feel, you're free to go. But I highly recommend you find another therapist. You need to continue treatment. Let me know if you need a referral."

On his way around her desk, he noticed a glass bowl with pink lollipops. He took one without asking. On his way down the elevator of the twenty-story business building, he unwrapped it and stuck it in his mouth.

Sugar was the preferred drug of most Americans, and he was no exception.

Outside, the bright sun caught him full in the face, and it took him a moment to notice a white plastic table set up to the left. He glanced at it, searching for a colorful fundraising sign and a gaggle of teenagers fundraising for vacations disguised as sports functions.

Instead, he found a simple, black-and-white sign on an otherwise bare table manned by one woman.

SLEEP ADVISOR. GUARANTEED SLEEP OR YOUR MONEY BACK.

It felt fortuitous and comical, because the woman appeared to have dark circles under her own eyes. Her short brown hair and long-sleeve dress gave her a practical

337

appearance, and she was staring openly at him but didn't attempt a sales pitch.

Curious, he wandered in front of her stand. "Hello," he said and gestured to the sign with his lollipop. "How much money are we talking?"

"Three hundred dollars," she said promptly. "I'm Amy. Do you have trouble sleeping, sir?"

He felt his face transform into a mirror of his therapist's from ten minutes earlier. *Sir?* She was probably in her late twenties or early thirties, and he bristled at her implied age difference.

"Yes." He paused and considered which phrase would be better. Did he have something, or was he something? He settled on the former. "I have insomnia."

He let the word hang in the air as a challenge, half-expecting her to tell him she only worked with the nominally sleep-challenged.

"I can help." She was quick to move around the table and offer him her hand.

His reaction was automatic.

"Gunnar," he introduced himself. Her hand felt hot in his, but then he'd been sitting in an air-conditioned office building for the past hour while she'd been standing in the sun.

Still emboldened by his abrupt end with the therapist, he opened his wallet and handed her three hundred-dollar bills. They both maintained eye contact, and the cash was exchanged through peripheral vision. She pocketed it and put down her sign.

"When can we start?"

"Right now," she replied, and kicked in the legs of her table. "I give my clients one hundred percent of my attention."

"Am I your only client?" his voice rose in surprise.

"Second."

"So he, or she, has zero percent of your attention now." Gunnar moved out of her way, and she loaded the table into the trunk of a lime green Prius parked on the curb.

"He's in Phase Two. He's stable. You're in Phase One,"

she said and slammed the trunk shut.

He wanted to ask, "How many certifications do you have?" but the words that came out were, "How many phases are there?"

"Four. I should also mention that you'll need to buy the necessary materials. Three hundred is just for my service fee."

"Necessary materials?" he repeated.

"Yes. Cell phone please," she said and extended her hand. "I'll put them all in your Amazon cart for you."

He hesitated, then punched in his pin. It took her about five minutes to finish skimming her fingers over the screen until she handed it back.

"When it arrives, give me a call." Before he could ask the question, she added, "It's already in your phone."

Gunnar pulled open his contacts and stared down at a circular icon with Amy's grinning face. He quickly scrolled through three more of her selfies in his photo gallery and looked up.

"And here you are," she said, holding her phone up for him to see. His contact photo was a picture of himself looking down at a trashcan.

"I took it when you were throwing away your lollipop," she explained.

Before he could protest and tell her to take a better one, she hopped into her car.

"See you soon! Better sleep ahead!" she said, and merged into a stream of cars just as a white and blue meter maid car crept up to the flashing red meter.

Inside the shade of his own car, he suppressed his ire as he scrolled through an $800 Amazon order. He reassured himself of the option to return it later. His tired mind turned over the probability that each random item would weave together into one harmonious miracle cure, and by the time he pulled the stick shift into drive, he abandoned the notion of science and decided this scenario would require an alternative mental muscle — faith.

339

"This is Rufus." Amy stood on his doorstep and took off a pair of boxy sunglasses. She wore a white blazer and long black pants, and her haircut was gelled into a sideways bob.

Gunnar's gaze darted down to the strange dog by her feet. The animal had tufts of fur on the top of its head, all four paws and the tip of its tail. He wondered if the dog had survived a mange attack and this was the fur that remained.

"Rufus is basically a therapy dog," Amy continued at Gunnar's lackluster reaction. "He's a Chinese Crested so he's mostly hairless. Shouldn't be a problem for allergies. This will take about an hour."

Amy spoke with a blunt and firm tone, and he imagined she'd been prepared for buyer's remorse. Had she read the vibes off of him? He'd been doubting himself these past few days, wondering what he had been thinking, launching into an expensive charade without any proof of her identity or accolades.

"To be honest," Gunnar began, "I wasn't myself when we met a few days ago. I was seeing a therapist for years, and that was my last day."

"It sounds like you were ready for a change. I'm glad, because this is going to work."

"How can you be sure? Are you a licensed therapist? Where do you work?"

"Here's my business card," she said, and presented him with a plain business card.

"This just has your name on it."

"That's right. Amy Greene, and I answer my cell 24/7. It can't be easy living on so little sleep. Three hours, was it? Don't worry. You'll be sleeping through the night in no time."

And just like that, what he wanted most was again confidently promised. He had wanted better sleep for so long. Did it even matter what her credentials were if it worked?

He led her inside.

"Beautiful home," Amy commented, and her words echoed under the twenty-foot ceiling and sparsely furnished living room. His parents had taken most of the furniture when they moved, leaving plenty of room to spread out the materials on a massive Turkish rug.

Amy planted herself over a stack of cream-colored jersey cotton bed linens. "We have a lot of work to do. But before we begin, I'm going to need a commitment from you."

"This isn't a commitment?" Gunnar countered. As she had requested, he'd unpacked every item and laid it out on the floor. He'd even broken down the boxes, confident that a return wouldn't be necessary. Even if he didn't find the purchases useful for sleeping, nothing was outright wasteful, and he knew he could count on his socialite mother to rehome them.

"Raise your right hand and repeat after me."

He hesitated, then raised his hand.

"I, state your full name," she led, "do solemnly swear that I will follow all of the steps to the best of my ability, and that I will not deviate from doing them for thirty days."

He repeated the words and dropped his hand.

"Perfect," she said and gave him her first smile of the day.

While she stooped to stash crinkly items in plastic sleeves and paper boxes in a wide duffel bag on her shoulder, he shifted from foot to foot and waited. He couldn't help it. He was going to ask.

"Was that in place of a contract?"

"What was?"

"The oath."

"Yes, I believe commitments can be made person to person, without any legal mumbo jumbo," she answered. "I will trust you until you give me a reason not to."

It was the first time she spoke with weight, and he felt like he needed to live up to the potential she saw in him.

"I'll follow you to your room."

The walk to his bedroom felt a mile away. He could end the visit anytime. "Thank you, but no thank you," was on the tip of his tongue, but he couldn't say it. He was a captive audience, watching her dance between playful and serious. He wanted to keep it going, even if it was only until the end of

341

today's visit.

She flipped off the light switch by his door, and they stood in silence in the semidarkness. The curtains blocked most of the sunlight, but their eyes adjusted after a few seconds. His heart beat faster.

"The Big Three," she announced and held up three fingers, "light, sound, and smell. First, you need complete darkness. You shouldn't be able to see the hand in front of your face," she directed. "You'd be amazed how fast that solves a lot of sleep problems before trying anything else. Also," she said and dropped a roll of tape onto the middle of the bed, "use the electricians tape to cover the light from any electronics."

She flicked the lights back on and he tried to resume normal breathing. His swallowing sounded too loud so he moved to the other side of the room. He yanked open one of the curtains while she set up an object on his nightstand.

"Second, you need constant background noise." Amy raised her voice and turned the device on. "This is a white noise machine. Flip through all of the sounds until you find one that's most pleasing. It needs to be on about the level of a loud conversation."

She gestured for him. "Come try it."

He rejoined her. She waited for a few minutes while Gunnar flipped through the sounds. Most were irritating, some annoying, and some seemed loud for no reason.

"I prefer complete silence," he said.

"You'll get used to it after a few nights. Turn it on and keep it on, all night, every night. Thirty days, remember?"

He murmured a noncommittal response.

"Third," she said, undeterred, "you need to associate sleep with a comforting smell." She took out a box of oils and handed it to him. "Put a bit on your wrist and see which one you like the best. Most people like lavender or vanilla. Mix it into the spray bottle with water and ten drops, spray it over your sheets and around your face, right before you lay down. Some people also like the smell of fresh air, so keep your window open if you like."

342

When he didn't move, she lifted the top off for him and plucked one out.

"Lavender," she said and held it under his nose.

He shuffled out of her reach. "What's your favorite smell?" he asked to soften the abrupt movement.

"Rose," she answered. "Don't skip these steps. A lot of people think it doesn't do anything, but your body will instinctively start to relax when you hear the white noise and smell the sleep scent you pick. Now, tell me the Big Three again."

He should have felt silly, repeating words for her like a schoolchild. But she had already pulled him into that dance of play and purpose since the oath, and it wasn't as awkward as he thought it would be. When he finished reciting them, she gave him three more.

"Mental, physical, and spiritual," she announced.

His hands felt empty, and he wondered if he was expected to write this down.

"For your mental health, write down your thoughts for at least ten minutes before you go to bed. Your brain has to do a data-dump, or you keep everything in your head and it's hard to fall asleep. If you've never journaled before, write down your high and low of the day and one thing you're grateful for. To make sure you write for ten minutes, one of your items is an alarm."

She handed him a blue leather book and a gel pen.

"Try it," she encouraged, and he opened the first page. He uncapped the pen to write the date and felt pleased by the silky flow of the ink on the textured paper.

"There's a lot you can do for mental health, but this is the cheapest and quickest way to do it."

"For physical health," Amy continued, "doctors always tell you to exercise, and that's good for you, but exercise is stress on the body. Pick something you actually like, even if it's walking or hiking. Just move the body and eat a Mediterranean diet."

He petted Rufus's head politely and bit back the comment that he could have bought a *Reader's Digest* if he wanted that

343

medical advice.

"Touch is the most overlooked part of physical health."

Gunnar looked up in surprise.

"People need to be touched. Hugs, handshakes, anything like that. And most of the time, it's not sexual," she added, giving him a sideways glance. "It's just comfort. Everyone wants to feel like they belong and they're accepted, and touch from people you're close to is reassuring. If you don't have that in your life, then pay for it."

He gaped at her.

"Get a monthly massage," she said, oblivious to his reaction. "Touch is touch and that still counts."

She shifted from her position on the edge of his bed and rose. "Spiritual health. If you don't go to church or believe in God, at least practice gratitude. You're just one tiny piece of the universe, and it's not all about you. Everyone has problems, but sometimes, you get to be someone's solution. Focus on that when it's tough in your life."

There was a natural pause as each considered the thought; Amy, wondering if he would remember everything, given that he had failed to take notes, and Gunnar, wondering what was tough in Amy's life. Why did she have a therapy dog?

On that thought, he looked at Amy. "Where'd the dog go?"

As if he knew he'd been called, Rufus appeared at the doorway and pranced in three circles, kicked his back legs against the floor, and trotted over to the bed.

"Wait here," Amy said with a hasty retreat out of the room. Gunnar waited patiently, deflecting Rufus's eager nudges against his shins for a few seconds before wondering what he was waiting for.

"Amy?" he called in the hallway. He took a few steps to the living room, toward the only other room Amy had seen, when the toe of his Allen Edmonds Oxford stepped onto something soft.

He looked down at the brown puddle of stool and froze. "Poop! Poop in the hallway!" he shouted.

Amy came running with a roll of paper towels and a bottle

of cleaning solution he didn't know he owned. "I'm so sorry! He must have eaten something he shouldn't have."

She touched the heel of his foot and lifted it out of the shoe and away from the offending pile.

"Here," she said, leading him by the elbow to the living room while he walked off-kilter, a half inch shorter on his socked foot. "Sit down, I'll clean it up."

He sat on the pink armchair his mother had favored for novel reading and marked the spot in his mind, burning the position into his memory so he could avoid it. He would have to take an extra-large step over the coral rose bloom on the hallway carpet until he could get the carpet steam cleaned.

"All clean," she said in a bright voice. She reappeared with Rufus tucked under her arm, and he was pleased that Original Amy voice had returned. Her business tone had disappeared, and he rose from the sofa chair.

"What's next?" he said weakly.

He followed her around the house as she listed off a few other tidbits, always in a new group of three.

"Don't watch TV or look at your phone an hour before bed. Set your phone on silent after 8 p.m. Finish your evening with a hot shower, a hot tea, and a book."

"I'm not a granny," he replied. "I'm a working professional, and people contact me at all hours."

"Then set some boundaries. You're probably not that important. Doctor?"

"Well, technically," he started, glancing at the framed PhDs hanging in the study, then dropped it. He knew that wasn't what she meant. "No."

"Don't leave clutter laying around, keep your house tidy, which I see you already do," she said, roving from room to room. Her rubber Crocs made squelching sounds on the marble floors in the kitchen, and he had to work hard to redirect his focus on what she was saying.

"Get some plants, they help with oxygen, and it's healthy to see some life in the house. But if they start dying, get rid of them."

They ended back in the living room, where all of the sleep

345

improvement items had been redistributed elsewhere, mostly to his bedroom.

"Last bit for today. Keep the house cool, at least 70 degrees or lower, and use the new sheets and blankets. Any questions?"

Gunnar glanced at his watch. Two hours had flown by.

"So I do all these things, and then what?"

"Thirty days, follow the plan. You can start taking the magnesium and calcium supplement today. And here's your cheat sheet. Everything we talked about."

He took a folded piece of paper from her and looked it over. The bullet points were accented with clip-art photos of smiling moons and cartoon sheep.

"Trust the process. This will work," Amy reassured him. "I have a good feeling about this."

When her green Prius had disappeared from sight, he felt uncertain, and his heart ached with a hollow feeling. Fortunately, she'd given him a distraction, and he returned inside to superglue magnets to his bedroom curtains and walls so they would eliminate outside light. His mother would kill him if she knew he was ruining the luxury drapes she custom ordered from France. "Get an eye mask!" she'd tell him, and he wondered why Amy hadn't recommended it.

She had her reasons, he was certain of it. But, he thought he'd better send her a text just to make sure.

Fifteen texts later, he had arrived at the first hour of the new routine. Eight p.m. on the dot, he gently placed his phone into the charger and set it to silent. He made sure to end his last text to his new sleep advisor with a good-night greeting, sensing it was appropriate to wish her luck in her own sleep endeavors even though she was clearly well-versed in the ways of the well-rested.

Although he'd already showered in the morning, he stepped into his mosaic tiled bathroom and turned on the Moen rain shower head to a degree hotter than he'd normally like. He toweled himself dry and grabbed the morning newspaper, the only non-academic reading material in the house. The *Dear Abby* column provided him with mildly entertaining scenarios of in-law faux pas, and he wondered if he should write in to ask about the Rufus accident debacle of the afternoon.

He found himself adding ten drops of rose oil to the water spray bottle, thinking of Amy as he directed a streak of water onto his pillow before correcting the dial to mist mode.

He settled on a muffled fan noise, and with a sigh, he propped himself against the headboard and leaned over the empty journal page.

"Dear Journal," he wrote. "It's been a crazy day. I'm in bed earlier than any man my age should be, although I still have some papers to grade. My high of the day was learning from my new sleep advisor. My low of the day was her dog. I'm grateful for hope. I hope this works."

It had taken him all of two minutes, and he stared at the alarm, ticking down the seconds left. What could he write about for eight minutes? He realized that he had spent every thirty seconds glancing at his phone for the telltale blue flashing light that meant he'd received a text.

He knew he shouldn't, but he grabbed his phone and checked again. No new messages from Amy, and he was disappointed. He wanted to send a message, but then she'd know he hadn't followed her rule. He couldn't fail on the first night.

It took him twenty minutes of shuffling from his side to his back until he found a way to ignore the white noise and get into his usual habit of replaying the day in his mind. He recalled the conversations, reconsidering his words and revisiting unfinished thoughts and actions. It took another hour before he felt tired enough to consider sleep, and eventually, he drifted off.

At 4:42 a.m., he woke.

At 7:00 a.m., he called Amy.

"It didn't work," he reported.

"Good morning to you too," she replied.

He gripped the phone a little tighter. "Thirty days right?"

"That's right. You can do it."

"What happens after thirty days?"

347

"Let's just get to thirty days."

When he arrived at the university later that morning, he felt like doing something different. He was going to start the day with a pun instead of finish with one.

Dr. Rose shuffled a stack of graded papers together and greeted his class.

"Did you hear about the houses falling in love? It was a lawn-distance relationship."

He relished their early morning groans, and with a smile, he thought about how he could work the pun into a text to Amy. Maybe he could lump it together with a question about tea.

Normally he let his teaching assistant log the graded essays, but today, he felt like doing it himself. He pulled up the first blue exam sheet and opened it up. The name *Amy Greene* jumped up at him, and he dropped the sheet back onto the stack.

He hoped it was a coincidence. With over 600 students, he couldn't be expected to know them all. But one thing was for certain; he had to find out. This complicated things. Or did it? It was about sleep, and their relationship was strictly an exchange of information.

Reassured, he stood and called for his teaching assistant. He didn't feel like logging grades anymore, but he didn't feel like sending Amy the pun either, in case she'd already heard it. He suddenly felt very tired and found himself wishing he were back in bed. He took it as a positive sign and wondered if his days being sleepless in San Diego were numbered after all.

The Bed

Amy Wall

The page was torn out from the want ads, *Queen Sized Mattress, $10,* circled in red crayon. Amy's mom found it on her desk.

"What's this?"

"Me and Carrie are saving up to buy a bed."

Amy tucked her brown hair behind her ears and went back to the project she was working on, gluing macaroni to a picture of a poodle carrying a handbag. It was a present for Santa. When she looked up, her mom's feet were still there, green shag carpet peeking through the cracks between her toes.

"Since when did you and your sister want to share a bed?"

"Never. I don't wanna share a bed with her," she said, counting the pieces of macaroni left to glue.

In the corner of her eye, she could see her mom's feet in the same place.

"So why on this God-given earth would you want to buy a queen bed?"

"Thirteen, fourteen, fifteen." Amy counted the remaining pieces. She squeezed dots of glue one at a time on the macaroni, then placed them on the flap of the handbag in the picture. Her mom's foot began tapping, waiting for an answer.

"Oh." Amy paused, "'Cause you and dad won't let us jump on your bed."

"You are buying a bed to jump on?"

"Uh-huh."

Amy shifted to the other side of the picture, nudging her mom's legs to indicate she wanted her to move.

"Where are you planning to put it?" Amy's mom asked while taking a step back.

She put glue on the last six pieces, then placed them quickly before they dried.

"Do you think Santa will like it?"

"Amy, I asked where you plan on putting it."

"I'm giving it to Santa."

"Not your picture, silly. The bed. Where do you plan on putting it?"

"Oh that? In the front yard."

* * *

Two weeks later, Amy woke up at 5:47 a.m. She stayed in bed watching the clock, waiting for the hour and minute hands to stretch out on opposite sides, indicating it was finally 6:00 a.m. That was the earliest the girls were allowed to get up on Christmas morning. When the second hand finally hit the 12, she flew out of bed and sprinted out of her room.

Carrie opened her bedroom door at the same time and the two nearly ran into each other in the hallway. Her golden hair, normally smooth down her back, was twisted and knotted from a rough night of sleep. Neither were concerned about grooming as they sprinted through the house to the front room.

In the living room, the tree stood, covered in ornaments and silver tinsel. The girls gasped when they saw how many presents spilled out, in, and around the tree. They weren't allowed to open them yet, but they started counting and organizing them.

As the morning sun rays began to peek over the hills in the east, the darkness faded into a pre-sunrise glow. Amy looked out the window and spied something on the front lawn. It was sitting there as if it dropped out of the sky, maybe even out of a sled—a brand new trampoline.

She gasped, pulled Carrie's shirt and pointed outside. They both screamed—half jumping, half running toward the door. Just before turning the handle, Amy grabbed her sister's face, noses almost touching and said, "I told you Santa likes macaroni."

Perspectives from a Zen Garden

Judith Lief

Ten plump crows guarded the pilgrim's path like samurai as my husband and I walked toward the Ryoanji Zen Temple in Kyoto, Japan, to visit its famous rock garden. Torrid afternoon sun penetrated my light cotton clothing. Tired, irritable, I questioned what possessed me to insist we visit despite an intense day of sightseeing.

Three walls surrounded the dry garden and its wooden veranda viewing platform. Fifteen large rocks arranged in five groups perched atop moss on raked white pebbles. When I looked at the garden from any place on the veranda, I saw only fourteen of the fifteen rocks. Each time I changed my vantage point, one rock disappeared and a different one replaced it.

Although its message eluded me during my visit, on reflection, the garden provided a metaphor for life itself. Standing on the veranda, I saw the groups of rocks but remained unable to see all of the rocks at the same time. Each change of position shifted my perspective the same way that my perspective changed looking back at my life from different time frames. Though I perceived the garden through space, I viewed my life through time. Neither the garden nor my life revealed itself in its entirety. While viewing the garden, I wondered when I left the veranda if I would be able to see all of the rocks and fully understand their interconnections. The same conundrum held true for my life. The aesthetics of the garden and the richness of my life seemed to intensity with the shift of position and the passage of time. Some believe enlightened beings see the fifteenth rock while still on the veranda viewing platform.

I've been blessed to look back at experiences in my life which caused pain, and later understand how they helped me grow. Often those things I once viewed in a negative light, hardships that I faced and overcame, now appear as gifts. The more perspectives I see, the more complete my understanding of my life will be. But even so, the completion appears hard to fathom. The shifting views of the garden are part of the continual process of its creation. That is also true of my life.

I did not fully appreciate the aesthetics of the garden during my visit. Many other tourists filled the veranda. It was difficult to find a place to sit or stand undisturbed. That in itself may say a lot about how I lived my life, becoming stressed by outer turmoil because I was not calm inside. I have not fully valued the life I have been given or appreciated its unique aesthetics. It seemed much easier to focus on the external. I remember what the garden taught me, and then I forget, only to remember once again. My life is an unfinished book which I must edit while still writing.

I never imagined that a few hours at the most renowned dry rock garden in Japan would shower me with life-enhancing lessons.

Contributors

(Numbers in parenthesis reference author's contributions.)

LAURIE ASHER (108, 202, 316) started her writing career after retiring from Real Estate. She has written one currently unpublished children's book in honor of her nephews, and is working on two other novels - adult and youth, and has a picture book in progress. Her work has been performed onstage at the San Diego Writers Ink's Memoir Showcase in downtown San Diego. She has her certification as a memoir writer and has assisted a noted client in San Diego with her memoir. She has been published in the San Diego Writers and Editors Guild's Anthology for the past four years with an eclectic mix of stories. Her favorite 'literary' quote is: "Everything stinks until it's finished." — Dr. Seuss. Laurie served as Secretary of the SDWEG's board of directors, is a member of SD Ink, and the San Diego Memoir Writers Association.

KELLY BARGABOS (204) Kelly's memoir, *Chasing the Merry-Go-Round: Holding on to Hope & Home When the World Moves Too Fast*, was a 2018 Nautilus Book Award Silver winner and a finalist in the National Indie Excellence Awards. Her work has also appeared in literary journals, anthologies and news publications. Her fiction won third prize in the 2017 Fiction500 contest and in February 2021 another story was published in the San Diego Decameron Project. She holds a certificate in Creative Nonfiction from the Downtown Writers Center in Syracuse, New York. Kelly is currently hosting two podcasts, *All There Is* and *Here to L.E.A.D.*, and serves as a board member for the San Diego Writers and Editors Guild. She loves to write about the things that move her, with the hope they move you too.

GERED BEEBY (113, 312) Gered is Past President (2003) of the San Diego Writers and Editors Guild and remained on the Board as a Director-At-Large for many years. His suspense-thriller novel of industrial espionage, *Dark Option* (2002), was nominated for a PMA Benjamin Franklin award in the category, Best New Voice—Fiction (2003). He has written two screenplays. "The Bottle Imp" is a deal-with-the-devil story based on Robert Louis Stevenson's 1892 classic tale. Gered has also written "Dark Option" for the screen. He has contributed several short stories and essays to *The Guilded Pen*. As a registered professional engineer (PE) in California, Gered serves as a Subject Matter Expert for the California engineer licensing Board. In this capacity he performs detailed analyses for the Board's technical advisory unit.

M. LEE BUOMPENSIERO (200) is the author of *Sumerland*, winner of the 2017 San Diego Book Award, Best Published Mystery. Writing under the pseudonym "Loren Zahn," Marcia also publishes the Theo Hunter mystery series: *Dirty Little Murders* (2009/2017), *Deadly Little Secrets* (2015), and *Fatal Little Lies* (2018). *Deadly Little Secrets* received a "highly recommended" rating from the SDWEG Manuscript Review Board and was a finalist in the 2015 San Diego Book Awards unpublished manuscript division. She writes nonfiction magazine articles about the history of San Diego's Little Italy. Marcia serves on SDWEG board of directors as co-Treasurer and is a managing editor of *The Guilded Pen*. SDWEG recognized her efforts to further the impact of the Guild in the writing community and honored her contributions by presenting her with a *Rhoda Riddell Builders Award* in 2018 and is the founder of Grey Castle Publishing greycastlepublishing.com.

LAWRENCE CARLETON (118) has published or otherwise presented scholarly work in philosophy, cognitive science, and software development, thereby putting to some use his advanced degrees in computer science and philosophy, and his post doctorate in cognitive science. He took up writing when Parkinson's disease ended his hobby as a jazz trumpeter, and currently amuses himself and, he hopes, others, by writing short stories with interesting characters in unusual situations. A contributor to several anthologies including *The Guilded Pen,* he's particularly proud of his book, *I'm Not Roger Blaime and Other Curious Phenomena,* which contains twelve of his best stories. lrcarleton@gmail.com Facebook: Lawrence Carleton.

ANNE CASEY (121) Since its inception ten years ago, Anne has been a frequent contributor to The Guilded Pen. She is a past editor of the SDWEG newsletter, of the Sharp Memorial Guild Auxiliary newsletter Sharp Notes, and the student newsletter for David N. Myers College, Cleveland. She also assisted foreign graduate students and post-doctoral fellows with the English grammar needed to write their scientific manuscripts, fellowship research papers and grant research documents. Anne holds a degree in Literature/Writing from UCSD which she obtained after she retired. She writes short stories, poems, creative non-fiction and anything that interests her. Current projects are the ever-in-progress Hungarian recipe book, "First You Steal One Chicken" and an autobiography,"The Juniper Street Lemonade Stand". A few historic and scientific projects are percolating.

AL CONVERSE (30) is a 1965 graduate of Boston University, served as a Naval Officer in the Vietnam War 1965-1968, earned an MBA from the University of Connecticut (1969), worked many years in the finance industry, and retired as Chief, Finance Division, US Small Business Administration, San Diego District. Since retiring, he has published eight novels, *Bitch'n, Die Again, Boston Boogie, Baja Moon, News from the East, Flagship, Hornwinkle Hustle,* and *Jack Blue.* His short stories, "Warrior's Stone," "The Marble Game," "Drippy Pants," "The Woods," "The Wake Up," "A Rose for Mrs. Delahanty," "One Soldier," "Old Kim," and "Kitchen Help" appeared in different editions of the Guild's annual anthology.

JANICE COY (14, 136) is the author of six suspense novels, a scuba diver, a hiker (successfully reaching the summit of Mt. Kilimanjaro), and an animal lover—all elements that enrich her stories. An award-winning former journalist and freelance feature writer, Coy has always been curious about people's motives. "Now I get to create motives for my characters," says Coy. Her books can be purchased through her website www.janicecoy.com or on Amazon.

E. M. CRIMAN (211) grew up across the street from a forest in a small Oregon town where she watched the trolls and fairies in the forested meadow. The trees whispered to her, the forest beckoning, animals watching, imagination waiting. And as the breeze spoke, the story began. E. M. Criman works at a prison during the day and is a student, speculative fiction novel writer, copywriter, and a voice over artist at night. She loves nature and books and believes they should be appreciated equally, with copious amounts of chocolate. She currently resides in the deserts of southeastern California with her dog and three cats, and her very kind and patient muse, her husband. Although she is not currently published, she always has work to be edited, finished, or started. The story is always waiting.

NICK DI CARLO (297) Born in a small upstate New York town, Nick Di Carlo now meanders about a southern California hamlet. He has taught literature, writing, and educational psychology in universities on both east and west coasts as well as in Skidmore College's University Without Walls programs in New York State medium and maximum security correctional facilities. Also, he has served as instructor for a cross-country student journalism summer program. He has published feature news articles. His poetry and short fiction have appeared in small magazines, and most recently his flash fiction story "What Comes Around" has been accepted by the online literary journal *Shotgun Honey* to be published in September 2021.

J. DIANNE DOTSON (151) dreamed up other worlds and their characters as a child in the 1980s in East Tennessee. She formed her own neighborhood astronomy club before age 10, to educate her friends about the universe. In addition to writing stories, she drew and painted her characters, designed their outrageous space fashions, and created travel guides and glossaries for the worlds she invented. As an adult, Dianne earned a degree in ecology and evolutionary biology, and spent several years working in research. She published *Heliopause: The Questrison Saga®: Book One* (2018) and its sequels *Ephemeris: The Questrison Saga®: Book Two* (2019), *Accretion: The Questrison Saga®: Book Three* (2020) and her last novel in the saga, *Luminiferous: The Questrison Saga®: Book Four* (2021). Dianne is also a science writer, content writer and manager, short story writer, watercolorist, and illustrator. She lives with her family.

BOB DOUBLEBOWER (222) was born in Philadelphia, raised in the southern New Jersey town of Lindenwold, and attended Villanova University where he received a bachelor's degree in Civil Engineering. Beginning his engineering work with Bechtel Power division in Washington, DC, his career has taken him to Colorado, Arizona, Virginia, and, finally, California where he now maintains a consulting engineering practice, Regional Shoring Design, in San Diego County. Bob has been published in *The Guilded Pen* since 2012 and is currently working on a horror novel, *The Circling Bench*. Bob is past president of the SDWEG board of directors and currently serves as vice president.

CHLOE KERNS EDGE (230) is currently her husband's primary caregiver as he battles Leukemia. She is writing to remain sane. Her works include *Birdcage Review* (1982) and *Maize, Volume 6* (1983); a published book, *Tattoo (1988)*, for women in prison; poems; nonfiction; and, has been published in *The Guilded Pen since 2012*. She is currently working on a memoir and a sarcastic book for addicts who don't want to stay clean called *Crime Lessons*, based on the notion: "No matter what, don't get caught!"

HR GOOLD (32) is a recent high school graduate and is excited to have her second ever published work featured in SDWEG's 10th edition of the annual anthology. Now presenting a short story, she shows her talent in both human interaction, dialogue, and environmental personification to weave a storyline made to make you think. Hannah hopes that this work will be received as positively as her last, and she is looking forward to writing and sharing more as she begins her college courses with a focus on writing and editing.

JANET HAFNER (238) spent most of her professional career in language acquisition both in educational institutions and the corporate world. Her written work focuses on writing for children in the middle grades. She is dedicated to telling her life story. Her memoir essays appear in anthologies, and she has been published in *The Guilded Pen* since 2015. Janet serves on the board of SDWEG, and is a member of several writing organizations and critique groups. Janet is an all-time optimist who loves to laugh and understands the value of tears. Visit wwwjrhafner.com or Jrhafner19@gmail.com

PEGGY HINAEKIAN (244) owes her love of books to her grandfather who owned the largest private library in Egypt. She is an internationally recognized artist and author who lives and works in the United States and Switzerland. Her short stories have appeared in the anthology since 2016. Her novel, *Of Julia and Men,* available on Amazon.com and Audible.com, appeared in the *New York Times Book Review Magazine,* Discover New Titles — Great Stories, Unique Perspectives. Peggy designed the book cover

358

illustration, plus twenty-six interior images. In 2020, Peggy's work was featured on "Living Your Dreams," (Mara Brown), airing on Los Angeles TV. She was awarded 3rd Place by the Writers Workshop of Asheville, NC, for her 5000-word memoir *My Apartment in Heliopolis.* Peggy published two other books in 2020. *The Girl from Cairo - A Memoir,* covering her life between 1940 and 1960 in Cairo, Montreal and the U.S. and *Collection of Short Stories and Essays — Of Humans and Animals —* comprised of quirky stories taken from her experiences and illustrated by her. Visit: www.peggyhinaekian.com and www.peggyhinaekian.artspan.com

DORA KLINOVA (37, 307) is an award-winning writer and poet. In 1992, Dora emigrated from the Ukraine and left behind her profession as an engineer-designer in the movie industry. America recreated Dora. Her thoughts flooded onto paper like a rushing stream. To her own surprise, the torrent of words was in English, not her native Russian. In March 2003, the International Society of Poets presented Dora a Silver Cup- Merit Award for her poetry. Dora's works have been published in newspapers and magazines, performed in many theaters in San Diego, and were published in many anthologies: *Hot Chocolate for Seniors, Hot Chocolate for Senior Romance* and *The Guilded Pen* yearly since 2018. Dora wrote three books, all of which have achieved worldwide success. Her first book, *A Melody from an Immigrant's Soul,* is a collection of heartfelt stories. The second book, *The Queen of the Universe,* is translated into Japanese, Russian and Spanish. The novel, *Did You Ever Have the Chance to Marry an American Multimillionaire?* is Dora's personal story. www.doraklinova.com.

LEON LAZARUS (20) grew up in Apartheid South Africa. Recognizing the brutality of the regime at a young age, he arrived at Rhodes University in 1986 as an anti-apartheid activist. By the start of his second year, Leon had formed an eleven-piece non-racial band, destroyed student radio with a show called *The Hallucinogenic Wasteland,* and published three controversial student magazines. He graduated as a journalist in 1991. Leon spent the intervening twenty-eight years in marketing and communications, holding senior positions in both corporations and agencies. Today, Leon consults on projects that interest him, but writing remains his first love. He has written and illustrated children's picture books, is querying a middle grade chapter book and a YA speculative fiction novel, and looks forward to completing *Barking At Dogs,* a collection of creative non-fiction short stories describing life in Apartheid South Africa. His podcast featuring South African music and musicians is available to stream at www.TuneMeWhat.com.

RICHARD LEDERER (63, 156) is the author of more than 50 books about language, history, and humor, including his best-selling *Anguished English* series and his current title, *Richard Lederer's Ultimate Book of Literary Trivia.* He has been profiled in magazines as diverse as *The New Yorker, People,* and the *National Inquirer* and is founding co-host of "A Way with Words" on KPBS Public Radio. Dr. Lederer's column, "Lederer on Language," appears in newspapers and magazines throughout the United States, including the *San Diego Union-Tribune*. He has been named International Punster of the Year and Toastmasters International's Golden Gavel winner. He was awarded the San Diego Writers and Editors Guild's Odin Award in 2019. Website: www.verbivore.com

TOM LEECH (106) is the author of multiple books covering a variety of topics. His most recent is among the high-culture level, that is *Titillating Tales from the Outhouse*. Just before that was *FUN ON THE JOB: Amusing and true tales from Rosie-the-Riveters to Rocket Scientists at a major (San Diego-based) aerospace company*. Garnering attention is Tom's book, *On the Road in '68: A year of turmoil, a journey of friendship*, about his travel experiences during that wild year, fifty years ago. His years as Forum Editor for *San Diego Magazine Online* led to his book, *Outdoors San Diego: Hiking, Biking & Camping*. Other current books include *Say It Like Shakespeare: The Bard's Timeless Tips for Successful Communication*, 2nd ed. and *The Curious Adventures of Santa's Wayward Elves*, with coauthor and wife, Leslie. His AMACOM book, *How to Prepare, Stage & Deliver Winning Presentations*, is in its 3rd edition and has been acclaimed by many relevant publications. His poems have appeared in many anthologies and journals.

JUDITH LIEF (98, 352)is a lifelong writer of fiction and memoir. Her short stories have appeared in *Active Voices* and in *Journal of Crisis, Illness & Loss*. Currently she is writing a travel memoir about her trip to Central Europe to do healing work at concentration camp sites. She enjoys being a grandmother of three teenage boys. Judith shares her passion for minerology with her husband of 52 years. Often she can be found in her La Jolla, California garden placing crystals next to plants.

CARY LOWE (42) is a San Diego writer and political activist. A retired land use lawyer and planner, he has published over seventy essays on environmental and urban planning topics in the *Los Angeles Times*, *San Diego Union-Tribune*, and other major newspapers, as well as articles in professional journals. He also has taught courses in law and urban planning at UCSD, UCLA, and USC. His book *Becoming American*, published in 2020, is a political memoir describing his experiences growing up as a child of Holocaust survivors in postwar Europe, immigrating to the United States, serving in the US Navy, having a career in law and academia, and becoming involved with prominent political causes and candidates. Additional information on his writing may be found at www.carylowewriter.com.

JEFF MASON, MD, MHA, FACP, MSHA (186) has more than 40 years' experience as a practicing physician, with physician organizations, and California Health Plans. He most recently served as Senior Medical Director for UnitedHealthcare in California where he developed policies, procedures, and infrastructure for numerous commercial ACOs in California. Jeff is a graduate of New York Medical College, a fellow of the American Academy of Physicians and earned his Masters in Healthcare Administration from the University of Colorado. In 2017 Jeff retired and moved to San Diego where he has started a second career as writer, bicyclist, and attentive grandparent. He is polishing his first novel, a story about a young doctor in training and hopes to share more of his work.

ROBERT MULLER (160) After earning a bachelor's degree in Education from the University of Wisconsin-Milwaukee, Robert took a teaching job in Las Vegas, Nevada. He taught in the classroom for a few years, was a school librarian for over twenty years, and got married. He has always been interested in American History and historical fiction. When his grandson asked me to help him do research on Al Capone for a school project, I was surprised to learn that Capone had six brothers and that his oldest brother became a lawman in the Midwest during the Prohibition Era. At the time, he this would be great material for a story but did not start working on it in earnest until he and his wife, Ann, retired and moved to Carlsbad. *To Baltimore and Back* is just one part of the story of *The Brothers Capone*.

PENNELL PAUGH (170) has published extensively in nonfiction newsletters and magazines in the fields of mental health, corrections, speech and hearing. *Thrift Store Luck* is her debut fiction story. She has written two fantasy novels; one for 9-12-year-olds and the other for young adults. She joined SDWEG in 2020 and has been part of its marketing team.

RICHARD PETERSON (47) has written magazine articles and was a former staff writer for "Wholistic Living News." He authored the article "Stained Glass Television" in the Journal of Popular Culture (Vol. 19 No. 4); a chapter called "Electric Sisters" in *The God Pumpers: Religion in the Electronic Age* (Bowling Green State University Popular Press); and has been published in *The Guilded Pen* since 2012. Rick formerly served on the Guild's board of directors as membership Chairman, and has been a judge for the San Diego Book Awards since 2008.

TY PIZ (66, 182, 268) was born and raised in Colorado where he water skis in cold mountain lakes, scuba dives, and snow skis. He raced Motocross and Flatrack from 1972 through 1979. In 1980 he switched to road racing until retiring in 2004. He has won three regional championships, and twice finished Top Ten overall in the AMA Superbike Series onboard a Yamaha TZ-250 Grand Prix motorcycle. Ty has three amazing daughters that have raised him quite well. He is a Paraeducator, working in the public-school system with elementary students that have a wide range of special needs. He feels great to share his passion for life with these loving, caring young people. He also instructs new riders as they pursue their dream of street riding. He has been published in *The Guilded Pen* yearly since 2012.

FRANK PRIMIANO (274, 319) retired from academic and industrial careers in which his writing was required to be strictly factual. Now, he gives free rein to his imagination and concentrates primarily on fiction and creative nonfiction, some of which has appeared in local anthologies, including *The Guilded Pen* (annually since 2015) and San Diego Writers, Ink's, *A Year in Ink*. He has been a finalist in the San Diego Book Awards' Unpublished Novel and Unpublished Short Story categories. Frank is a Philadelphian who lived for over thirty years in Cleveland, Ohio. He and his wife, Elaine, moved to San Diego in 1998 in search of the sun.

CYRIL ROSEMAN, PhD (139, 257) is rounding the turn into his third career as a writer, his first, a university professor and his second, a financial advisor and retirement planner. While he continues to satisfy financial clients and has never really given up on being a professor, he is now increasingly engaged as a writer, focused primarily on drawing Personal Dramas and Fables out of his searching soul. Cy says, "To be a writer is, first and foremost, to have something philosophically important to say; second, to be drawn to storytelling as an art form; and, third, to execute the assignment in the same way a baker fashions his pastries and breads — using tools and techniques to generate an appetite for delicious morsels." Cy is currently engaged in combining a baker's artful presentation with the confectioner's talent for stimulating salivary expectations.

PATRICK ROSS (329) has been a professional writer and editor for more than thirty years, including a decade as an award-winning investigative reporter. He earned an MFA in Writing from the Vermont College of Fine Arts and is the author of a literary memoir published by Black Rose Writing titled *Committed: A Memoir of The Artist's Road*. An award-winning creative writer, Patrick has been published in numerous literary journals and has also taught creative writing through The Loft Literary Center and at The Writer's Center in Bethesda, Maryland. He and his wife relocated from Washington, D.C., to San Diego in 2017. They love coastal living (except May Gray and June Gloom), and always look forward to a visit from one of their two adult children.

MARDIE SCHROEDER (68) published her debut novel, *Go West For Luck Go West for Love*, in 2015. In 2019 she received the Rhoda Riddell award for her contributions to the Guild. She has contributed to *The Guilded Pen* since 2014, and has served as president of the SDWEG from 2017 to 2020. Website: www.mardieschroeder.com.

SHUJEN WALKER-ASKEW (75, 143) is a poet, journalist, editor, writer, and author of the novel "Across All Skies." She explores a variety of genres and writes short stories in fiction and creative nonfiction. Her works are published in literary magazines at Mesa College, Grossmont College, San Diego Writers & Editors Guild, San Diego Writers Ink, and other local anthologies. She made the top 10 in the San Diego Decameron Project and had her short story performed by a professional actress. ShuJen won first place in the NYC Midnight Short Story competition and honorable mention in the Screenwriting competition in her category. She is an Electrical Engineer, a busy wife, and the mother of a four-year-old son and a six-year-old daughter. ShuJen loves writing and hopes one day her kids will read her works.

AMY WALL (93, 277, 349) is the Senior Vice President of the Western Region for one of the country's top M&A firms. She is also a writer and editor for Runner's Life magazine. In addition to writing articles about running, she loves writing about health and fitness as well as anything on her mind. Her work has been featured in magazines like The Startup, The Writing Cooperative, In Fitness and In Health and others. Besides magazine articles, Amy loves writing general fiction and poetry. Some of these works have been published in literary journals and anthologies. She currently lives in San Diego with her family after living in Australia and New Zealand for almost a decade. Together they have traveled to over 30 countries (and counting). Her other interests include running, hiking, backpacking, gardening, and anything that takes her outdoors.

RUTH L. WALLACE, PhD, (91) retired from clinical practice in dietetics and self-published *Linking Nutrition and Mental Health.* A second book, *Nutrition and Mental Health,* was published later by Taylor and Francis. She contributes to the Behavioral Health Nutrition dietetic practice group's newsletter and educational webinars. Ruth has been published in *The Guilded Pen* since its inception in 2012 and has served as Assistant Editor of the anthology. She served as president of SDWEG and edited *The Writer's Life* for five years. While president, Ruth initiated the SDWEG Marketing Support Group and Open Mic Night. She is currently developing a collection of short stories as a nontraditional means of teaching nutrition. Ruth has contributed several chapters to nutrition textbooks.

NICO WATERS (286) is a published children's book author currently focusing on historical fiction. She also writes and indie-publishes sweet, clean romantic comedy fiction, available under her pseudonym at www.RenePenn.com.

JOHN YAMADA (1) is an aspiring young adult fiction novelist. He enjoys stories that involve characters who must overcome inner turmoil while navigating the external challenges of extraordinary circumstances. Besides writing, he enjoys all kinds of games, delicious foods and quality time with his beautiful wife Lara, their daughter Zoey, and their Pomeranian Zumi.

LARA YAMADA (334) is an aspiring young adult fiction novelist. She loves lap swimming, exploring new cities and parks, and chilling at home with her husband John, their baby Zoey, and their furbaby Zumi. She recently completed six years in the U.S. Navy and is ready to spend more time writing!

KEN YAROS, DDS, (281) is an alumnus of Albright College, received his DDS degree from Temple University. He spent six years serving with the Air Force and seven years serving with the Connecticut Air National Guard, attaining the rank of Major. Now semi-retired after 45 years of practice and teaching Dental Hygiene, he has turned his hand to writing short stories both nonfiction and fiction. He has been a contributor to *The Guilded Pen* since 2013 and was published in the national *OASIS Journal* 2014. Ken often writes under his pen name: KAY Allen and is putting together an anthology of short stories for Kindle publication. Ken served as a director at large on the SDWEG board.

SANDRA YEAMAN (83) spent the first twenty years of her life trying to figure out how to get away from Minnesota. She spent the next forty years living in twelve countries, as she worked first as a teacher, then as an engineer, and finally as a diplomat. While she thought those exotic locations and occupations would provide her with plenty to write about, she finds the topics she draws from most often in her writing are her childhood and her home state. Sandra serves on the Board of Directors of the Guild and as webmaster and social media manager. She has had works included in *The Guilded Pen* each year since 2013. In 2018 the Guild awarded her with the Rhoda Riddell Builders Award for her contributions to the Guild.

CPSIA information can be obtained
at www.ICGtesting.com
Printed in the USA
BVHW092307141121
621672BV00014B/364